HOW TO COOK
BOUILLABAISSE
IN 37 EASY STEPS

HOW TO COOK
BOUILLABAISSE
IN 37 EASY STEPS

Culinary Adventures in Paris and Provence

Diane Shaskin & Mark Craft

Photographs by Mark Craft

Cover & Illustrations by Russ Willms

Une Coupe de Champagne et Pistaches Chauffées / 1

The Beginning / 3

The First Noël / 11

The Best Cheese Ever / 21

Searching for Françoise and Laurent / 35

Happy Good Year! / 45

La Quincaillerie / 57

Dr No's Hideaway / 67

In the Summer, When it Sizzles / 81

Christmas in Provence / 93

Of Bread and Ideas / 107

The Cheese Shop of Belleville / 117

The Prince of Côtes du Rhône / 127

La Femme Chocolat / 137

A Day in Champagne / 147

Sunday Lunch in the Country / 161

A Glass of Wine in Paris / 171

The Markets of Paris / 183

Culinary Boot Camp / 193

Cookin' at the Ritz / 205

Réveillon / 217

Truffles. To Die For. / 227

Close Encounters of the Parisian Kind / 235

The Four Chefs *Plus* One / 247

The Elevator on the Right Bank / 259

How to Cook Bouillabaisse in 37 Easy Steps / 273

La Carte de la Maison
AMUSE BOUCHE

Pistaches Chauffées / 1
Warm Pistachios

Foie Gras Sliders / 8
Yes, you read that right!

Pâte à Choux / 9
Puff Pastry

Chèvre et Tomates Séchées / 16
Provençal Goat Cheese Dip

Provençal Tapenade / 64
Provencal Tapenade

Pain d'Olive de Nyons / 65
Olive Bread from Nyons

Scones au Citron Parisienne / 113
Parisian Lemon Scones

Boule / 114
French Rustic Bread

ENTREÉS

*Soupe aux Lentilles, Croûtons
Maison & Crème Fraîche* / 17
French Lentil Soup with Homemade
Croutons & *Crème Fraîche*

Salade de Chèvre Chaud / 19
Warm Goat Cheese Salad

Quiche Lorraine / 131
Authentic French Quiche

Pâte Brisée / 133
Pastry Dough

Salade Maison / 191
Diane's House Salad

L'Omelette Parfaite / 232
The Perfect Omelet

*Polenta Soufflé au Chèvre
à la Crème* / 242
Polenta Soufflé with
Goat Cheese Cream

Coquilles Saint-Jacques / 244
The Famous French Scallop Dish

Crème de Tomate en Croûte / 268
Tomato Soup in Puff Pastry

PLATS

Poulet Braisé à l'Ail / 31
Braised Garlic Chicken

Polenta Crémeuse au Jambon / 32
Creamy Polenta with Ham

Ragoût de Boeuf avec des
Panais Rôtis / 41
Rosemary Beef Stew with
Roasted Parsnips

Soupe Vietnamienne au
Poulet et Nouilles / 76
Vietnamese Chicken Noodle Soup

Poulet à la Citronnelle / 77
Lemongrass Chicken

Pavé de Saumon Grillé / 103
High-Broiled Salmon

Pommes de Terre Rôtis au Four
aux Pistaches / 104
Oven Roasted Potatoes
with Pistachios

Chou-fleur Gratiné / 105
Cauliflower Gratin

Bifteck au Échalotes / 124
Steak with Shallot Sauce

Sole Meunière / 156
The Most Famous French Fish Dish

Purée à l'Ail / 158
Garlic Mashed Potatoes

Tomates Confites / 166
Slow Roasted Tomatoes

Pâtes Fraîches Maison / 168
Fresh Homemade Pasta

Steak au Poivre / 179
Pepper Steak

Asperges Rôties au Four / 190
Oven Roasted Asparagus

Cardamome Poulet / 202
Cardamom Chicken

Magret de Canard aux
Sauce de Cerises / 211
Duck Magret with Cherry Sauce

Sauce aux Cerises / 213
Cherry Reduction Sauce

Polenta Poêlé / 214
Pan-fried Polenta

Thon au Poivre / 223
Pepper Ahi Tuna

Champignons à la Crème / 231
Mushroom Pasta Sauce

Bouillabaisse / 280
The Famous French Fish Soup

Desserts

Tarte Rustique aux Pommes et Amande / 53
Rustic Apple and Almond Tart

Brioche au Miel / 54
Honey Brioche

Glacée au Crème Fraîche et Amandes Grillés / 125
Toasted Almond & Creme Fraiche Ice Cream

Gâteau au Grand Marnier / 134
Grand Marnier Cake

Profiteroles à la Fleur de Sel Sauce au Chocolat / 143
Profiteroles with Chocolate Sauce

Truffes au Chocolat / 144
Chocolate Truffles

Molleux au Chocolate / 180
Warm Chocolate Cakes

Macarons Noix de Coco / 224
Coconut Macaroons

Caramel au Beurre Salé / 257
Caramel Butter Sauce with a Touch of *Fleur de Sel*

Gâteaux aux Miel et Amandes / 270
Almond Honey Cakes

Crème Brûlée Infusée au Miel de Lavande / 279
Lavender and Honey Crème Brûlée

Une Coupe de Champagne et Pistaches Chauffées
A TOAST TO FRANCE

A glass of Champagne, a bite of warmed pistachios. What better way to begin a tale of food adventures in France? It's no secret to my friends that Champagne is my favourite drink of all. In France, whether you're in a local bistro or a three-star restaurant, the natural start to any meal is *"une coupe de Champagne, s'il vous plait."*

Over a dozen years and too many visits to count we have delved into the food, the wine and the culture of Paris and Provence. We've learned how to cook bistro classics in the kitchens *Le Cordon Bleu* and the Ritz. We've baked bread with a Parisian *boulanger* and discovered the secrets of baking a perfect, crisp baguette. We've tasted our way around the 56 French AOC cheeses. And of course, we have made bouillabaisse in Avignon from an eccentric chef who is the recipient of *Le Charte de la Bouillabaisse Marseillaise.*

And now, we want to share our adventures with you. So let's raise a glass to the journey ahead. *À votre santé!*

2 oz roasted pistachios in shell, about 48 nuts 1 tsp extra-virgin olive oil ½ lemon	Preheat oven to 225°F. Shell and hull the pistachios, then toss them in a very small amount of olive oil. You want them only lightly coated, so they shine. Place them in a small baking dish and squeeze a little lemon juice over them. Heat the pistachios in the oven for 10 to 15 minutes. Serve them individual portions while still hot, in the smallest serving bowls you have, about a dozen nuts per person.

THE BEGINNING

The story starts with me crying in a restaurant. On my birthday. The best stories all start with tears.

At the time, we were living in a winter city famous for its giant mall and although we had a home and a successful business I knew the Canadian prairies were not where I was meant to be. There is no tradition of food or wine, and I hate hockey and winter time. For years we had been escaping to Napa Valley and had even found a real estate agent in the cute town of St. Helena. But, on March 4, over lunch, I was trying to convince Mark that we just had to go to France.

"France?" Mark couldn't keep up, "I thought you wanted to put all of our energy into California," he said, treading carefully. It was my birthday after all.

"I do, but once we get busy there, we won't have any time or money to go to Europe, and you know it's my dream to go to France with you. Remember?" I tried to sound logical, but tears were beginning to form.

"I just don't think that's a good idea right now," said Mark, as calmly as he can.

⟡

Crying, it seems, is how you get things done. June 4, exactly three months later, I'm sipping Champagne at a bistro in the 6th Arrondissement, a stone's throw from the Seine.

Writers, artists, and expatriates have expounded on the loveliness and charms of Paris. I feel the same, Paris is magical: the banks of the Seine, the museums, the lovely cafes, the narrow streets to explore, the broad avenues to promenade. The city seems to exist for my pleasure. I am in love with Paris.

And tonight we will have our first meal together in a Paris restaurant, a small bistro recommended by people in the know!

⟡

"Can we go in there?" The narrow storefront with one small window is intimidating, not at all like restaurants I'm used to. I double-check the address and Mark checks our map. "Is this it?" I ask in consternation. I almost back away, but Mark opens the door and we step in.

The small room is crammed with little tables, each butting up to its neighbour. A woman approaches and I say something like, *"Nous avons réservations,"* hoping she will understand. She smiles and leads us to a table, and returns a moment later carrying a chalkboard with the day's menu; it's like looking at hieroglyphics. It is our first restaurant meal together in Paris, at a bistro close to Place des Vosges, and I'm feeling a bit nervous.

A waiter comes to take our order, but I'm still trying to acclimatize to the crowded room and the chalkboard menu. I don't yet know that useful phrase *"pas encore,"* not yet, so I have to mime that I need a little more time. Then Mark and I begin to study the menu carefully, whispering to each other and referring to a dictionary we have hidden beneath the table.

I pick out a *chèvre* starter because we think we know what that means; goat cheese, right? We seem to remember that *raie* is a fish, so I choose that as well. Mark deciphers *canard* and we're pretty sure that means duck, so he decides to try it, taking the chance that *confit* doesn't mean feet or brains. This takes a long time.

You can't hide in a Paris restaurant, you are part of the scene. Neighbouring diners squeeze past us to get to and from their tables. Waiters pass dishes over our heads. I feel under the spotlight when I place our order; I'm convinced that everyone within earshot (and there are a lot of them) is snickering at all of my French grammatical errors.

While I wait for the *entrées* I take in the surroundings. Compared to the Napa Valley restaurants we have been visiting, with their high-end décor and plenty of space, this is foreign and intimidating. I've been weaned in a different kind of restaurant: lavish entries with huge displays of flowers, waiters explaining the menu in culinary poetry. This is the distilled version, stripped down to the essentials. Hemingway vs. Tolstoy.

The biggest technological advance is found in the closet-sized bathroom: a self-cleaning toilet seat. After every flush the seat rotates a full 360 degrees as it is washed and sanitized. It's so marvellous that I visit the bathroom three times; or maybe it's just nerves. Heading back to my table, I pass the incredibly small kitchen, smaller than the bathrooms in most California restaurants. Yet two chefs are at work, back-to-back, in the tiny space, producing three courses for fifty meals a night.

Seated next to us are a pair of men from San Francisco, so close in the packed room we have to be careful not to poke each other with our elbows. They tell us that when they come to Paris they always bring their own coffee because, as everyone knows, the best coffee comes from the Bay area. Mark and I give each other a *look*.

Our meals arrive and Mark finds, to his relief, that *confit* does not refer to brains or feet or, indeed, to any body part, but is the manner of preparing the leg and thigh of duck. The crispy brown skin covers meat so tender it falls off the bone with the touch of a fork. It comes with goose-fat fried potatoes. The *raie* (it *is* a fish, skate) comes seared, almost caramelized; exquisite with a black butter sauce. To accompany all this we drink a rustic, flavourful wine from the southwest of France. I always imagined French cooking to be complicated and fussy, but here are simple high-quality ingredients, simply combined to a delicious effect.

This is my first lesson in Parisian dining, close quarters and tiny tables with diners jammed into every cranny; yet the room is remarkably quiet. I notice how the diners stay within their private, small spaces and speak softly to each other. Every customer greets the hostess upon entering, *"Bon soir, Madame. Une réservation pour M. Leblanche…"*, and on leaving every diner says a courteous farewell to those on either side of them, *"Bonne nuit,"* even though they may not have spoken before. Understanding the customs is like unlocking a code. I am learning the passwords and look forward to becoming full a initiate.

༄

We spend a week living *la vie Parisienne*: discovering the food markets, sampling croissants, sipping Champagne. Too soon it's time to board the TGV, the high-speed train, for our next destination, Provence. We picked the town of Vaison-la-Romaine randomly out of a book about charming French hotels. While Mark was showing me a hotel in Sisteron on page 218, I looked on page 219 and saw exactly what I was looking for in Vaison-la-Romaine: a bell tower, a fountain and the distant French countryside. "Let's stay there," I said impulsively.

The TGV is quiet, luxurious, and speedy. At the sleepy station of Orange, our car isn't waiting at the *gare* as promised, so we walk through the humid, misting rain to find the Avis office. Orange seems a plain town with only the Triumphal Arch to make it mapworthy. I'm hot and tired, and decide that a slice of this Orange is enough. It isn't horrible, but it's missing something. Quaint beauty? Charm?

Once we leave Orange, driving towards Vaison-la-Romaine, the fear sets in. What I see around me is flat, gravely farmland. Sure, the crops are mostly grapes, but this scenery isn't what I had expected. I don't say anything, but I begin to worry that we have made a terrible mistake. Where is the beautiful Provençal countryside of legend and literature?

Suddenly green hills rise up around us and we are following a river. The flatland is behind us and we are among vineyards and fields that climb the swelling hills, dotted with ancient villages, with views of distant mountains.

The curving river road takes us into Vaison-la-Romaine. I manoeuvre our petite car through narrow streets and up the hill toward Vaison's *haut ville*, the medieval town built on the peak, until we come to a stone archway with a red sign that reads *"Sauf Riverains."* Something to do with river dwellers?

"Can we go up there?" I ask nervously, looking at the sign and the constricted lane in front of us. "Will our car even fit?"

"Let's try," Mark says, and I inch the car forward up the steep slope.

It's a bouncy ride on the cobblestones, well worn from centuries of feet, carts and cars, but a couple of tight turns later we arrive at our pretty hotel, surrounded by vines, spectacular views, a bell tower and a gurgling fountain. Our room is decorated with the colours of Provence and has views on three sides: one overlooking the town below, one looking out onto the small square with the fountain, and one facing the *beffroi*, or bell tower. Just like on page 219. We look out over the Ouvèze river valley with its Roman bridge, the tree-lined streets of the modern town, and the splendour of the hills that surround Vaison.

At the reception desk I learn that *"Sauf Riverains"* means "except residents," but the cars of hotel guests are allowed. Relieved that we're not breaking the law, we leave the car at the hotel and explore the *haut ville* on foot, walking the maze of narrow cobblestone streets that wind up to the base of the *château*, the abandoned stronghold that once dominated the area.

I feel at home immediately and, almost as quickly, the California wine country becomes only a pleasant memory. We spend days motoring across the gorgeous landscape, just when the grape leaves are bursting forth from the vines; big, verdant, covering the countryside. I am enchanted by the number of hilltop villages dotting the landscape, each within hiking distance of another; the outdoor markets once or twice a week in every village; the plane trees on the *places*; the Provençal light. I easily adopt the relaxed pace of life, *la vie provençale*.

I am discovering a new world, a new type of life. But just as I'm becoming familiar with the region, its towns and specialties, it ends. It is time to go home. But I know I will be back. And as soon as we are home I begin to plan our next trip: our first Christmas in Provence.

Foie Gras Sliders
YES, YOU READ IT CORRECTLY!

I could eat an entire meal made of *amuses bouches* (literally "mouth amusements"). Come to think of it, I've done exactly that on more than one occasion! This little starter has a way of waking up your appetite, preparing you for the meal to come. Here, *foie gras* is treated like a slider or as they say in France, *le 'amburger.*

1 *pâte a choux* per person (see separate recipe)

3 ounces thawed slices of *foie gras* (I buy mine from our local fine food store)

1 T extra-virgin olive oil

Fleur de Sel
    sprig of fresh parsley

Cut each *pâte a choux* in half like you would a hamburger bun and set aside.

Dry the *foie gras* slices by gently patting with a paper towel.

In a small skillet, heat the oil until it's sizzling. Add the *foie gras* slices and fry on each side for about thirty seconds depending on the thickness. Remove from the heat.

Slice the *foie gras* on a diagonal and place a slice of the cooked *foie gras* inside one half of the *pâte a choux* and add a sprig of fresh parsley on top with a few grains of *Fleur de Sel.*

Place the other half of the *pâte a choux* on top and serve immediately. Serves 4 as an appetizer and two as a main course.

Pâte à Choux
PUFF PASTRY

This basic recipe can be used in so many delicious ways: in profiteroles or as the "hamburger buns" in tiny *foie gras* sliders as well as for *éclairs*. Or, add a cup of grated *gruyère* to the recipe and you've got *gougères*, glorious cheese puffs.

1 egg yolk, beaten
½ cup water
¼ cup butter
½ tsp sea salt (only if the butter is unsalted)
½ cup unbleached flour
2 eggs

Preheat oven to 400° F.

In small bowl, beat the egg yolk and set aside.

In a medium heavy saucepan, mix the water, butter and salt and bring to a boil.

Remove the pan from the heat and add spoonfuls of flour, mixing until all the flour is incorporated. After the flour is completely blended, return the pan to medium heat. Stir constantly until the mixture becomes sticky and pulls away from the sides of the pan, about two to three minutes.

Remove from the heat, cool for a minute, and then stir in the eggs, one at a time, completely mixing before adding the second, beating vigorously. The dough is now ready to be baked. Using a teaspoon or tablespoon, depending on the size you want, spoon the pastry onto a prepared baking sheet.

Just before baking, brush the tops with the beaten egg yolk to give them a glossy appearance. Set the baking sheet on the middle rack, reduce the heat to 375° F. and bake for 20 minutes or until they have puffed and are firm and golden brown.

Remove from the oven but do not remove them from the tray. Using a small knife, cut a slit in the side of each puff to release the steam, (otherwise they will become soggy). Turn off the oven and open the door. Return the pastries to the oven, (with the door open) and leave them for another ten minutes to dry out. Cool on a rack.

THE FIRST NOËL

"*Braang.*" French phones sound different. "*Braang.*" Like cats jumping to dig their claws into the ceiling. The golden glow in our hotel room is the first sign that it is not 8 o'clock. Madame, our charming concierge, is on the phone asking when we are going to leave because, after all, check-out time *was* noon.

We have missed our train.

Yesterday, we arrived in Paris, ready for Christmas dinner at our favourite restaurant, *La Régalade*. We dropped our bags at the hotel, jumped on the Metro, ordered up two *coupes de Champagne*, and celebrated the fact that we were back in France only six months after our last trip.

La Régalade was founded by Yves Chamborde, one of a new generation of independent-minded French chefs. Housed in an unlikely location far out in the 14th Arrondissement, next door to a 24-hour Laundromat, it became one of the hottest addresses in Paris. In June we had eaten our last Parisian meal there, and we immediately became Chamborde devotees. Now we couldn't wait for one of the best Christmas presents ever: dinner at *La Régalade*.

We knew we were at the right place when the communal *amuse bouche* was plunked on our table. A heavy ceramic pot, the size of a cookie jar, filled with *pâté campagne*, served with *cornichons* (bite-sized homemade pickle) and what I swore was the best whole grain bread I've ever had.

Nine o'clock and the place was hopping. We ordered a lively bottle of *Côtes du Rhône* from *Domaine Gramenon*, with notes of pepper and blackberry. Then the fun began. *Calamares en beignet*: crisp, tender calamari served on a bed of black ink risotto. Fresh oysters on ice with hot, small pork sausages. Marinated tuna, sliced in a round, served on a few pieces of phyllo with *asperges têtes noires*. *St. Jacques à la coque, endives meunières à l'orange*: large, fat, grilled scallops served with grilled endive in a sea foam sauce with a touch of orange.

The meal finished with two of *La Regalade's* signature desserts: *pot de crème vanille avec langues de chat,* tiny pots of chilled custard with sugar cookies or "cat's tongues"; and *riz au lait au caramel,* caramel rice pudding in a giant black cauldron with a wooden spoon for serving, accompanied by little jars of marmalade. This was a meal worth travelling seven thousand kilometres for.

It was midnight by the time we slurped up the last of the wine and caught the Metro back to our hotel in the 6th Arrondissement. Our concierge met us at the door, hair effortlessly piled on top of her head, perfect makeup, and a simple outfit that whispered French chic. She greeted us like old friends, wished us *Joyeux Noël* and sent us to the best room in the hotel, *chambre 36,* decorated in salmon tones, with dark antique dressers, a lovely white tiled bathroom, and, most importantly, serenity.

We had been travelling for nineteen hours, been awake for thirty hours, and had just finished a three-hour meal. However, our train didn't leave Gare de Lyon until 11:24, and we imagined ourselves waking up early, having a leisurely *café crème* and heading over to the train station. We couldn't wait to get to Provence.

༄

"Braang." Madame takes control as we stumble into the lobby fifteen minutes after her call. Setting her priorities, she first orders strong coffee and croissants for us. Then she is on the phone: to the train station to rearrange our travel, to a taxi to get us to the Gare de Lyon, to the car rental company in Orange to change our pick-up time, to restaurant *Le Brin d'Olivier* in Vaison-la-Romaine to reschedule our dinner reservation.

She bustles us out of the hotel to get us to station in time to catch our new train. Arriving at Gare de Lyon, I go to the ticket booth to pick up our new reservations.

I hear the agent say something that sounded like "four" and *"francs".* Taking a good guess, I hand him two twenty-franc notes. The agent gives me a look and hands back one of the twenties plus sixteen francs in change. It costs only four francs to change our reservation, less than a dollar. Ahh, France.

⌒

"Bonnes Fêtes"

These are the first words I see on our first Christmas in Provence. Spelled in fat rose-coloured bulbs across the top of the gate to the château in the village of Camaret-sur-Aigues.

After our concierge got us to Gare de Lyon things went smoothly. The TGV left Paris exactly on time; two hours and sixteen minutes later we arrived in Valence, where we transferred to the local train heading south to Orange. This time our rental car was waiting for us and now, a few minutes later, we are speeding through the Provençal night.

We have only driven these roads in daylight, but now the sky is dark; the road, if anything, is darker. Suddenly, one more curve brings us into the welcoming light of Camaret and its holiday message.

"Joyeux Noël" a second sign greets us as we turn the corner into the village. I feel as if I am coming home.

We pass through the village and leave the lights of Camaret-sur-Aigues behind as we drive back into the darkness, on the way to our town of Vaison-la-Romaine.

⌒

This was the beginning of our lasting love affair with France. It was just Mark and me, but friends and family would soon join us, summer, winter, spring and fall, in Paris and Provence, to share our obsession. As we returned year after year we discovered a place broader and deeper than monuments and museums: the country, the people, the food, the *joie de vivre*.

The adventure began with our first Christmas in Provence, but it got even better. We didn't know that in just a few years we'd have our son, Alexandre, to share it with us.

NOËL EN PROVENCE

Every town and village in Provence lights up the December nights with signs proclaiming *Joyeux Noël* and *Bonnes Fêtes*. But, in the French way, there are rules. *Les Provençaux* begin hanging their lights in late November, but, keeping with tradition, the decorations remain unlit until December 4, when the season officially kicks off with the feast of *St Barbe*.

La Saison des Fêtes is all about the food; the festivities carry on with special meals on Christmas Eve, Christmas Day and New Year's Eve (*La Réveillon de la Saint Sylvestre*). It's the time of year where *foie gras*, Champagne, and roast duck are part of many celebratory meals. At our favourite bakery in Vaison, in the days running up to Christmas, the tables groan with mounds of special orders.

All through December people prepare for the celebrations. Annual *Marchés de Noël* are held in many towns and villages on the town plazas, where you can buy local and seasonal arts-and-crafts, often from stalls built to look like log cabins or mangers.

The height of the celebration begins on Christmas Eve with the *Gros Souper,* the Big Supper. Despite its name, the *Gros Souper* is today a simple meal of several meatless dishes. The meal ends with the well-known *treize desserts*, the Thirteen Desserts of Provence: a combination of dried fruits, nuts, candied fruit, nougat and *calisson*, a marzipan candy from Aix-en-Provence.

A celebration of the season centering on food, family, and friends is a satisfying way to end a year. And, in Provence, it's a moment of pure pleasure to drive out of the total darkness of the countryside into the welcoming Noël lights of a small village.

Oysters: *Pourquoi pas?*

During our very first Christmas in France we learned to love platters of fresh oysters, cracked open and served on a bed of ice with seaweed garnish, slurped down with a crisp *Sancerre*. French oysters simply taste better.

The French eat their way through about 130,000 metric tons of fresh oysters every year, and about half of that is consumed during the *Saison des Fêtes*. Oysters are as traditional to the French at *Noël* as turkey is to us.

At the wine cooperative at Beaumes-de-Venise we read a poster with a picture of oysters piled up to look like a Christmas tree, and the slogan, *"Noël sans Huîtres? Pourquoi pas sans arbre, pendant que vous y êtes!"*

It took us days and a serendipitous phrase in a dictionary to translate it as: *"Christmas without Oysters? Why not without a tree, while you're at it?"*

Chèvre et Tomates Séchées
PROVENÇAL GOAT CHEESE DIP

When I am in Provence my kitchen becomes filled with my favourite ingredients, including goat cheese, Nyonsais olives and *Herbes de Provence*. This delicious appetizer makes the most of the small jet-black olives from Nyons, but you can use another type of black Provençal olive.

2 garlic cloves, minced

½ cup fresh basil

½ cup black olives from Provence

½ cup sun-dried tomatoes in olive oil

1 tsp *Herbes de Provence*

2 T extra-virgin olive oil

8 ounces soft goat cheese log

Preheat oven to 350° F.

Mince the garlic cloves and tear the basil leaves into small pieces. Set aside in a small bowl.

Prepare the olives by squashing them with the side of a broad knife to remove the pits, then chop. Drain the oil from the sun-dried tomatoes and chop into chunky pieces. Set aside.

In a small skillet, heat one tablespoon of the olive oil at low and sauté the garlic at a low temperature. Stir in the *Herbes de Provence*. Do not let the garlic brown, but look for a light golden colour. Remove from the heat and let the mixture cool for about ten minutes.

In a small bowl, gently mix together the basil, sun-dried tomatoes and cooked garlic. Let this mixture rest for 15 minutes at room temperature to allow the flavours to blend.

In a small, shallow ceramic baking dish, spread the goat cheese about 1-inch thick. Pour the herb mixture over the goat cheese and spread evenly. Sprinkle with the chopped black olives.

Bake for less than ten minutes. The dip should be just warm, be careful not to over-bake or it will become too soft and the cheese will melt.

Just before serving drizzle with the remaining one tablespoon of extra-virgin olive oil. Serve with baguette slices. Serves 4 to 6.

Soupe aux Lentilles, Croûtons Maison & Crème Fraîche
FRENCH LENTIL SOUP WITH HOMEMADE CROUTONS & *CRÈME FRAÎCHE*

Dark olive in colour, firm textured and tiny, *lentilles du Puy* (or French lentils) turn any lentil recipe into a sophisticated dish. With just minutes to put together, this soup will be on the simmer and with a few added touches, like the fresh croutons, *crème fraîche* and dill, it is elevated to a stunning first course or main meal. Be sure to add the sherry vinegar before serving. It instantly livens the flavours of the soup.

1 T extra-virgin olive oil
2 T butter
1 potato, 1/4" dice
1 carrot, 1/4" dice
2 celery stalks, 1/4" dice
2 cloves garlic cloves, chopped
1 yellow onion, chopped fine
1 cup French lentils (*lentilles de Puy*)
8 cups water or chicken stock
½ tsp sea salt
freshly ground black pepper
1 T dill, dried
1 T fennel seeds
2 T sherry or red wine vinegar
fresh croutons (see separate recipe)
2 T fresh dill, finely chopped

Rinse the lentils in water and prepare the vegetables.

In a soup pot, sauté the vegetables in the melted butter and oil until soft. Add the lentils, stock, salt, pepper and herbs and simmer partially covered for 30 minutes. Add extra water if the soup is too thick. Adjust the seasoning by adding salt, pepper and the vinegar to brighten the flavours.

I like to use a hand blender to pulse a few times, leaving a smoother texture. If you don't have a hand blender take a few cups of the soup and process in a blender or food processor.

To serve, add a small handful of croutons to the bottom of a soup bowl. Pour over the hot soup. Add a dollop of *crème fraîche* to the top and a sprinkle of freshly chopped dill.

HOMEMADE CROUTONS

3 ounces baguette or bread

2 garlic cloves, minced

1 or 2 T extra-virgin olive oil

Cut the baguette or bread into small cubes.

In a heavy bottom skillet, heat the olive oil and sauté the minced garlic for about thirty seconds, until the garlic is golden brown.

Add the cubed bread and sizzle until golden brown. It's important to keep stirring the croutons so they brown evenly but do not burn. Remove from heat, drain on paper towels and serve immediately.

THE BEST CHEESE EVER

"**T**his is *cheese!*" he proclaims. "We don't have cheese." He says it in the way you might say our entire culture is a failure.

It's the night before New Year's Eve in the candlelit dining room of *L'Auberge de la Bartavelle* on the Place de Sus Auze in Vaison-la-Romaine. Mark is making a point to our new best friends, Tom and Jos, whom we have known for 48 hours.

"This is cheese," he says again with less force, as if he has indisputably made his point.

I knew what he means. Coming from the Prairies I have never been exposed to the variety and creaminess found on the cheese cart in this small restaurant in Vaison. "This is the best cheese ever!" I say in turn. Tom, the quintessential low-key Brit, is amused by our enthusiasm for the cheese course. "The best *ever?*" he asks with humour.

"*Ever*", I repeat.

It's day four of our first Christmas in Provence and we're revelling in a five-course dinner at our new favourite restaurant. Although Tom and Jos have been coming to Vaison-la-Romaine for nearly ten years, they've never dined here before. I noticed the restaurant on our first night in town: the ochre-coloured exterior with its big windows and the peachy-rose walls, crisp white tablecloths and candlelight. Mark noticed the Marcel Pagnol inspired *carte*, with menus named after characters from Pagnol's memoir of his childhood, *My Father's Glory*. One could choose from the *Oncle Jules* menu, or the *Augustine*, or the *Tante Rose* menu. Even the name of restaurant is from the book. *Bartavelle* is a game bird famous in Provence: *Le Roi des Gibiers*, "the king of game" as Uncle Jules calls it.

We are covering a lot of new culinary territory in this meal. I learn that the only civilized aperitif is *une coupe du Champagne*. Here the *coupe* is generous and decorated with a plump gooseberry dangling off the side. Thousands of fine bubbles rise from the bottom of our glasses and reflect the warm colours of the room.

I start with *escargots*: plump snails in a garlic and butter sauce. Jos shows Mark how to dig out the chewy meat from a myriad of tiny shellfish, with tools ranging from a miniature fork to a large pin. They each have ordered the *méli-mélo* seafood platter with fresh oysters, mussels, snails, and cockles on a large tray with ice and tangled seaweed. Tom's *coquille St Jacques* salad has the red foot attached, which is common in France to assure the diner that the scallop is genuine and not a cut piece of cod. His scallops are grilled and laid over a handful of greens.

Next, to tide us over until the main course, a tiny serving of *oeufs brouillés*: fluffy scrambled eggs served in an eggshell with slivers of truffle.

My lobster stew is creamy and served in the shell. The luscious chunks of fresh lobster meat are lightly flavoured with fennel. *Confit de canard*, crispy and smoky, is Mark's choice, the beginning of what will be a lifelong affair with things *canard*. Tom's knowledge of *Côtes-du-Rhône* wines from the restaurant's list is impressive; the table fills with bottles from Vacqueyras and Gigondas, wine villages we've visited during the last three days. I had no idea the Brits could handle so much wine with their dinner! After the main course, a small refreshing *sorbet du marc*, the strong local spirit, cleanses the palate.

With a rumbling of wheels on tiles, the imposing cheese trolley is rolled to our table. We have eaten, talked and laughed for nearly four hours and we have yet to eat the cheese course. I have never seen this many cheeses, all ripe and luscious, on one tray and don't have a clue where to start. But our server, the owner of *La Bartavelle*, recommends cheeses to me, including the Roquefort. As I bite into it, I taste the entire culinary history of France. It *is* the best cheese ever!

૭૦૭

Only two nights ago Mark and I sat in the pizza place in the *haut ville* of Vaison-la-Romaine. Over a thin crust *quatre saison* pizza we talked about how we *had* to spend more time in Provence and wondered how we were going to do it. During the meal my eye was drawn to the only other English-speaking couple in the room. "Quit staring!" Mark whispered.

"They are *so* British." I watched as the ruddy-complexioned man played with the salt and pepper shaker while his blond companion ate her salad. The rest of the restaurant was filled with dark *Provençaux*.

As the British couple rose to leave, the man stopped and asked us, "So, how do you like Vaison?"

"We like it," I proudly answered, "In fact, this is our second visit in six months." I was feeling quite worldly.

"Oh, we've an apartment here, just up the hill", he said nonchalantly. That was it; clearly these were people we needed to get to know.

"Can we buy you a glass of wine and talk about the area?" I boldly asked.

A bottle of red later, we had set a date to meet at the market in the morning, have lunch at their apartment, and then set out on a tour of their favourite wineries.

⁓

A matchmaker could not have done better. The four of us share a distinct sense of humour, a love of France, and an appreciation of food and wine. Tom and Jos have owned an apartment in Vaison for almost a decade and make the trip from The Cotswolds every chance they get.

Tom describes himself as "Britain's oldest schoolboy", still working on his PhD dissertation in urban studies at an age when some men are contemplating retirement. He is big and tall with a great sense of humour. When he's serious he adopts a professorial tone, but he loves telling funny stories and holding court, laughing in anticipation of his own jokes.

Jos is an inspector of schools. Although she's the more serious of the two, the rebellious streak from her youth still shows through: she travelled solo in Europe, taught at international schools and even followed a boyfriend to Saskatchewan. Petite and precise, she loves long walks, whether at their home in The Cotswolds or in the high country behind Vaison.

⁓

I am up early and walk around the streets and *places*, watching the vendors arrive and set up stalls. Tuesday is market day in Vaison-la-Romaine and has been so since the 15th century. I've been waiting to see the famous Vaison market since our visit in June, when we arrived on a Wednesday and left on a Monday. This will be my first market.

The entire central part of the town is closed to traffic at 6:30, but it isn't until 9:00 that the market really gets going. We meet up with Tom and Jos as planned. It is strange and wonderful to run into friends at a market in France. We exchange the three air kisses of Provence and stroll the streets of Vaison, now filled with the booths of a wondrous variety of vendors: vegetables, fish wagons, piles of coarse country sausages, freshly cut flowers, hardware booths, the sewing machine vendor, Provençal fabrics and linens, the honey merchant, the boisterous cheese seller, spices displayed in small burlap bags, clothing, shoes, knives, and giant skillets filled with paella. Tom leads us to the rotisserie chicken vendor's stall, where there are two large ovens roaring, each with thirty chickens sizzling, rotating and dripping fat onto the crisp potatoes cooking in the bottom tray.

"*Un poulet rôti s'il vous plaît,*" Tom says with confidence, or at least something very near that. The vendor shrugs and shakes his head and says something in French, with lots of hand gestures. A lengthy explanation by a chicken roaster is beyond us. Just then Jos steps in and speaks with the chicken man, using her excellent French. "*Ah, oui, monsieur,*" she says. "*Je comprends bien.*" She motions us to walk with her.

"The gentlemen was explaining that it is necessary to reserve a chicken. You can't expect to just walk up and buy one. Tsk, tsk."

But, we're in a land of food, and there are a lot of vendors to choose from in the market. Soon, laden with our purchases – olives, cheese, bread, sausage, wine, but chickenless – we follow Tom and Jos up the hill to their small apartment in the *haute ville*.

As we cross over the first-century stone bridge, built by the Romans, the depth of the history of the place strikes me. People have lived in this beautiful valley forever; our "discovery" of it is only made possible by a thousand generations of those who live here and built here. On the slopes of the hill above the river, looking down on the bridge, we walk on narrow cobblestone streets, past houses and monasteries built at a time when the heights were the only safe place to live and stone was the only building material available. Our friends' apartment is in a new building, designed to fit the style of the medieval village, perched on the very edge of the rock that once protected Vaison. We eat lunch overlooking the river Ouvèze while Tom maps out the wineries we will visit in the afternoon.

∽

The road to Crestet clings to the side of the mountain, curving all the way. The curves don't stop at the top, either. The narrow road twists back on itself and we turn first right then left through the *Dentelles de Montmirail*. Tom suddenly comes to a stop and asks, "Are you all right, Diane?" He must have seen my green face in the rear-view mirror. I thought I could tough out a lifetime of motion sickness but I am close to losing my *fromage*. Once I swap seats with Mark and sit in the front I feel better and can enjoy the magnificent place we're driving through.

Tom takes us over the top of the *Dentelles* at the scenic village of Suzette population 150, where we stop to take in the 360-degree view. We're in the original Jurassic park, for that's when the limestone layers that make up the *Dentelles de Montmirail* were formed then thrown upright towards the sky, where the now-horizontal peaks were left to the ravaging of wind and rain to become the dramatic jagged ridge that I'm looking at now. *Dentelle* means "lace", the closest comparison the people who named this ridge could think of, although to me they look more like the spine of a monstrous dragon skeleton.

We drive down the other side of the *Dentelles* to the wineries that will become our favourites. At *Château de Montmirail*, in the village of Vacqueyras, Tom and Jos are treated like friends. The winemaker speaks to Jos with both respect and humour. "Here I want you to try this" and "this one is special" as the two of them sip and gossip in French. I watch with jealousy as Tom loads up the boot of his car with cases of *Montmirail* to take home to their apartment in Vaison and to their cottage in The Cotswolds.

But the best is still to come, and it is the last winery of the day that captures my heart. We drive to the village of Beaumes-de-Venise and take another small road that rises above the village until it breaks through to high, rolling countryside. Jos cries out in excitement, "Look, isn't this the most fabulous view in the world?" as we ride along the ridge that divides two valleys. "It's my dream to live here. I never tire of this view."

It's exhilarating to be right up among the jagged limestone outcrops of the ridge. Tom stops the gold Volkswagen in the middle of road, right on the great divide. We take in the incredible scene. In all directions are vineyards, rolling hills, patched fields, the distant Rhône River; even in winter, all tinged with green.

Finally we arrive at *Domaine de Durban*, where, Tom tells us, his favourite sweet *muscat* is produced. From the terrace of the winery we look over the stunning panorama of the *Dentelles* and the valleys below before going inside.

In the tasting room a young woman, dressed in a simple cashmere sweater, greets us and begins setting out glasses for a tasting. Then, through the door that connects the tasting room to the owners' residence, the Madame emerges.

"Ah, comment ça va, Madame Gill?" It seems everywhere we go Jos is treated as a special guest. Madame takes over the pouring. "Please you must try last year's vintage of the *blanc*. It has delicate notes, and will be superb with fish."

After the white vintages we sample a couple of reds before we come to the grand finale: the *Muscat de Beaumes-de-Venise*. Tom looks at the bottle and grins. "Ah, yes, Monsieur," says Madame, "this is perhaps the best muscat I have made here. You will be pleased."

The wine has a colour lighter than honey, and a bouquet of fresh fruits and limestone. I breathe it in and hold my breath. The aroma of the wine in this quiet, reverent tasting room hints at what Provence has to offer. What, I think, could be better than this moment?

We buy the two bottles we'll be allowed to carry home on the flight while Tom fills the last spaces of his car. The visit to *Durban* has affected me in an unexpected way, some sort of transformation has taken place. This, then, is how life can be lived. Perhaps even how life should be lived.

This beautiful, delicious wine will become an important part of our lives when, two years later, Mark and I and all of our guests will toast our wedding vows with a glass of *Muscat de Beaumes-de-Venise* from *Domaine de Durban.*

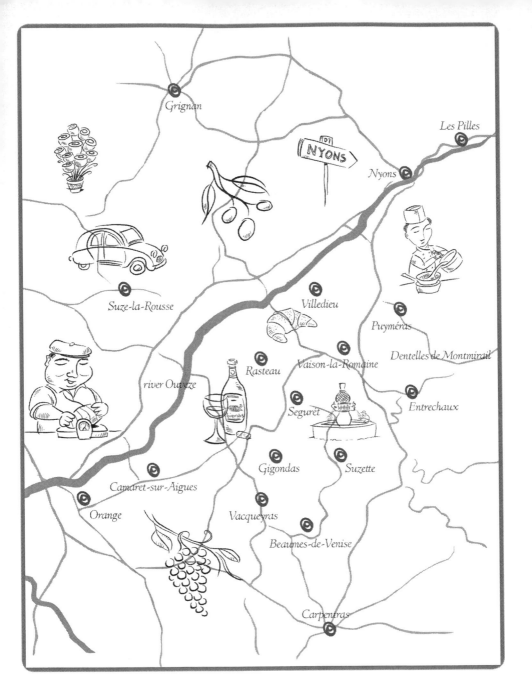

THE VOCONCES

Provence is used to describe a large area of southern France, from the Mediterranean of Nice and Marseilles to as far north as Valence.

My Provence, however, is a much smaller area. Draw a circle around the Dentelles de Montmirail encompassing Beaumes-de-Venise to the south, Rasteau to the west, Entrechaux in the east, and Vaison-la-Romaine to the north. Then add another large circle with Vaison in the south, Les Pilles in the northeast, and Grignan in the northwest.

These may just be names on a map to many people, but to me these circles represent my Provence: olive groves, wineries, mediaeval villages, abandoned châteaux, winding roads, spectacular views.

The area is called *Les Voconces*, after the Celtic people who made Vaison their capital at the end of the fourth century BC. These people, the *Vocontii*, were conquered by the Romans in about 120 BC, but retained a certain amount of authority under Roman rule.

There are other beautiful areas of Provence: Arles, St Remy, Nice, the Luberon, Avignon, Orange. But for me, the Voconces is the essence of Provence.

THE LIGHT OF PROVENCE

It's the light that first got to me, as it got to Cézanne, Matisse, Van Gogh. The sun coats everything it touches in colours of gold, red, green and yellow. The sun conspires with grape vines and plane trees and jagged limestone rocks to create fantastical shadow pictures.

The winter light in Provence is even more captivating than the summer light. The low sun shining through mist, trees, and vines; stretching along stone walls and streets; illuminating ancient buildings, casts a spell over the region. The beauty is especially pronounced on the days around the winter solstice, when Provence shows off the amazing special-effect of layered hills stretching into the distance.

Poulet Braisé à l'Ail
BRAISED GARLIC CHICKEN

This recipe uses braising to make a delicious French-inspired dish, for a true bistro special, serve it with creamy polenta.

Braising (from the French *braiser*) is a combination cooking method using both moist and dry heat. First the meat (or vegetable) is seared at a high temperature and then finished in a covered pot with liquid until it thickens. Think *Coq au Vin*.

1 whole chicken breast
6 garlic cloves
2 T extra-virgin olive oil
1 T butter
½ tsp dried thyme or *Herbes de Provence*
½ cup white wine
1 cup chicken stock
2 small hot peppers
1 medium yellow onion, sliced thinly

Remove the chicken skin and bones and cut the meat into pieces. Peel the garlic cloves and trim off root ends.

In a 4-qt chef's pan or heavy skillet with a cover (set aside the cover for now), cook the garlic cloves in a little butter and olive oil until they just start to brown. Remove them from the pan.

At a medium-high heat, in the same pan, sear the chicken pieces on all sides, adding the thyme or *Herbes de Provence*.

Return the cooked garlic to the pan, add ½ cup white wine, ½ cup of the chicken stock, the hot peppers and the sliced onions. If you are serving this with *Creamy Polenta with Ham*, add any ham trimmings to the pan as well.

Now braise the mixture: cook covered until the liquid thickens and the chicken is done, about 25 minutes. Check frequently and add extra chicken stock as needed, don't let the mixture dry out. At the end, remove the ham trimmings and the hot peppers.

Spoon some of the polenta onto warmed plates and place some chicken pieces alongside. Spoon the cooked juice and onions onto the polenta. Serves 2 to 4.

Polenta Crémeuse au Jambon
CREAMY POLENTA WITH HAM

This is another one to add to your essentials list. Despite its reputation, polenta is not hard to make or particularly time-consuming, this one is done in an half hour, start to finish. A great side dish, it goes particularly well with *Braised Garlic Chicken* or *Duck Magret with Cherry Sauce*.

1½ cups ham

1 T extra-virgin olive oil

1 small yellow onion

2 cups chicken stock

1 cup polenta

½ cup *Parmigiano-Reggiano, Ossau-Iraty*, or your favourite cheese

Peel and chop the onion and dice the ham.

In a heavy pot cook the diced ham in olive oil. As it browns add the chopped onion. Sauté until onions are "toothy" but not browned.

Add 5 cups of liquid to the pot. It can be all water or a mixture of water and chicken stock. When the water starts to boil, whisk in the polenta. Cook 20 to 25 minutes, stirring frequently. Don't let the polenta stick. A heavy whisk works well, or a wooden spoon. I like to put a lid, slightly ajar, on the pot when I'm not stirring it.

Grate the parmesan. If you're using an optional diced cheese, cut it up now. When done, stir in the cheeses and serve hot.

O.N.F.
Suzette 2,6km
Crestet 6,2km
Séguret 9,7km
Vaison 10km

D 7
NYONS

SEARCHING FOR FRANÇOISE AND LAURENT

"*Bonjour, Madame*," I say to the 78-year-old pump jockey. *"J'ai besoin de pétrole."* She is wearing slippers and a headscarf and has emerged from the gas station no more than seven or eight minutes after we parked at the pump. She shuffles over and begins to fill the tank of our Ford Ka. Mark whispers to me, "If anyone knows, it's her."

We're running on empty after spending the day searching for Françoise and Laurent. We know they live near Puyméras and we've spent hours scouring the landscape in all directions from that point. Now we are back in Puyméras, at the gas station, the only fueling stop in the area.

∾

We met Françoise and Laurent on our previous trip to Provence. It was a warm evening in June and our last night in Vaison-la-Romaine before leaving the next morning for Italy. We were dining at *Le Clos Saint-Germain* on Cours Taulignan. Mark and I shared a *Niçoise* salad, very good with a herbaceous olive oil. I ordered a pasta *pistou*, delicious and light on sauce, while Mark had sea bass with eggplant ratatouille. For some reason, I remember that were drinking a *Domaine Saint Claude Côtes-du-Rhône*, 1995.

But even more memorable was the scene taking place at the table next to us. It seemed a mismatched foursome, speaking a combination of fractured English and French. One woman was speaking the most amazing, Texas-accented French I've ever heard; her companion was clearly British. There was an older woman speaking a form of English in what I assumed was a German accent. There was also an elderly man with beautiful white hair who said hardly anything. I thought there were four strangers thrown together in a tour group and sharing an uncomfortable evening.

"J'adore fromage! I love cheese! It's so good. I love French cheese. English cheese is good too. Sometimes it is orange." Here was a classic, awkward conversational French course played out in real life.

Mark and I took a pause before dessert and stepped outside for a breath of fresh air. By then it was ten o'clock and the foursome passed us as they left the restaurant. I couldn't help myself, I said to the Texan, "Tough work, huh?"

She laughed. "We're used to it. We've been friends for a long time. Ten years now." Her British companion nodded agreement. So much for my insightful observation about strangers thrown together!

We exchanged introductions. Jean and Paul lived in Greenville, South Carolina; she was originally from Texas, Paul from England. Their friends were Françoise and Laurent, longtime residents of Provence.

Françoise smiled and said, "You are English, our friends are English, you must come for coffee." I thanked her and explained that, while we were leaving the next morning at 5:00, we'd love to visit her on our next...

"Now," she said. "You must come to my house *now.*"

So we paid our bill, left our dessert, and a few minutes later found ourselves navigating the dark Provençal roads toward Puyméras, a nearby village. On the drive I learned about their amazing tale and how this unlikely foursome ended up together tonight.

Françoise and Laurent were in their mid-70s with ten grown children and a multitude of grandchildren. A decade earlier one of their daughters was living in Greenville, where their grandson had been diagnosed with leukemia. So Françoise and Laurent flew to South Carolina for an extended stay to help their daughter and her family.

Jean told me this during the speedy drive through curves and darkness, which ended at the country home of Françoise and Laurent. Within minutes, Françoise had hot black coffee served in tiny cups for us. "I love coffee at night," she declared. "It does not keep me awake, but it must be Arabica!"

Jean continued their story while Françoise got out a scrapbook of newspaper clippings showing her teaching a group of Carolina church ladies how to bake baguettes. Other clippings featured photographs of Laurent playing with his grandson in a local park. It seemed that wherever this outgoing couple went they met new people and developed lasting friendships, including Greenville locals Jean and Paul.

In the ten years since, Jean and Paul had spent each summer in Provence with Françoise and Laurent. For ten years, they had endured difficult dinner conversations and awkward translations, but it all made sense when you spent a few minutes with this special couple. Unlike the French stereotype, there was no reserve; Françoise's blue eyes simply sparkled.

Laurent's family had lived in Puyméras for centuries, and he had been born there. As was common after World War II, Laurent moved to Paris for work, where they raised their large family. Each summer, the family would return to the small estate in Puyméras and would renovate and add new rooms to accommodate the growing number of children. When Laurent retired they moved to Puyméras full time.

He gave us a tour of the house. It seemed modest from the outside but he led us through what felt like endless bedrooms, two indoor kitchens, an outdoor kitchen and a hidden room that you could get to only via a secret exterior stairway. Once the children had grown, Françoise and Laurent moved into a new wing of the house with bedroom, bathroom, kitchen, and salon.

In another scrapbook Françoise showed us family pictures, including one of their extended family at their 50th wedding anniversary. With all ten children, grandchildren and spouses, it looked like the graduating class at a junior college.

She told us the story of when they met. She was sixteen years old, beautiful, robust, like a country milkmaid. She still talked about that time with stars in her eyes. Francoise's and Laurent's devotion to each other was unmistakable. She was very proud of Laurent, often pointing out how handsome and spry he was: "He's so healthy, he still walks five kilometers a day!" We saw pictures from a recent trip to Vietnam to visit their son, who was an airline pilot based in Hanoi. There they were in a canoe, with Laurent paddling them down the river.

By the end of our visit they had given us a card with their name and phone number and invited us to come and stay with them on our next trip.

Paul took us outside for a tour of the grounds. "Laurent has the best view in Provence," he said, gesturing toward the dark silhouette of Mont

Ventoux, the second highest peak in France. Within a few months, Paul and Jean would themselves buy a run-down house in the nearby town of Nyons.

Long past midnight, we bade our farewell. We had to find our way back to our hotel, pack and be on a morning train to Milan.

∞

Now, six months later we've decided to pay a surprise visit to Françoise and Laurent. The trouble is we only have a vague idea where they live, having only been there in the dark with someone else driving. Worse yet, we don't have the card Françoise had given us, and we don't even remember their last name!

We set out in the morning from our base in the *haute ville* of Vaison-la-Romaine. How hard can it be? We're pretty sure we passed through the village of Puyméras on our last visit, so we start there. The road on the other side of Puyméras splits and we take the fork that winds around a small hill, where it splits again. We stay right and pass through vineyards. On this winter day the leaves are long gone, but branches haven't yet been trimmed and a golden-orange sea covers the hills around us. In the distance ahead there is a cone-shaped hill with buildings on top. We head toward it.

We aim our car up hills on narrow roads that drop off sharply to one side. It's full-attention driving; one lapse and the farmers will be harvesting us next season. Near the top of the cone we come upon a sign advising us that the access to the village is for residents only. We drive on past a single tower perched on a mound that overlooks acres of golden vines.

Up here the wind is strong. An older couple walking along the road leans sideways into the gusts. We see nothing we recognize, and no clues leading us to our friends. Our little car is buffeted in the wind, so we head downhill and try other roads. Finally, after driving around for hours, we spot a gas station near Puyméras . We haven't found our friends, but we have seen some beautiful countryside and breathtaking scenes.

At the gas station Mark coaxes me, "We have to ask somebody for directions. I'm sure this woman will know where Françoise and Laurent live. Go ahead, ask her."

While I look through the dictionary preparing my question, Mark pays for the gas. The woman says to him, "Something, something *francs, s'il vous plaît.*" Now, in his defense, I have to say that the gas pump is ancient and the display is hard to read. He glances at the amount on the pump, reaches in his wallet and hands her a twenty-franc note, saying, effectively, "Here you are, my good woman."

She blinks at the note a couple of times, then gestures toward the gas pump. Finally Mark understands. The gas costs not twenty francs but two hundred francs. Sheepishly he finds the right amount and hands it over.

I call up my Canadian high school French *"Excusez-moi, Madame. Je cherche mes amis Françoise et Laurent,"* is about all I can manage. I keep thinking, if they are our friends wouldn't we know where they live? Or at least their last name!

By now the poor woman thinks we are complete idiots. She blinks again, takes a breath and says, very s-l-o-w-l-y in French. "You see, in France, people have a first name, and they have a last name. Laurent's last name is Janvier. Françoise also has a last name, and it, too, is Janvier."

Then she begins to pick up speed as gives me driving directions for about two non-stop minutes. I listen, nodding my head. I listen some more, and then thank her very much for her kind help.

I jump in the car and Mark asks, "What did she say?"

"Something about a tree," I reply.

OUR TOWN IN PROVENCE

Vaison-la-Romaine is a real working town where locals shop, eat and live; a town with history: Roman, medieval and modern.

In the early years of the first millennium Vaison was an important Roman centre, *Vasio Vocontiorum*, with around 10,000 inhabitants. Remains of Roman structures can still be found there: the oldest extant Roman stone bridge, the excavated Roman streets and houses, and a large outdoor amphitheatre still used for events and concerts.

Although in centuries past the medieval town, built on the hill that dominates, and once protected, Vaison, was the centre of town life, today the *haut ville* is mostly homes carved out of the original stone buildings, with a few scattered galleries and craft shops, and a small weekly market on Sundays in the summer.

In the valley on the north side of the river is the part of town where most of daily life now happens; stores, *les places* (town squares), houses, and, these days, a couple of big parking lots. Though it's a modern town Vaison still wears its history. Walking through the town you're aware of the traces of Rome beneath your feet, and, far above your head, the *château* is always in sight, as if it is still keeping watch over the town.

Vaison is just big enough to have a cosmopolitan feel. There is a spicy mix of outsiders living among the natives. As the month of December moves closer to the *Saison des Fêtes* you begin to see more stylishly dressed people sitting outside the cafés on the warm days. And it's no wonder; during the winter months, Vaison gets more than twice as many sunny days as Paris.

There are smaller villages nearby, some more charming, but it's Vaison's vitality that makes it our town in Provence. We've spent time in other areas of the Vaucluse and the Drôme, but it's always feels good to come back home.

Ragoût de Boeuf avec des Panais Rôtis
ROSEMARY BEEF STEW WITH ROASTED PARSNIPS

During my very first Christmas in Provence I learned about long-simmered stews and daubes, often made with wild boar (*sanglier*) or deer (*chevreuil*). Back at home I found myself longing for those flavours so I devised this recipe to recreate the velvety sauce and the meat that could be cut with a fork.

I was amazed how slow cooking transformed the red wine into thick, rich gravy. Don't be tempted to add potatoes, or carrots. The simplicity of the dish will be lost, instead serve with roasted parsnips.

1 large yellow onion
3 garlic cloves
3 lbs boneless beef
½ cup unbleached flour
2 T extra-virgin olive oil
2 cups red wine
1 tsp sea salt
½ tsp black peppercorns
3 T fresh rosemary, chopped

Peel and roughly chop the onion and garlic cloves.

Trim the beef by removing excess fat and cutting into 1½-inch cubes, then dry the cubes with paper towels.

Dredge each piece of beef in flour, either in a paper bag or on a plate. If you're using a plate, use a pair of tongs to handle the beef; forks will pierce the meat and you don't want that. Personally, I enjoy the dredging method, but the paper bag method is faster. Shake the pieces to remove the excess flour and set aside.

In a heavy pot, heat a tablespoon of olive oil over medium heat and add the roughly chopped onion and garlic cloves and sauté until the onions are translucent, about 3 minutes.

Using a slotted spoon, transfer the onion and garlic to a large plate. Increase the heat to medium-high, add the remaining tablespoon of oil and then the beef, a few pieces at a time. Brown on all sides, about 5 minutes careful not to overcrowd the beef. It's best to brown the beef in batches.

The point to browning is to sear the exterior and keep the juices locked inside, so don't be afraid to cook the pieces until they develop a nice browned exterior crust on all sides. Don't pierce the pieces with a fork as that will allow the juices to escape. As they are ready, transfer the browned beef to the plate holding the onion and garlic.

When all the meat is browned and removed from the pot, pour in 1 cup of the wine and deglaze the pan. After the juices and wine are bubbling, add the rosemary, salt, pepper and remaining cup of wine.

Return the beef, onion and garlic and any collected juices to the pan. Reduce the heat to low, cover tightly and cook for one hour, stirring from time to time.

Cover and cook, stirring occasionally until the meat is tender enough to cut with a fork and the sauce has thickened, 1½ to 2 hours longer. Taste and adjust the seasonings.

Transfer to a warmed serving bowl or serve directly from the pot. Serves 6.

ROASTED PARSNIPS

1 lb parsnips

2 T olive oil

½ tsp sea salt

Preheat oven to 400° F.

Peel and wash the parsnips. I like to keep them whole if they are small but they can be cut into diagonal slices if they are larger. In a shallow baking tray, drizzle the oil on the bottom and add the cleaned parsnips.

With your hands, cover the parsnips with the oil. Sprinkle with sea salt.

Place in the oven and bake for 30 to 40 minutes. Turn them every 10 minutes to ensure even browning. Remove and serve alongside the beef stew.

HAPPY GOOD YEAR!

Abead of sweat runs down my forehead and drops from the end of my nose onto the white tablecloth. Next to us a heavy-set man, face red with the heat, is tugging at his collar in an attempt to cool down. It's New Year's Eve at *Le Restaurant d'Éric Frechon,* a place that is hot in both senses of the word. For this, our first celebration of the New Year in Paris, I discovered that Eric Frechon's is the place to be. Later Eric will go on to greater fame at *Hôtel Le Bristol,* where he will win three Michelin stars and be awarded the *Légion d'Honneur,* but tonight he is cooking at his own restaurant in the far-flung 19th Arrondissement, and he is the talk of the town.

The condensation that coats the windows reminds me of the steam room at the YMCA, and the restaurant seems to be at the same temperature. The waiters are oblivious to the stains beneath their armpits as they race around with loaded plates, and not a customer complains about the heat. This is something I notice about Parisians, they never complain about hot, stuffy spaces, no matter how uncomfortable, but the slightest chill is like a call to arms. I take off my dinner jacket and watch our heavy-set neighbour eyeing me, wishing he could too, but I suspect his wife in her Chanel suit is not open to such a lowering of standards.

The heat wasn't as noticeable when we arrived because the first thing that caught my attention was the price on the *Menu du Réveillon,* triple the usual fare. I didn't know that most restaurants present special New Year's Eve menus, always at a premium. After the initial shock, I try to forget we are on a budget and settle in to enjoy the experience.

As the restaurant fills with people the temperature and humidity steadily climb. After the *amuse-bouche (cannelloni de saumon fumée et huître, crème acidulée au caviar)* is cleared I can't take it anymore. We are the only non-Francophones in the room, but I summon the waiter and do my best to ask about the heat. Our neighbour is eavesdropping.

The waiter shrugs and says, *"C'est la chaleur de la cuisine, que puis-je faire?"* The heat is from the kitchen, what can he do? Well, if you can't turn down the heat, I ask, how about turning on the air conditioner? The man next door nods his thanks as cool air begins to fill the room.

The restaurant becomes more comfortable during the pasta course (*raviole de langoustine cuite dans son bouillon parfumé aux morilles*) and the seafood course (*poêlée de céleri-rave et St Jacques aux copeaux de truffe et parmesan*), but with the *plat* things begin to go wrong as the room heats up again, condensation running down the windows. Before tucking into the *pigeon à l'étouffe de truffe et foie gras cuit en fine croûte* I call the waiter over and ask why the air conditioner has been shut off. Well, he shrugs, the customers seated near the *climatiseur* have complained about the cold. What can he do? *"Que puis-je faire?"*

The service is slow with plenty of time between courses, so I step outside to cool down and to see if there are any signs of celebration in the streets of the 19th Arrondissement. Our neighbour excuses himself to his wife and follows me outside, where we strike up a conversation about the heat in the room, business and Biarritz.

Back in the restaurant, before sitting down again, my red-faced friend glances at his wife, shrugs, and boldly takes off his jacket. This single act starts a buzz in the room and soon other men are nodding in agreement and removing their jackets. And so, with our comrades in heat, we bring in the New Year with *Vacherin servie à la cuillère*, a delicious soft cheese from the Jura region (with an AOC, of course!) and a *délice de l'An neuf au marron et whisky*. Who knew that chestnuts and whisky would be one of my favourite combinations?

Despite the heat, the food is so amazing that I'll later follow Eric Frechon to the restaurant at *Le Bristol*. Even though its prices are atmospheric, the staff at *Le Bristol* do know how to use the thermostat.

The long Metro ride back to our hotel is surprisingly quiet. Next to us, a group of Spanish tourists are mystified by the lack of celebration. "In Madrid, we know how to throw a party!"

Olé!

Cannelloni de saumon fume et huître, crème acidulée au caviar
Cannelloni of smoked salmon and
oysters, sour cream with caviar

Raviole de langoustine cuite dans son bouillon parfumé aux morilles
Lobster ravioli cooked in broth flavoured with morels

Poêlée de céleri-rave et St Jacques aux copeaux de truffe et parmesan
Pan fried scallops and celery root, with
shaved truffle and Parmesan

Pigeon à l'étouffé de truffe et foie gras cuit en fine croûte
Pigeon with truffle and *foie gras*, cooked in a thin pastry crust

Vacherin servi à la cuillère
Vacherin cheese

Délice de l'An neuf au marron et whisky
New Year's delight of chestnuts and whisky

❧

Brilliant flashes of colour explode above the ruins of the Forum. The Romans would have done this, I think to myself, if they had invented gunpowder instead of running water and flush toilets. But this is the last day of the twentieth century in Vaison-la-Romaine, and the town is celebrating the advent of a new millennium with fireworks in the Roman ruins.

Place du 11 Novembre, normally a huge parking lot, is filled with many of the town's 6,000 inhabitants. Mixed in are a few visitors like ourselves. Everyone is drinking the Champagne provided by the *Mairie*, the town hall. Back in our neck of the woods, that would mean something like Baby Duck served in little plastic cups. Here in Provence, though, welcoming the millennium means the real stuff served in real Champagne glasses to an entire town.

After the fireworks I toast my fellow townspeople (that's how it feels, at least) and then, still holding our Champagne glasses, we walk over to *L'Auberge de la Bartavelle* for New Year's Eve dinner.

The *patron* greets us at the door and shakes our hands; he's happy that we're back. We've been here five times in the last couple of years, including our memorable first dinner with Tom and Jos, and Mark's birthday party with Joe, Françoise and Laurent. It still hasn't lost its charm for me, with its warm colours and Pagnol-themed Provençal menus.

Tonight the room is filled with fellow townspeople, in couples and families. It's Bartavelle Classic, made special by the fact that this is the last meal of the millennium, the last chance to eat for a thousand years.

The familiar generous *coupes* of Champagne arrive at our table, delivered by a handsome young man decked out in formal wear for the occasion. It's a delicious pleasure to be able to sit back and relax over this meal that is playing out like a familiar piece of music.

An *amuse bouche* comes to accompany the Champagne. The *surprise d'oeuf* is a bit of scrambled egg with a drop of truffle oil on top. Seeing as it's the last night of the millennium and all, I'm going to have oysters next. This decision is easily made, adopted from my standard playbook, "Seeing as it's [*insert any day*] and all, I'm going to have oysters." Oh, luscious lusciousness!

As usual at the Bartavelle we are the only English speakers in the room. At the table next to us is family with a 12-year old boy who runs outside every few minutes to wave noisemakers around the *place*. He returns panting with excitement.

The *plats* arrive and I've chosen a filet mignon with a mustard sauce. With the main courses comes a bottle of Gigondas, deep red and rich. Mark takes a sip from his glass, winces, and summons over the *patron*, who gives it a quick sniff and abruptly takes away the bottle and our glasses in one swoop.

"What's going on?" I ask.

"The wine was corked," Mark tells me. How can he tell when a bottle of wine is bad? "Well," he says, "it smells like a skunk inside of a gym bag." I'm impressed. Our host brings us a new bottle and fresh glasses, and harmony is restored at our little table.

I'm just noticing that the bread is very good with a slightly higher salt content when a murmur arises in the room. Everyone is checking their watches; it's almost midnight! Suddenly I hear noises from outside on the *place* and the lights in the restaurant go out. It takes me a few moments to realize that this is how the *patron* is acknowledging the New Year.

Everyone gets out of their seats and wanders around the dark room to greet the other diners. This is great! I get up and join the milling crowd. There is plenty of cheek kissing and *"Bonne Années."* When the mother of the 12-year old realizes we are English speakers she says, "Happy Good Year!"

I assume most of the diners know each other, but they treat us like neighbours, too. After there's not a cheek left to be kissed the lights come back on and everyone resumes their meals.

It's gentle, low-key, convivial; not the hype and hoopla I've come to associate with New Year's Eve. The fireworks and the civilized glass of Champagne on the town *place* were the extent of the hoopla. The celebration is marked by the menu, the courses, the conversation: things that have been going on like this for centuries in France.

We finish with some *Roquefort*, and then a dense *moelleux*, a flourless chocolate cake with a scoop of vanilla ice cream. And, of course, a glass of *Muscat de Beaumes-de-Venise*.

There's something deeply satisfying about being in a country, centuries old, bringing in a millennium without commotion and frenzy. It's just another century after all, just another millennium.

∽

"Restaurateur gives up three Michelin stars!" It's the top story in Paris, and major culinary news everywhere. Alain Senderens, chef at restaurant *Lucas Carton* for twenty years, has renounced the Michelin star system to allow himself more freedom in the kitchen. This is extraordinary and brave. No one gives up Michelin stars! In fact, recently another chef,

Bernard Oiseau, took his own life when he heard a star might be removed from his Burgundy restaurant.

I was piqued. With his stars gone, the prices at his restaurant on *Place de la Madeleine* will plummet. Well, maybe plummet is too strong a word, but they will definitely be down in the stratosphere.

The news is too deliciously scandalous to ignore, so I promptly set out to make reservations for New Year's Eve dinner at the restaurant, renamed *Alain Senderens*. This year we are a force; a tribe of six English-speakers gathering in Paris to ring in the new year. It's a tradition for us, but for our friends this will be the first *fin de l'année* celebration in the City of Lights.

We meet on *Place de la Madeleine* with hugs, handshakes, and kisses all round. It's wonderful to meet up with old friends and new friends and introduce them to each other and to Paris. We are ushered into the restaurant where the staff take our coats while we admire the beautiful room. But, instead of seating us here, the *chic* hostess leads us upstairs, past a number of small rooms, and into a private oval salon with soft pink walls, surrounded with white sheer curtains and with an arched window overlooking the *place*. The large table, also oval, is set for six and decorated with candles and a blanket of rose petals. Mary-Lynn actually gasps at the beauty!

Champagne is poured and we toast Paris, the evening and each other. I read the menu and discover that Chef Senderens has created a special meal for our salon, with wine paired to each course. I have no idea how we warrant a special menu, but I act as if I'd planned it all along. Nothing, I proclaim, is too good for my friends.

We have three staff to serve us; it's a good ratio for six people, I think to myself. They bring us *foie gras de canard*, sublime with exotic fruit, on a bed of edible rose petals. The wine they pour, a *Gewurztraminer* from the Alsace region, is woodsy and sweet and a great complement to the *foie gras*.

With each course we savour and delight and discuss flavours and presentation while we catch up with each other's stories. With each glass of wine we learn a little more about each other. At midnight car horns honk on the *Place de la Madeleine* and more Champagne is popped. We wish each other *Bonne Année* and make the rounds of the other rooms to greet the less fortunate diners in their plain surroundings. As soon as we can, we hurry back to our pink-hued corner room to look out over one of the most famous squares of Paris, now a year older.

I'm not sure how we're going to get home. It will impossible to catch a taxi and the few Metro trains running will be packed, but I'm not worried about that right now. For the moment I'm happy to be in this magical restaurant with friends. And I'm glad that Chef Senderens gave back his three stars.

Louise Pommery Rosé 1996
Amuses bouches

Gewurztraminer Vendanges Tardives 1999, Cave de Pfaffenheim
Foie gras de canard de Landes rôti aux
fruite exotiques et pétales de rose
Roasted *foie gras* from Gascony, with
exotic fruit and rose petals

Meursault 2002, JF Coche-Dury
Homard à la vanille Bourbon de Madagascar, cheveux d'ange à
la chlorophylle de cresson, quelques feuilles de tétragone et d'oseille
Lobster flavoured with Madagascar Bourbon vanilla;
watercress angel hair pasta with sorrel and tarragon leaves

Chambolle-Musigny Vielles Vignes 2003, D. Geantet-Pansiot
Perdreau rouge rôti, gâteau de choux verts
truffé (confit 3 heures au four)
Roast partridge with slow-roasted cabbage

Sauternes, Château Doisy-Dëne 2002
Fine dacquoise au poivre de Séchouan, marmelade
au citron confit, glace au gingembre
Layered almond cake with Szechwan pepper,
lemon confit and ginger ice cream

DECEMBER 19, PARIS

A patch of blue sky welcomed us as we came out of the Metro. The rain has finally stopped and today we went over to Châtelet where we mingled with bundled Parisians in their colourful woolen scarves promenading on streets decorated for Christmas. It was like a dream about Paris, or a painting by Gustave Caillebotte.

But we weren't there for a walkabout, we were there for a Sunday concert. *Le Théâtre du Châtelet* is a magnificent structure from the 19th century. The interior is like a child's version of a classical opera house, on the gilded stage are the words *"danse, faerie, musique, drame, comédie."* Hordes of parents and children frantically searched for the best places in a madcap French version of rush seating.

"Mesdames & messieurs, je vous présente le quartet s'appelle Le Quator," the show began. This classically-trained quartet, who fiddle, dance, sing and perform acrobatics, integrated Bach, Hendrix, Tchaikovsky and Cab Calloway in a show called *Rap, Rock and Rachmaninoff*. The show was witty, physical, and musically perfect.

The children loved it. By the time the concert ended the stage was littered with shredded paper, a burnt manuscript, shards of shimmering metal confetti, a wine bottle, an overturned chair and four pairs of blue scuba flippers.

After the performance, we wandered to the *Hôtel de Ville* where a skating rink had taken over the square in front of the city hall. Next to it, an old-fashioned carousel was lazily spinning around, fueled by the cries of delighted children. Crossing the Seine we headed to my favourite winter eating spot, *Brasserie de l'Ile St. Louis*.

The *Brasserie* was packed with wine-guzzling, pork-chomping Parisians out for Sunday brunch. The is the place for *choucroute garnie*, the real thing: a pile of Alsatian sauerkraut with chunks of pork and sausages served with waxy yellow potatoes and a biting mustard. Dessert was a plum tart that would make any Granny weep.

The light was lovely as we walked back to the apartment. The low winter sun struggled to illuminate the city, casting long shadows everywhere. It was a perfect Sunday in Paris.

Tarte Rustique aux Pommes et Amande
RUSTIC APPLE AND ALMOND TART

Rustic fruit tarts are one of my favourite desserts. The French love twice-cooked fruit in their desserts; the double cooking makes the fruit far more juicy. Although I've used apples, this recipe is so versatile that you can use any seasonal fruit: apricots, plums or pears.

2 lbs apples
¼ cup butter
¼ cup sugar
thawed puff pastry or
   honey brioche dough
   (see separate recipe)
¼ cup sliced almonds
1 T sugar for topping

Preheat oven to 375° F.

Peel and core the apples, then slice them into 8 sections.

In a heavy skillet or cast iron frying pan over medium heat, melt the butter and sugar together until bubbling. Add the sliced apples into the pan and gently stir to coat evenly with the butter and sugar mixture.

Let the apples cook until they are somewhat soft and starting to caramelize, about ten minutes. Turn off the heat.

On a marble board, place a grapefruit size disc of the thawed puff pastry dough or brioche dough. With your hands, gently push it into a circle and then, using a rolling pin, roll it out into 1/8-inch thickness.

Transfer the rolled-out brioche dough to a pizza baking tray or cookie sheet. Spoon the cooked apples and sauce in the centre of the rolled out dough. Spread the fruit out, leaving 3-inches of pastry at the perimeter for folding. Starting at one place, fold over an edge and then another until the crust is encircling, but not completely covering, the fruit.

Sprinkle on the sliced almonds and one tablespoon of sugar. Bake for about thirty minutes, until golden brown and bubbling. Serve warm or at room temperature. Serves 6 to 8.

Brioche au Miel
HONEY BRIOCHE

This brioche is made in minutes without using a mixer and without kneading. I've adapted the recipe from *Artisan Breads in Five Minutes*. The dough can be used for my rustic apple and almond tart.

You can make individual brioche using brioche tins, a muffin tray, or use a larger baking dish to make a medium or large brioche. Just ensure that all baking containers are well buttered. Any unused portion can be stored in the refrigerator for up to a week.

½ cup butter
4 eggs
¼ cup honey
¾ T baking yeast
¾ T coarse salt
1 cup lukewarm water
4 unbleached flour
1 egg for the wash
1 T water

Preheat the oven to 370° F thirty minutes before baking

In a small pan, melt the butter and honey. Set aside.

In small bowl, lightly blend four eggs.

In a large mixing bowl, with a spatula, mix the yeast, salt, and water. Add the eggs and the honey and melted butter mixture. Mix gently together. Using a wooden spoon, mix in the flour, one cup at a time, until all the flour is incorporated.

Cover with a tea towel, or plastic wrap and set aside for about two to three hours. Ensure that that the dough can breathe, so don't make the cover airtight.

After two to three hours the brioche will have risen considerably, but it will be too soft to bake. Place the bowl into the refrigerator for one hour to allow the dough to firm up.

With floured hands, and with extra flour available, grab a piece of dough (smaller than the bakeware as it will rise to almost double in size) and cut it off with a sharp knife. Roll the dough into a smooth ball and place into the bakeware. Make an indent into each ball of dough and then grab a smaller piece of dough; small-marble size for muffin tins, large-marble size for larger brioche; and roll into a ball. Place it on top of the indented brioche.

Set the prepared brioche dough aside and cover with plastic wrap or a tea towel for another forty-five minutes. This will allow the dough to rise again. Just before baking, mix the egg with a tablespoon of water. Gently paint the brioche with the egg wash to give it a glossy finish.

Bake in the heated oven for about 30 to 40 minutes (depending on the size) or until the brioche are golden brown.

Remove from the oven and let the brioche cool for a few minutes before gently removing them from the bakeware and onto a cooling tray. This is an important step, if you don't remove the brioche from the bakeware the bottom will become soggy. And no one likes a soggy brioche bottom!

La Quincaillerie

The bell tower rings nine times. I dangle my foot from under the covers and detect a cold front. Not a good sign. I nudge Mark, he usually can fix anything, but he sleeps on. The bell tower rings out a second set of nine, as they do in Provence. I wrap a blanket around myself and go off to explore.

The indigo bathroom is as cold as a meat locker. I let the faucet run a few minutes in the hope that hot water will somehow miraculously appear, it being Christmas and all. I slip on a pair of shoes and go down the four flights of stairs in darkness.

I try the lights in the kitchen. Nothing. I mean nothing: no heat, no lights, no hot water, no electricity for the stove, the tea kettle, the radio. It is December 20 and we are in our rent-free house in the south of France.

We faced a dilemma in October as we began thinking about our holiday plans. For us, Christmas means Provence, but this year we were starting a new business and trying to adopt a baby from Vietnam. We just couldn't afford a trip to France.

We started out with a simple plan for the holiday season; we'd stay close to home, maybe rent a cabin in the Rockies. But then I thought, if we were going to have to drive for five hours, we might as well fly to San Francisco for the same amount of time and money. But then I thought, the Canadian dollar is being battered in the US, we might as well go to France. Again. Just the name evoked memories of sitting in cafés and visiting my favourite villages in Provence.

I converted the ephemeral asset of air miles points into airline tickets and stretched the boundaries of casual friendship to ask to borrow our friends' house in Nyons. Jean and Paul's generosity astounded me. In return for staying at their house we have agreed to look after some final renovation tasks: contacting the architect, calling some trades, finding some bedroom furniture.

Nyons is a bustling, working town in the *département* of the Drôme surrounded by vineyards, apricot orchards, and some of the last olive groves in France. When we arrived yesterday one of my first stops was the *Nyonsais* growers' cooperative, where the best of local products are found. I bought good wines at incredible prices, olives, olive oil, and what I swear is the best apricot jam I've ever tasted. *Ever.*

We are the first winter visitors in 13 Rue de la Liberté since Jean and Paul finished restoring it; the tall townhouse was still closed up after the last of the summer visitors: power and water shut off, windows locked and shuttered. We let ourselves in and followed Paul's instructions for turning on the electricity, which is used for everything: lights, heating, cooking, hot water.

There is nothing that feels colder than an unheated stone-and-rubble house. But we opened a bottle of wine and waited for the house to warm up. And waited.

                                        ❧

Now the only thing for me to do is to get dressed and go out into the street for morning baked goods and coffee. Where Mark excels at fixing things, my talent is finding food.

I step out onto the narrow Rue de la Liberté and look high above the five-story townhouses to see a brilliant blue sky. The street is barely two metres wide and I nearly run into the house opposite gawking at the slit of blue above.

Just twenty paces to the right is the *pâtisserie*, a playhouse-sized shop with yellow and white striped awnings and a tinkle bell that rings when I enter. A pastry case is filled with an array of *tartes* glistening in the morning sun. *Citron, poire, framboise*; shelves groan under the weight of homemade chocolates, cookies, local jams and preserves; walls display photos of the local soccer team and a framed picture of a *croque-em-bouche*, the famous towered French wedding cake. The tiny space contains enough goodness to last a lifetime.

I choose a golden-yellow pear-and-almond tart decorated with the name of the patisserie, *Jean-Pierre Gavet*. As I walk out with the tart I feel that the day is already warmer and brighter.

I take a few more steps to the *boulangerie*. In the strict French fashion, this bakery makes only bread; cakes and pastries are found in *pâtisseries*. This tradition of specialization is one of the things that makes France so appealing.

Already there is a line-up that snakes out into the courtyard. The shop is so small that only two people can stand next to each other without bumping into the bread stacks. The rest of the valuable real estate is filled with an assortment of bread: baguettes; *boules, grande et petit* depending on your appetite; bread shaped into sheaves of wheat; whole grain, rye and my favourite, sourdough.

I study the selection and practice placing my order in French, muttering under my breath. The woman next to me to eyes me suspiciously and hugs her purse a little closer to her body. When it's my turn I choose a giant *boule* (a hearty country loaf) and of course, a few buttery croissants. The *boulanger* wraps them in brown paper. When I pick up the loaves the paper crinkles against the hard crust, sounding as delicious as the bread tastes.

Nyons represents what town life should be. Everything I need to make my life fulfilling is found in the centre of Nyons. Walk out the front door and I find the patisserie, and then the bakery, and then the butcher. Turn around and there's a flower shop, a book store, a camera shop. Just through the arches beyond the *place* are other shops packed with both essentials and extravagances: chic dress shops, children's clothing stores, a produce store; banks, realtors, linen shops and shoe stores all within a five-minute walk. And every Thursday and Sunday there is even greater choice as the market comes to town. In Nyons you don't need a map, it all flows naturally, as a town should.

My last stop is the *Petit Casino*, where the sight of fresh oysters, piled high in wooden cases, bits of seaweed peeking out, smelling of brine and the sea, stops me in my tracks. *Petit Casino* is a chain of convenience stores found throughout France, but it's like a Seven-Eleven in heaven. You don't find rows of machines dispensing Super Slushies. What you do find is crates of oysters, Christmas displays with cases of Champagne, a fine choice of cheeses, a smattering of local produce, and the basics: butter, eggs, toilet paper. I know I'm in a food culture when I see eggs, sausage and oysters displayed openly, instead of in antiseptic packaging. I stock up on yogurt, coffee and milk for our first breakfast.

Back at the Ice Palace, I find Mark and a lanky American in the dark wine cellar examining the breaker box with a flashlight. The man is Wayne Marshall, who lives just up the street. Wayne and his wife Lydie Marshall, the French cookbook author and teacher, divide their time between Provence and New York City. Lydie conducts cooking classes in their beautiful home carved out of a piece of the old Nyons *château*. We met them the previous summer when we were visiting Jean and Paul. It was thrilling to meet the author of one of my favourite French cookbooks, *A Passion for My Provence*.

"Just what I thought," Wayne explains, "There's not enough power to keep the house going in the winter. This breaker box is only good for summer living. You're going to need heaters to keep yourselves warm. I have one you can borrow, but you should buy more at the *quincaillerie*." Mark and I look puzzled until Wayne explains, "The hardware store".

∾

The *quincaillerie (can-ku-RIE)* in Nyons is about the most enjoyable one-stop shopping I have ever encountered. But, come to think of it, I also feel that way about the *Nyonsais* cooperative. And the local Petit Casino, for that matter! For a small store the *quincaillerie* is surprisingly fully stocked in the tidy French tradition. Mark quickly spots the regular hardware store supplies, but it's the multi-coloured pots and pans, space-age kitchen gadgets, and a beautiful display of dishware, vases, and home decor that catches my eye. My instinct pushes me toward a set of lemon-yellow cappuccino cups, but Mark pulls me toward the display of kerosene heaters.

Here's what they don't teach you in French language class, how to buy a kerosene heater for your frozen villa. I've been studying French for several years and was now as fluent as a native one-year old. As we admire the fleet of heaters on offer, a friendly employee asks us if we need help.

"*S'il vous plaît*", I reply in perfect French. So far, so good.

I cleverly say we need heaters. Monsieur responds with a dozen helpful questions: how big is the house, how much do we want to spend, what quality of oil do we want to use? I take a deep breath and slowly explain our dilemma. Monsieur nods solemnly. He hurries to the back room and returns with a catalogue. He flips through several pages and then, with a dramatic flair points to a picture of the heater perfect for our needs. Mark and I *ooh* and *awe* in unison, nodding to share his enthusiasm.

"The perfect choice," I say, "we'll take three, *s'il vous plaît, Monsieur.*"

"*Ah, malheureusement, ils ne vont pas à la vente jusqu'à vendredi,*" he says. They don't go on sale until *vendredi,* Friday. That means three more days and nights of cold weather for us. I explain slowly that *vendredi* is many days away. "Can we buy them today?" I meekly suggest.

"*Non, il n'est pas possible,*" he stands his ground. Minutes pass. It's like negotiating in slow motion. I know that the French use that phrase a lot, "it is not possible." I try to stay calm. After several minutes of consulting my dictionary and forming my rebuttal, I finally ask him, "*Pourquoi n'est-il pas possible?*"

"Because, Madame," he says slowly, as if speaking to a child, "this model will not be delivered until Friday. It is not in the store, therefore *il n'est pas possible!*"

"Aha," a giant light bulb goes on over my head. It isn't possible, because he only has the picture and not the actual item in stock!

I explain it to Mark but, by then, Monsieur understands that we are cold *now!* Quickly, he swings into action. He pulls three brand-new heaters of a different model off the sales floor and tells us we can use them now and return them on Friday when the other model arrives. He helps load them into our car, along with the kerosene we will need, and within minutes we are heading home with enough heat to keep a castle warm.

Remarkably, he does not ask us for a credit card, a deposit, where we are staying, or even our names. Knowing we are cold, he is kind enough to let us take hundreds of *francs* worth of merchandise without so much as a phone number.

As the heaters roar and the house becomes warm and cozy in preparation for our holiday guests I think fondly of *Monsieur de la Quincaillerie,* and the kindness of strangers.

THE THEME SONG FROM BEAUMES-DE-VENISE

Beaumes-de-Venise is the only wine I know of with a theme song. And I'll bet I'm one of the few people outside of the village of who can hum the melody. Beaumes-de-Venise is a village, an appellation, a song, and the wine growers cooperative. On weekends the cooperative parking lot is usually packed locals there to stock up on their favourite wines. Most shoppers leave the store pushing carts piled high with cases of wine.

One winter, after tasting numerous wines at the cooperative, we wandered into their small theatre where a film about the village and its wines was being shown: sweeping landscapes of the gravely terrain, the history of the wine, a velvet-voiced narrator, and a theme song that was played as often as *Lara's Theme* in *Dr. Zhivago*. We were so enthralled that we bought both the DVD and the CD, complete with lyrics.

Although the red wines of *Beaumes-de-Venise* are always good and, in some years, great, it's the *Muscat de Beaumes-de-Venise* that I adore. There's something magical in the gravely vineyards that make ideal conditions to grow Muscat grapes. In fact, this is the only place in Provence where the Muscat grapes are grown and where it is turned into a delicious, honey-coloured sweet wine that can be served before dinner, after dinner, or with dessert.

The cooperative produces three sweet *muscats*, but our favourite comes from *Domain de Durban*, perched high above the village along the dragon spine that is the *Dentelles de Montmirail*; on one side the valley below, on the other the ragged limestone peaks of the *Dentelles*.

We even used *Durban* at our wedding to seal our vows. We, along with all our guests, toasted our marriage and each other with a glass of *Muscat de Beaumes-de-Venise*.

December 29, Vaison-la-Romaine

One of the joys of returning to the same place year after year is revisiting favourite restaurants. There always seem to be a four or five really good restaurants, serving food that tastes of the region: the creamy, tangy olive oils; the bitter grassy flavours in *Herbes de Provence*; salads with fat, ripe tomatoes; thick, pungent stews of wild boar.

There's a base satisfaction in eating food grown in the soil I'm standing on. The wines taste of it. When I drink a Gigondas or a Vacqueyras, wherever I am, I can taste the hills surrounding those villages, and I'm back here.

Tonight, in a restaurant set on the banks of the river Ouvèze, on a chilly winter's night, the Champagne arrived in small parfait glasses along with a few creamy *amuses bouches*. One, a steaming hot *velouté* served in an espresso cup, took the bite of cold out of my body, right down to my toes. The *amuse bouche* is often a predictor of the meal to follow and I looked forward to the entrées.

The restaurant occupies the ground floor of a medieval house and spills into the attached courtyard in warm weather. I've always been attracted to the building: the warm colour of the stucco, the rustic metal gate, and the olive tree. The classic courtyard led to a large wooden door and then up a steep set of stairs to the two interior rooms, one small room with the fireplace and the larger room with more windows. We were seated in the smaller room with the fireplace.

Mark's thinly sliced salmon *carpaccio* came with a tumble of fresh herbs lightly dressed with lemon and olive oil. My *soupe l'oignon* was exquisite; the broth was light, perfumed and soothing.

The homemade thyme-scented bread rolls complemented the slightly flowery flavours of the white wine. And the *plats*! *Cuisse de confit de canard* served over creamy polenta on a caramelized vinegar and shallot sauce. Mark's *bouillabaisse* was steamy, flavourful and served in a pretty blue-and-white seafood embossed bowl.

The cheese course was equally considered: a small round of warm *chèvre*, broiled and placed on a handful of dressed watercress. The dessert arrived with the same thoughtful approach; my *crêpe* was presented as a tiny bundle filled with the lightest whipped cream mixed with ground almonds and a swirl of honey.

Another memorable Provencal meal.

Provençal Tapenade

One Christmas, I made giant vats of tapenade to give away as gifts. I could have started my own factory! The quality of the ingredients is very important, use black olives from Provence if you can find them. Serve as an appetizer with baguette slices, crudités or as a topping on pizza and flatbread.

½ lb black Provençal olives

1 tsp anchovy paste

2 T capers, drained and rinsed

1 clove garlic, peeled

1 tsp Grappa, *Marc de Provence*, or Brandy

2 T extra-virgin olive oil

To remove the pits from the olives, lay them on a cutting board and use a rolling pin (I have a marble one) to gently crush them. The pits will then be easily removed. Set the olives aside. Rinse and drain the capers to remove excess salt and water.

In a food processor, using the pulse mode, blend the olives, anchovy paste, capers, garlic and liquor until a paste just begins to form. Slowly add the olive oil in and mix until the tapenade is just blended but still retains a coarse texture.

The tapenade can be serve immediately and it stores well for a long time.

Pain d'Olive de Nyons
OLIVE BREAD FROM NYONS

This olive cake was inspired by a trip to the *Coopérative Nyonsais* when I bought more olives than we possibly use. Make sure to choose good quality olives and olive oil for this savoury quick bread. It's delicious served warm with a smear of soft goat cheese.

4 ounces black Provencal olives, pitted

1½ cups unbleached white flour

½ cup whole wheat or rye flour

1½ tsp baking powder

¼ tsp sea salt

1 tsp sugar

2 eggs

¼ cup extra-virgin olive oil

½ cup buttermilk

¼ cup fresh rosemary , chopped

Preheat oven to 350° F.

Pit the olives by squishing them beneath the side of a broad knife. The pits will easily slide out. Coarsely chop the olives and set them aside.

In a medium mixing bowl combine the flours, baking powder, salt and sugar. Toss the pitted, chopped olives into the flour mixture.

In another medium bowl, add the eggs, olive oil, buttermilk and rosemary. Beat until smooth.

Add the dry ingredients to the wet mixture. Stir with a fork or whisk until completely blended, but careful not to over-mix.

Prepare a small loaf pan (7 x 3½ in) by coating it with a small amount of butter and dusting with flour. Pour the mixture into the cake pan and put it into the oven. Test for doneness after 45 minutes. It is better to slightly over-bake than under-bake the cake. Serves 6 to 8.

DR NO'S HIDEAWAY

The restaurant walls are painted in the colours of Provence. The service is formally attentive and precise. A glance at the menu reveals that all the classic French dishes are on offer. I feel myself starting to unwind from the three hectic weeks I've just spent. Now it's time for a nice dinner for me, Mark, Jane, and two small babies sleeping in basinets. It's Jane's last night so Mark makes a toast. "We'll always have Hanoi," he says as he lifts a glass of Champagne.

We are at restaurant *Les Quatre Saisons in* the French quarter of Vietnam's capital city.

❧

"Cheers," I say again to Jane. We clink our glasses and settle back in the *chaises longues* overlooking the pool where the nannies are playing with the babies. A girl for her, a boy for me. Just beyond the pool the hillside drops steeply to the valley below. And then, across miles of vineyards, sunflowers and lavender, Mount Ventoux looms majestically.

Mount Ventoux, the second highest mountain in France and the backdrop to our vacation home in Provence. We're here for a celebration of our new families, to remember our adventures in Vietnam, and to get together with old friends and new friends.

I met Jane in Vietnam, when we were both there to adopt our children, and an instant bond was formed. Jane, a posh lawyer from London with a wry sense of humour, had been in Vietnam for a week before I arrived. Over two trips to Hanoi and a total of five weeks together in the country our friendship deepened. Now here we are, less than a year later, for a two-week holiday in the south of France, with husbands, children, friends, and nannies. Seven adults versus two babies; the ratio seems just about right. It takes a village, it seems, to vacation with a baby in France.

The house is a modernistic affair perched on top of a wooded hill that overlooks the valley of the Ouvéze River, the same river that runs through Vaison-la-Romaine, though here the valley widens to accommodate a riot of Provençal crops. The architect might well have been James Bond: the house is a number of white blocks, stacked and fitted together. When Jane first saw it she called it "Dr No's Hideaway" and the name has stuck.

From the mountain country of rural Vietnam to the French countryside, our two babies, Isabelle and Alexandre, share an exotic past and this, their first trip to Provence.

∾

I had been in Hanoi for fewer than twelve hours when I met Jane. I was there to make the long trip north to Lang Son, up against the Chinese border, to apply for approval at the provincial government office to adopt my son. It is a two-trip process: once to apply and meet the baby and then again, several months later, to finalize the adoption.

The *Hotel Claudia*, where I was staying, was known as the "adoption hotel". All the guests had the same nervous look in their eyes and shared a sense of excitement: they were all there to adopt a baby. Mrs. Tihn Di of the *Claudia* was our host and guide. The hotel was only eight feet wide, typical for Hanoi because taxation was once based on street frontage, not on the overall size of the building. The narrower the building, the lower the tax rate.

In a building eight feet wide the small breakfast room had barely enough room to change your mind. So, I couldn't help noticing the activity at the table next to me on my first breakfast. A man and a woman seemed to be caught in some sort of adoption intrigue. She was up and down ten times to use the phone at the front desk for urgent business.

"Have you done any shopping yet?" The man at the next table turned towards me while his companion was again on the phone. It was Jules, Jane's long-time friend from her Oxford days, who had travelled to Vietnam to lend his assistance.

By noon the three of us were having lunch in Hanoi's colourful Old Quarter, where an incessant stream of bicycles and scooters filled the narrow streets day and night. Over fresh spring rolls and Chinese beer we were discussing Jane's turbulent morning. She had been to the British consulate to visit a baby that just might be hers if all went well. International adoption is about as complicated as French irregular verb conjugation; the rules are different for different countries and can change on a moment's notice.

For the next nine days, in between phone calls, filling out forms, and meetings with the adoption agency, we explored Vietnam. In Hanoi we jumped on the backs of motor scooters and zipped around the city to restaurants, temples, markets and monuments. Mrs. Tihn Di arranged for us to visit breathtaking Ha Long Bay on the coast. We took a small boat to the island of Cat Ba, where we danced at a disco and ate mysterious meats that Anthony Bourdain would love.

Finally, just when I was wondering if anything at all was going to happen, I got the call to go to Lang Son. It was a bit of good luck that Jane's daughter was from the same province as my son and we would travel together on the grueling five-hour van ride north.

At the Justice Building in the provincial capital (also called Lang Son) we met the babies and their families. Thi Dau, a girl, was two months old and Van Nam, a boy, was two and a half months. As is required in Lang Son, we applied in person for approval to adopt these children. We were interviewed by officials, we filled out more forms, and after twelve hours, returned to Hanoi empty-handed. It would take more paperwork and another trip to Vietnam to be able to bring our babies home.

Two months and seventeen days later, with husbands in tow, Jane and I were back in Lang Son to attend the formal Giving and Receiving Ceremony at the Justice Building to formally adopt our children. The most important and rewarding part of the process was done, but there was still the matter of visas and passports to complete. Officialdom works at its own speed, so we had another two weeks spending time at the swimming pool, eating wonderful dinners, and getting to know each other and our babies.

On that trip, following Jane's lead, we were staying at a modern hotel. We could enjoy the wonders of Hanoi, but when the mid-summer heat reached temperatures of 45°, we could escape to our air-conditioned rooms, the swimming pool, and the kitchen in our large apartment-style suites. It was a magical time.

At last the Canadian embassy had our visa papers, our baby's Vietnamese passport was ready, and we had one last dinner with Jane and Chris. It was time for us to return to Canada, but Mark and I still hadn't chosen a name for our son.

While making our connecting flight in Hong Kong, just as we were about to board our plane, we passed by what I think of as *The Last Gift Shop in Asia*. On a spinner rack were common Western names, written in Chinese characters. We chose the five names we had been considering (which included Danny, Jean-Paul and Julian) and formed them into a fan. Mark held the cards up to our baby who looked them over then shakily stuck out his chubby arm and touched one. Alexandre had chosen his own name.

໖໐

Here in Provence it's warm, serene and beautiful. The hills fold away into the distance as we drive toward our favourite villages. We're on our way to buy wine. This will be different than other visits, though. In the past we might buy the one bottle we are allowed to carry home on the plane. But this time we'll need to buy enough wine and food to feed and entertain a house of seven adults, and various guests, for two weeks. It's the most fun I can imagine.

Dr. No's Hideaway is the first villa we've rented in Provence and it's complete with a modern kitchen, a large dining room, six bedrooms, numerous bathrooms, and a patio with a scenic view. The fact that it's filled with friends makes it even better.

Our first stop is the village of Gigondas, where we pay a visit to the cellar of the Brusset family sales room, makers of our favourite from this village, *Les Hauts de Montmirail*. Stowing a case of mixed local wines into our trunk, we aim our car downhill towards the village of Vacqueyras. The narrow road is bordered by stone walls with vineyards behind. It's June and the vines are straining toward the sun, reaching up with giant, leafy mitts of green. We pass by *Pierre Amadieu's* new winery building and then turn south on *department* road D7. We're in the flat lands of the Rhone Valley, filled with vineyards as far as I can see in every direction. Although we're driving at what I feel is a madcap pace, a car overtakes us and zooms past. It's a mom in a minivan, taking her two kids to soccer.

We're in the border territory between the appellations of *Gigondas* and *Vacqueyras*, and most wineries here offer both types of wine. *"Domaine Palon,"* a red and white sign reads, *"Gigondas - Vacqueyras - Côtes-du-Rhône."* The road we're on feels good: flat and straight, but with just enough curves and just enough gentle slopes to keep it interesting. The sky is blue with popcorn balls of clouds dancing in the breeze.

We make a detour to stop in at one of the winemakers introduced by Tom and Jos, *Domaine La Fourmone*, and we take away some of their *Vacqueyras* blend, *Trésor du Poète*; dark, spicy, and tannic. A few minutes later we arrive at Vacqueyras where we find *Château de Montmirail*, located in the village. The winemaker obviously saves his charm for Jos, but we pick up a couple of cases of the two famous local wines.

"Since we're this far," I say to Mark, "and Beaumes-de-Venise is only a little ways farther..."

That's all the convincing it takes and soon we're at the cooperative for more reds and then up, up, up above the village to *Domain de Durban* for a two-week's supply of their *muscat*.

When we get back to Dr No's, much later than we had promised, our little car is scraping bottom on the roughest bits of the unpaved driveway. It seems that we've bought more wine than I realized!

We begin to carry the cases of wine into the villa. With each new case Jane's eyes open wider in disbelief. "Are we supplying the entire village with wine?" she teases. When I ignore her humorous dig she says, "Come on, I want to show you something," leading me to the patio. Surrounding the outdoor table are pennants hanging on cords; the table itself is festooned with decorations. "Bunting," Jane says brightly. Today is the anniversary of the Queen's coronation, so Jane and her husband Chris, Brits to the core, have prepared the house for the celebration, with the nannies and the children assisting.

I feel it's important to test the *Beaumes-de-Venise Muscat* for quality, so glasses are distributed and toasts are made. It seems somehow right to introduce Alexandre to France while he's still one-year old. It's also fitting that he'll be meeting Tom and Jos, who are staying at their apartment in Vaison-la-Romaine, only fifteen minutes away. They're invited to this evening's celebration.

∾

"I hear there's a party going on here!" It's Tom and Jos, armed with gin and tonic to mock-celebrate the Queen's coronation, and with them two new guests: Bob and Elizabeth from New Mexico, who own the apartment above Tom's in Vaison.

Elizabeth, a tall and glamorous women, stretches out her arms to give us a hug, "I've heard there are some beautiful babies here. Where are they?" In that instant I know it will be a good group. Bob, less exuberant than his wife, but equally friendly, spent his work life travelling the world overseeing projects for the World Bank. Elizabeth and their two daughters often accompanied him. And although they love to travel, they avoid flying. They came to France on an ocean liner.

"Oh, flying is for birds," Elizabeth declares. "There's slow food so why not slow travel? I just adore taking our time to getting somewhere." Now, they spend half the year in Vaison and half in New Mexico.

As the sun is setting, we set the enormous patio table for eleven adults and two babies. The nannies feed the babies and whisk them away for playtime, while the other adults get settled for a feast.

To start the meal Mark has made one of his favourite Provençal creations, a salad of big, buttery leaves of lettuce topped with slices of fresh ripe tomato and *crevettes,* the cooked shrimp found in all the markets of France. I notice that Jane and Chris have looks on their faces that are somewhere between panic and disgust. "I just *can't* eat seafood," Jane confesses. Not to worry, I slice up some *pâté* I bought at the market and the two Brits spread it over slices of fresh baguette for their starter.

Next up are thick slices chicken breasts, stuffed with local goat cheese and cooked to a crispy goldenness on the outside, with some of the melted cheese oozing out.

Over dessert and even more glasses of *muscat*, as the setting sun lights the top of Mount Ventoux a rosy peach, we tell the story of our adoptions. Today is the first time we've seen Tom and Jos since we got Alexandre, so the story is new to them.

After we finish relating our adventures in Vietnam, we all sit in silence for a few minutes. Then Bob asks, "What was the city in the north where you finalized the adoptions?" We tell him.

"I spent a fair bit of time in Vietnam," Bob tells us. "I was supervising the construction of that road that runs from Hanoi north to the Chinese border; the road to Lang Son."

It sends a chill down my spine to hear that Bob built the road between Hanoi and Lang Son, the very road so momentous to Jane and Chris, Mark and I, as well as Alexandre and Isabelle. *C'est un petit monde.*

After dessert, Jane and I disappear to spend time with the babies and send them off to sleep. We both share a glance and thankful sigh for all our good fortune.

MARKETS OF PROVENCE

On my first visit to Vaison-la-Romaine I was struck by the small number of stores. Where did the Vaisonites buy the things they need? Was it necessary to drive to Avignon to buy a screwdriver?

The answer literally came to me on the next Tuesday. Vans, trucks, and trailers arrived early in the morning with spices, cheeses, sausages, bread, linens and sewing machines. Tables are set up, canopies are erected, goods are laid out and, at nine o'clock, the vendors begin selling their jet black olives from Nyons, fresh goat cheese, lavender honey, truffle oil and mountains of produce. The people of Vaison don't go shopping, the shopping comes to them.

The streets are closed to traffic and within minutes Vaison becomes a vibrant market place. There's a fairground atmosphere as people from Vaison and the surrounding area fill the streets carrying shopping bags and wicker baskets, testing the produce, talking to friends, selecting great slabs of salmon *pavé*, rifling through racks of CDs; buying flowers, hardware, fresh baking, ceramic pots, and Languiole knives. And it's been going on this way every Tuesday since 1483.

A weekly market is featured in many villages of the region, but Vaison's is renowned for its size and the variety of goods displayed. In Nyons, Thursday is market day. Here we like to shop for olive oil sold by small producers, for local goat cheeses, lavender honey, jet black olives and truffle oil.

The offerings change with the seasons. Fresh fruits and straw hats in the summer, root crops and scarves in the winter. And during the winter there are specialty markets like the Christmas markets and the truffle markets that run from November to March in towns like Carpentras, Avignon and Grignan. To be in Provence is to be surrounded by markets.

Avignon – every day
Beaumes-de-Venise – Tuesday
Cairanne – Thursday
Carpentras – Friday
Nyons – Thursday and Sunday
Orange – Thursday
Puyméras – Wednesday evening and Saturday
Sainte Cécile les Vignes – Saturday
Vacqueyras – Thursday
Vaison-la-Romaine – Tuesday
Valréas – Wednesday and Saturday

Soupe Vietnamienne au Poulet et Nouilles
VIETNAMESE CHICKEN NOODLE SOUP

When we were in the long process of adopting our son from Vietnam, I became passionate about Vietnamese cooking. As we waited for "the call" from Vietnam, I perfected several Vietnamese dishes. This soup is a winter favourite and I still make it today - it's simple, exotic and heart-warming.

8 cups chicken stock
1 ounce fresh ginger, sliced
2 sticks cinnamon bark
½ tsp coriander seeds, whole
3 pieces star anise
4 tsp fish sauce
8 shallots, thinly sliced
2 tablespoons oil for frying shallots
1 tsp sugar
1 tsp sea salt
1 tsp black pepper, freshly ground
½ lb rice noodles
½ onion, thinly sliced
4 to 8 ounces chicken meat, cooked
bean sprouts
limes, quartered
cilantro, chopped

In a soup pot, add the chicken stock, fresh ginger, cinnamon bark, coriander seeds, star anise, and fish sauce. Bring to a boil and then simmer for 15 minutes.

Meanwhile, in a small pan, heat the oil and fry the shallots until crispy brown. Drain and set aside.

After simmering for fifteen minutes, strain the stock. Return to medium heat and add the sugar, salt and pepper.

Add the uncooked rice noodles, onions and chicken and simmer until the noodles are tender and the ingredients are thoroughly heated, (about ten minutes). Taste the stock - it may need to have some rice vinegar, lime juice or salt and pepper to balance the flavours.

Serve in large bowls and top with browned shallots and fresh bean sprouts, limes and cilantro.

It's quick, it's special and delicious!

Poulet à la Citronnelle
LEMONGRASS CHICKEN

A Vietnamese grandmother taught me how to make this incredible spicy chicken dish. All the ingredients can be easily found in Asian markets and fine grocers. The first time I used lemongrass I was amazed by the unique citrus quality of this simple ingredient.

2 boneless, skinless chicken breasts

Marinade:
2 tablespoons fresh lemongrass, chopped
2 cloves garlic cloves, chopped
1-2 tsp Vietnamese hot chili sauce or:
½ tsp hot chili pepper flakes
⅓ cup good quality fish sauce

Tangy Sauce:
¼ cup sugar
¼ cup good quality fish sauce
¼ cup hot water
1 lime, juice and pulp
1 tsp Vietnamese chili sauce
1 garlic clove, chopped
4 tsp sugar
2 T oil

Place chicken breasts wrapped in plastic in the freezer for up to 1/2 an hour before preparation. The trick is to slightly freeze the breasts so that they can be easily sliced horizontally.

In a non-reactive bowl, mix together the marinade; lemongrass, garlic, chilli sauce or peppers and fish sauce.

While the chicken is in the freezer, make the Tangy Sauce. In a medium size bowl, add the sugar, fish sauce and water and completely dissolve before the next step. With a sharp, small knife, cut the lime into two halves. Carefully, juice the lime, capturing as much of the pulp as possible, using the sharp edge of the knife. Mix together and then add the chilli sauce and garlic clove. Blend together and set aside until serving.

After about twenty minutes in the freezer, the chicken breasts will be slightly frozen. Filet them horizontally into thin slices. Add the filleted chicken to the marinade for at least twenty minutes and up to two hours (in the refrigerator).

Just before cooking, caramelize the sugar. In a heavy bottomed pan, heat the sugar until melted. Watch carefully! When caramelized, turn off heat and remove from stove top.

Heat another heavy skillet with the oil and grill both sides of the chicken until cooked. Set aside.

Turn the heat to medium and pour the remaining marinade into the skillet and add the caramelized sugar, (it will be thick and syrupy). Blend together well.

Add the chicken back in the skillet and spoon over the sauce. Simmer for a couple of minutes. Serve the chicken over a bed of greens on a large platter - spoon some of the Tangy Sauce before serving and pour the remaining sauce into a serving bowl for those who want extra!

IN THE SUMMER, WHEN IT SIZZLES

"**Y**ou're going back again?"

It's my friend Sandra. Most people, she reminds, use their holidays to explore, to visit new places. But we keep going to France. "Haven't you been there, done that?" she asks.

I find her question puzzling. I haven't been to France for six months. Well, five if you count from when I got back. I mean, it's perfectly obvious, isn't it? Think of all the things I've missed during those six (okay, five) months. Parisian life is going on without me!

I remember that conversation as I wait for my taxi at Charles de Gaulle airport. Out here among the smokers and drizzling rain Paris does not look at all pretty. Taxis, busses, and shuttle vans roar past, echoing in the concrete cave that is the waiting area.

"Maybe Sandra is right," I think to myself as, jetlagged and exhausted, I am driven along the Universal Highway toward central Paris. "Why *am* I doing this again?" We pass sad modern hotels, the identical blue monoliths of Ikea and Castorama, miles of light industry. But a glimmer of hope rises in my heart at the familiar sight of the *Stade de France*, where France has won the World Cup in 1998.

Then, at *Porte d'Asnières,* when the taxi climbs off the *Périphérique* and turns through one of the former gates of a walled Paris, and we drive along Boulevard Malesherbes with its grand 19th century Haussmannian buildings, and I see the green flashing signs of the *pharmacies* (is it only me who sees the hidden message in these signs, *"Welcome to Paris, Welcome to Paris"*?), and we pass the familiar sight of the massive golden gates of *Parc Monceau*, and here I see a well-dressed man on a scooter, there an impossibly thin woman walking her dog. Then. Then I remember. We are now out of the Anywhere and into *La Vie*. It's Paris!

The city passes by in a delicious rush: the *fleuristes*, the arches, the *places*, the parks, the *boulangeries*. I can't wait to get to our apartment, drop the luggage and run out into the streets to buy my first baguette. Seeing it like this, from one side to the other, reminds me that Paris is not just one city, but many cities. So many that you could spend years and not experience them all, not even discover them all. Paris is a multiplicity of experiences. The editors of the *Michelin Green Guide* agree, "Ask a few Parisians: each has his Paris. Each has his Parises, one might say, insomuch as Paris is multiple, changing, contradictory." Every part of Paris, every Arrondissement, every avenue and boulevard, interests me and is a place I want to experience.

☙

Paris is an ancient city, but the city as we know it today was largely formed in the nineteenth century. It was Napoleon (it's *always* Napoleon, isn't it?) who started recreating Paris in the early 1800s with the building of Rue de Rivoli and it was his nephew, Louis-Napoleon, who carried on with the reforms until late in the century. In fact, the very layout of Paris, broad boulevards, large parks, twenty Arrondissements, and even the sewer and water systems, is the result of the work of Georges-Eugène Haussmann, the prefect of Paris from 1853 to 1870.

In the 1890s Auguste Escoffier perfected and codified *haute cuisine*, at the same time he was helping his friend Cesar Ritz to open his famous hotel. Many other enduring names in Parisian foodstuffs rose up in this period: *Debauve & Gallais chocolatiers* in 1800, *Dalloyau* in 1802, *Hediard* in 1854, *Fauchon* in 1886. The *grands magasins*, the famous Parisian department stores, were also founded: *Printemps* in 1865 and *Galeries Lafayette* in 1896.

The *Arc de Triomphe* was completed in 1836; *Palais Garnier*, then home of the Paris Opera, in 1874. The Eiffel Tower arose in 1889; the *Hôtel de Ville*, the city hall, was rebuilt in 1892; the grandiose *Pont Alexandre III*, the *Grand Palais* and the *Petit Palais* all in 1900. It was an explosion, a dot-com boom that didn't crash.

In 1800 Paris was still a medieval city, with narrow, unpaved streets and parks reserved for royalty. By 1900 it had been transformed into the

City of Lights. But even with all the changes, the older Small Paris still lived on within the new Big Paris.

ᑶᕽ

Everyone is familiar with Big Paris, it's the stuff of movies, travel brochures, and about a million photos on Flickr (200,000 of the Eiffel Tower alone). Big Paris is monumental and public: towers, museums, parks and *champs*. Small Paris is narrow streets, neighbourhood *boulangeries,* wine bars, pocket parks with children playing in them, and thousands of individual apartments. I love them both, and Paris needs both to be Paris. I keep returning to get more of each, to delight in the contrast and in the discovery.

Place Dauphine is one of my favourite places to stop and rest in Paris. The quiet *place* with its restaurants and *Bar du Caveau* is smack in the middle of Big Paris, but *Place Dauphine* is definitely Small Paris. Surrounded by the Seine (which is itself Big Paris) it shares the *Ile de la Cité* with the such monuments as the *Conciergerie*, Sainte-Chapelle and Notre Dame. And right next door, facing Place Dauphine, is Big Paris in the form of the grandiose *Palais de Justice*. At the *Bar du Caveau* you can enjoy a typical *tartine*, thin slices of ham and cheese melted on Poilâne bread, with a glass of flinty *Sancerre* for less than ten euros while watching the activity at the *Palais de Justice*. Fans of Inspector Maigret (he's the French Sherlock Holmes; without the addictions, but with a fondness for food and drink) know that this was his headquarters. Maigret often had his lieutenant run down to *Place Dauphine* to gather up some sandwiches and beer when an interrogation was underway.

Big Paris is the restaurant at *Hôtel Le Bristol*, with its coterie of specialized staff. One to serve you bread, one to pour Champagne, one to give you a stool for your purse, and one to guide you to the washroom when required. (By the way, always use the washroom in these places. The décor, ambiance, and accoutrements are not to be missed.) At *Le Bristol* there are separate dining rooms for each season. The Winter Room is just off the main lobby while the Summer Room adjoins the courtyard, open to the sky. The Winter Room is done in dark woods, heavy drapes, subdued lighting; the Summer Room is cool, in blue tones and light furniture, looking out on the green courtyard. Whatever the season you are presented with a multitude of miraculous courses, intricate food presentations, and a hefty tab at the end. Dinner at a four-star hotel restaurant in Paris is the best theatre around.

Restaurant Le Cinq (at *Hôtel George V*) is as much spa as restaurant. As they tuck cushions behind my back and arrange my feet on the velvet stool to the perfect chiropractic adjustment, my attendant notices I look chilled. Within seconds, he is wrapping a cashmere Pashmina around my shoulders. I suppose food was served, but all I remember is my relaxed shoulders and a sense of rejuvenation as I leave.

Small Paris is the compact wine bar near Madeleine where I sometimes lunch. The owners, a friendly couple in their 70s, prepare sandwiches and salad (the only items on the menu) using the worn cutting board and antiquated toaster oven that is their kitchen. The tiny room, with only three tables and a bar, is warm and welcoming. I drink a red *Auvergne*, which seems the perfect wine in this *caveau*. It's like eating at your grandparents' house; after lunch I want to clear the table, help with the dishes and look at a family photo album.

I thoroughly enjoy the experience of Big Restaurants, but, oddly, I never really remember the food. I know it was good, but I can't recall the specific flavours. The meals I've had in small restaurants leave strong flavour memories: the smoky, crispy *confit de canard*; the zingy salad dressing; the creamy goat cheese; the smoothness of the *crème brulée*.

❧

On my way with Mark and Alexandre to the Jardin du Luxembourg I stop off at my favourite Big Paris experience, and the best food show in town, *Le Grande Épicerie de Paris*, the grocery store attached to *Le Bon Marché*, Paris' high-end department store. It's a food lover's dream, a gourmet extravaganza, a Coliseum of comestibles. It's a place to watch Parisians, wearing cashmere and *Lacoste*, buying glorious foodstuffs: cheeses, meats and sausages as far as the eye can see, meticulously displayed behind sparkling glass; towers of elegantly boxed chocolate and bonbons; fresh apple, pear and raspberry tarts for appetites of all sizes. The selection runs from the ordinary (mustard and condiments) to the specialized (*foie gras* sandwiches, twenty different kinds of sea salt). I mingle with the crowd like an invisible visitor from another planet; nobody seems to notice me.

The lighting is low key; sexy halogen spotlights that show off the product, not the flooring. It's more like a food fashion show than a *hypermarché*. No rows of long, straight aisles here, the themed gondolas direct you this way and that. It's a place where I can slow down, be surrounded by great food, take a chance to think and to plan my meal; an oasis from the often frantic pace of Paris. I pay for my purchases and hurry to catch up with Mark and Alexandre.

∽

Children's voices cry out as they run and laugh and climb on the enormous rope pyramid in the play park at the Jardin du Luxembourg. Alexandre is at the very top, challenging the other kids, his new friends-for-a-day, to reach him. I wait for him to come down so we can eat lunch at the outdoor café.

When I first came to Paris, many years ago I stayed in a small hotel near Jardin du Luxembourg. Every morning I joined the runners who circled the perimeter of the park. I would pass the chess players and the tennis players and the children riding the miniature ponies that plodded back and forth along the garden's main walkway. I imagined coming here with my own children and letting them ride the ponies. After my run I would go out the garden gates for café crème and almond croissants at *Dalloyau* where, from the windows of the tea room upstairs, I looked down on the fountain in the *place* and the black and gold gates of Luxembourg.

Although the Jardin du Luxembourg is the garden of the French Senate, which is located in the Palais du Luxembourg at one end of the park, it is truly a people's park. Parisians and tourists alike come everyday, families, couples and individuals, to use the tennis courts, stroll along the shady pathways, or simply sit around the central pond on the iconic green chairs, shifting them around to face the sun, the pond, or their friends. Even on the hottest days there are cool places to sit among the trees and fountains of Luxembourg.

Leaving Mark and Alexandre, I promenade. In the chess corner, men lean over the boards in intense concentration while their cohorts look on in silent attention. Nearby, the *boules* courts are filled with middle-aged men playing the traditional game involving tossing heavy metal balls around. I watch a Johnny Halliday wannabe preparing his shot. Next to me another spectator, whom I immediately label the Professor because of his taped-up glasses and pocket-protector, nods to me and motions to the game in progress. "Do you know the rules?" he asks. I give a noncommittal shrug that he interprets as an invitation and, using his three English phrases, he launches into an explanation of the principals of the game. Johnny winks at the Professor sharing an inside joke, perhaps about picking up English chicks courtside.

As it turns out Alexandre has no interest in the ponies of Luxembourg but loves to climb the rope structure, play around the pond, and simply be with other kids. *Gendarmes* keep an eye on the kids as they run around the park. It's France, so there are rules. Sitting or walking on the grass is prohibited; there's only one strip of grass where lounging is allowed and, in the summer, it's as crowded as a sandy beach on the Côte d'Azur. To ensure that children keep to the rules *gendarmes* patrol the park in pairs. And they are vigilant: no climbing trees, no playing in the water, no sitting on the grass. Like other North Americans I first thought there were too many: too many police, too many rules. But, as I've spent more time here, I realize this is one way they keep Paris... well, Paris.

HAUSSMANN

Early one morning in 1854 residents of Parisian neighbourhoods were wakened by sounds of destruction. Their city was being changed.

Six months earlier Louis-Napoléon Bonaparte, now rechristened Emperor Napoleon III, had appointed an engineer and civil administrator by the name of George-Eugène Haussmann to recreate Paris. Haussmann, who called himself "Baron", wasted no time in drawing up plans that would change Paris forever. He envisioned the creation of broad, straight boulevards, lined with uniformly grand buildings; parks and open spaces; and a modern water and sanitation system.

Paris in 1853 was a morass of narrow, twisting medieval passageways, so it was remarkable how much of Haussmann's dream was accomplished in the next fifteen years, creating the Paris we know today.

Before Haussmann, Paris was known by both residents and visitors as a dirty city. There was a lack of hygiene, with sewage running down the middle of the streets in open ditches; there were hundreds of streets, alleys really, where two horses could barely squeeze past each other; there was darkness and dankness.

Haussmann's rebuilding began with the destruction of many of the city's streets and thousands of its houses. Wide boulevards were plowed through existing neighbourhoods, displacing the residents, and uniform five-storey apartment buildings were constructed. As many as 20,000 buildings were destroyed and 40,000 were built during the period of redevelopment. Haussmann also oversaw the construction of a sewer and fresh water system, with massive underground reservoirs.

Limestone for the massive construction projects was quarried from a spot in northeast Paris. The resulting excavation was then filled with horse dung collected from the streets, shaped and landscaped to become Parc Butte Chaumont.

It's because of Haussmann's work that we have modern Paris. But, he is not without critics. During the work thousands of low-income Parisians were forced out of their homes and relocated to Belleville and the Paris suburbs. Neighbourhoods that had existed for hundreds of years as socio-economic units were destroyed by the road building and the city was then redefined by twenty artificial Arrondissements that often cut through the ancient *quartiers*.

On the map of Paris it's easy to identify Haussmann's work. All those straight, wide streets, the *Grands Boulevards* – Boulevard St Michel, Boulevard de Montparnasse, Boulevard Haussmann – that slice across an older plan remind us that he was the architect of the Paris we love today.

I LOVE PARIS

It's easy to make a connection with life in Paris, to feel part of *la vie parisienne*. The sidewalks and streets of Paris are constantly flowing rivers of human contact. People are always going somewhere. In Paris you shop for food daily and on foot. And since Paris apartments are much smaller than our homes you need to go outside for space.

Although it's a big city, people tend to live in their neighbourhoods, their *quartiers*; Paris truly is a collection of villages. In Paris streets have names, not numbers, and names bestow personality and a sense of humanness to one's locale. Parisian have more of a connection to where they live.

Doing Christmas shopping at the *grands magasins* I am amazed to see autumn leaves still on the trees that line Boulevard Haussmann. But why are they sparkling? A closer look reveals that the leaves have been replaced, one-by-one, with shiny metallic stars in gold, oranges, reds and yellows. Subtle lighting makes them sparkle.

Summers Paris brings the beaches to you, and what a grand spectacle it is. *Paris Plage*, the four weeks in summer when main traffic arteries along the river banks are shut down and the Seine transposes into an improvised beach, complete with sand, sun chairs, volleyball and umbrellas. Showers dot the banks, spraying fine mists of cooling water on Parisians pretending to be on the Côtes d'Azur.

What makes Paris the most visited city in the world, the icon of elegance and good taste, is not just its tangible connection to history, but the miracle of an éclair, the hundreds of thriving cheese shops and *chocolatiers*. That the city's magnificent art museums are free. That a baguettes cost only a single Euro. That kissing on a park bench is *normale*. Paris brings out the romantic in everyone.

Salade de Chèvre Chaud
WARM GOAT CHEESE SALAD

I fell in love with this salad on our first night in Paris at *Bistrot Baracane*. I could eat this salad practically every day and sometimes I do! For added interest and flavour, I like to add toasted nuts and sliced strawberries or whole raspberries. A two ounce serving of goat cheese is ideal for a starter course; double it for a main course. A piece of unflavoured dental floss makes a great tool for slicing the goat cheese.

8 ounces soft goat cheese
½ cup breadcrumbs
½ tsp sea salt
freshly ground pepper
1 egg
salad greens, freshly
   washed and rinsed
¼ cup maple balsamic
   vinaigrette, (see
   separate recipe)

Preheat oven to 420° F.

Cut the goat cheese into two-ounce pieces. Using the palm of your hand, gently flatten each piece until it is shaped into a disc.

On a large plate, mix together the breadcrumbs and sea salt and freshly ground black pepper. On a deep sided plate or bowl, break the egg and beat. Dip the goat cheese into the egg mixture on each side and then lightly press into the breadcrumbs so that both sides are completely covered. Once the goat cheese is prepared, place in the refrigerator for about ten to fifteen minutes.

Line a baking tray with parchment paper and transfer the goat cheese on it. Place in the hot oven and bake for ten minutes.

In a large salad bowl, dress the greens with the vinaigrette. Place the goat cheese pieces over the greens and drizzle a small amount of the reserved dressing over the cheese. Serve with a crusty baguette.

Le Vinaigrette Balsamique
MAPLE BALSAMIC VINAIGRETTE

This vinaigrette has been a standard in my kitchen for close to twenty years. The trick is to not use too much maple syrup, just a dash mellows the flavour of the balsamic vinegar.

Always taste the vinaigrette before tossing with the greens. It may need a dash of salt or a drop more maple syrup.

1 clove garlic, minced
1 tsp Dijon mustard
pinch sea salt
freshly ground black
  pepper
¼ cup extra-virgin
  olive oil
1 T balsamic vinegar
1 tsp maple syrup

In a small bowl, blend together the minced garlic, Dijon mustard, salt and pepper. Slowly drizzle in the olive oil and whisk in until it is well blended.

It's important to keep blending until the ingredients are completely integrated.

Add in the balsamic vinegar and maple syrup and keep mixing until all the ingredients are well blended. Adjust the seasoning to taste.

CHRISTMAS IN PROVENCE

The room breaks out in applause as the two young women promenade the enormous turkey around the dining rooms. They're carrying the bird on what amounts to an avian stretcher, sagging with the weight of the giant roasted fowl.

It is Christmas Day and we are at Restaurant St Hubert in Entrechaux.

It was Tom who first told us about the *St Hubert*. "*Pichets* of Châteauneuf-du-Pape." He looked at each of us in turn, to make sure that this amazing fact sank in. "Can you imagine? The house wine is *Châteauneuf-du-Pape*. Served in pitchers." And then he went on to explain the specialties of the restaurant, as if he were talking to young children about school safety.

"You see, *St Hubert* is a game restaurant, with license to hunt and serve wild game like venison, boar, rabbit. The meats are slow-cooked in wine until the sauce is like chocolate and the meat falls from the bone."

"And the seafood platter," chipped in his helpmate, Jos. "Filled with fresh oysters and wonderful little shellfish like winkles and *bulots*. But only on special occasions," she added.

Tom told us that the restaurant had been owned by the same family since 1929. "We eat there every time we're in Vaison-la-Romaine. And we never miss the special Christmas Day dinner."

Alas, we first heard these glad tidings on December 30. Now we had to wait twelve months.

Three-hundred-fifty-nine days later, on Christmas Eve, we are back in Vaison-la-Romaine, in Tom and Jos' apartment, nibbling on carrot and celery sticks, talking about the next day's feast. Tom lays out the game plan for us.

"It's about pacing," he tells us. "Christmas dinner at *St Hubert* is a multi-course affair. We'll arrive at noon and probably not leave until sunset.

"No one can predict what will be on the menu. There's something new each Noël." But, he says, he can guarantee that there will be *foie gras*, "and, of course, there will be *gratin de cardons du pays*," he says, with a kind of flourish.

"What's that?" I ask. He explains that *cardon* is the traditional winter vegetable of Provence, a big celery-like plant that grows on the side of the roads and in gardens.

"So, it's a kind of ditch weed?" I ask.

"Well, yes, but it's delicious," Tom replies.

"You know," Tom leans back in his chair and scratches his chin, signals that he is moving into his professorial mode, "this is a perfect example of how the French differ from the British, and probably from you Canadians, too. In France, Christmas is not meant to be spent in the kitchen all day. It's the time to get into your finest clothes," I glance down at his worn, checked pants, "go out to a good restaurant, and spend time with friends in an enjoyment of food, wine, and life."

"You see, it's all because France had a revolution and we, in Britain, did not… " When he gets to the part about France being a hexagon, he notices our eyelids drooping. Smartly, he gets back to the matter at hand.

"Right, we meet here at 11:30 sharp. It's important to arrive on time," the Commander-in-Chief orders. Jos nods agreement.

∽

The next day we are in Tom's car, racing out of Vaison for the nearby town of Entrechaux. As we travel the road south the heights of the *Dentelles de Montmirail* are to our right, beautifully lit by the low December sun.

Just below the village of Crestet we turn toward Entrechaux. Green, rounded hills dot the landscape, rolling out eastward from the *Dentelles*, eventually growing into Alps in the unseen distance. In front of us, above the road that runs like an arrow toward Entrechaux, rises the single, rough peak that the village is built around. The ruined château at the top completes the picture. The château and the peak once provided protection and status to the town, today they provide a craggy beauty. The road skirts the peak and, a couple of curves and a traffic circle later, we are in Entrechaux.

Entrechaux is a small town, with limited services: the *Bar du Midi*, essential to any village; the abandoned *Café de France*; the charming *Mairie*, the town hall, with a perfect *petite place* in front. Tom pulls into the parking area in front of the restaurant: a plain, blocky, two-storey building with the simplest of signs: *St Hubert*.

We enter the restaurant grounds through a large gate, open to receive guests, and pass through a courtyard used for *al fresco* dining in the summer. But now the tables and chairs are stacked in a corner; red and green leaves cling to the trellis of vines overhead. Hanging by a rope from a second story window, is the skinny, sad, stuffed *Père Noël*, ubiquitous in Provence. He seems to be holding on for dear life. Just beside the door is the Provençal version of the Christmas tree, a few sparse branches that Charlie Brown would recognize.

Inside the restaurant we are warmly greeted by the owner, her daughter and her *belle-fille*, or daughter-in-law. The proprietress addresses Jos as *Madame* and we are introduced. The restaurant is filled with *les Français* settled in for the holiday feast. The large front room and the smaller side room are both heated by fireplaces and decorated with heads of deer, boar and other game; presumably from animals that were eaten in these very rooms.

We are seated beneath the head of a stag whose antlers are gaily decorated with tinsel and garlands. There is a gentle murmuring of voices, in marked contrast to the level of noise in restaurants in San Francisco or Calgary. The room is hot, but the French seem not to mind.

We start with a refreshing *coupe de Champagne* and review the list of courses that reads like something out of Tolstoy.

This is not the Christmas dinner I grew up with; one woman cooking for hours to serve the extended family. This is life, food and celebration of an entirely different sort. Course after course, each full of flavour; hearty, speaking of tradition, and wonderful. Nothing is rushed, the meal slowly extends through the afternoon, allowing time to appreciate food, the company and the day.

Yet I still feel like part of a family. Madame runs the room and serves tables, as do her daughter and her *belle-fille*. Their men are in the kitchen, as this family has worked for generations. Being surrounded by other

French families adds to the feeling. Like us, they are here to spend time together in an enjoyment of food, wine, and life.

Tom was right. By the time we leave the restaurant the sun is setting. And the *cardons* were wonderful.

Huîtres chaude gratinées, sauce royale, saumon fumé
Gratin of hot oysters with cream sauce and smoked salmon

Millefeuille de foie gras, betteraves rouges en folie sauce balsamique
Terrine of *foie gras*, served with red beets in balsamic sauce

*Filet de rouget barbet pane au sésame, panisse de
poix chiches au beurre, sauce bouillabaisse*
Sesame-coated red mullet filet with chickpeas
in butter, and a bouillabaisse sauce

Sorbet au marc de Provence
Sorbet with *marc* (Provençal liquor
made from grape pressings)

Dinde fermière rôtie au feu de bois, marrons confit
Wood-fire roasted turkey with candied chestnuts

Gratin de cardons a la crème
Cardons gratin

Brie de Meaux truffé, petite salade verte a l'huile d'olive
Cheese course: Brie with black truffles,
green salad with olive oil

*Nougat glace en coquille au chocolat, glace a
la châtaigne, coulis de maras des bois*
Two kinds of ice cream, nougat and chestnut,
served with a wild-strawberry sauce

Treize desserts
Platter of thirteen desserts

಄

Fleur de Thym

The chill has moved through the bottoms of my leather boots and sunk into my bones. It is one of the coldest winter seasons on record. The weekly outdoor market in Nyons is sparse in vendors and in shoppers; everyone is wrapped in silly scarves and hats. Seeking warmth, I walk to the top of the market to my favourite yellow patisserie. Although cold, the day is sunny and after a few minutes inside, I start to thaw.

"Aimez-vous de chocolat?," the lady behind the counter asks, seeing me eye the dessert case.

"Bien sur," I reply, using my favourite French phrase; of course I like chocolate! She launches into a detailed description of her favourite chocolate dessert and adds that it will be hot out of the oven in ten minutes. Whatever it is I will gladly wait.

"Pourriez-vous me recommander un bon restaurant pour le déjeuner à près d'ici?" I'm looking for a place for lunch. She carefully writes down a name with directions: *La Charrette Bleue* in the village of Les Pilles, on the route to Gap. She's been in the restaurant business and is fussy about her food. I trust her.

I know my trust is well-founded when I see the *gâteau au chocolat*. It's a dense, flourless chocolate cake shaped into a gold bar and decorated with gold flecks. She proudly wraps it and wishes me *bon appétit*.

The road to Les Pilles heads northeast from Nyons. I have never driven this way before and it seems like a new part of France. The curvy road follows the river Eygues through hills covered in trees. I catch glimpses of the river as we turn this way and that. There are fewer villages, fewer houses, more trees.

Les Pilles comes and goes in the blink of an eye. It is made up of a few buildings along the main road, a second street of deserted businesses, and a bridge connecting the south side of the village. The flaking stucco and weathered shutters are lit by the low winter sun. The effect is magical.

We go through the tunnel my friend at the bakery mentioned and, a couple of kilometres further, arrive at the restaurant, just on the side of the road. But the parking area is empty, not a good sign. Sure enough, *La Charrette Bleue* is closed for the holidays. We turn around and head back towards Nyons. It's time for Plan B. For me Plan B means "keep on going and hope something good happens". Which, come to think of it, is not a bad approach to finding a restaurant in France.

"Wait," I say, *"there's* a restaurant!" But it's too late to stop and we carry on through the tunnel. We're practically back in back in Nyons before we can stop and turn around. Then it's down the road, back to Les Pilles and through the tunnel again, before we finally pull into the parking lot. There in front of us, in a stone building on the small hill, is a restaurant. And it is open!

A very pregnant young woman wearing denim overalls greets us a the door. The room is modern and warm, with a large river-stone lamp in the centre and a wood stove in the corner. I stand beside the stove to warm myself while Madame readies our table. It's a new restaurant for us and I wonder what lies ahead. We're the only diners and that's often not a good sign, but I like the decor and the table settings. I notice the tall, wide-rimmed wine glasses and feel better. The menu is promising, too; a four-course lunch for 28 euros called *Balade des Moulins*. Besides, I am freezing and starving and I'm not going to leave until I am warm and fed.

Denim overalls recommends the *apéritif maison*. I taste the delicate Champagne cocktail, there's a touch of peach and a hint of the tropics, and I know we are in the right restaurant.

Each course confirms that we are at one of the best tables in France on this cold Thursday afternoon. At the side of the road. In Les Pilles, population 249.

La sucette de fois gras d'oie, au pain d'épices,
d'olives verte et noires, AOC de Nyons
Foie gras shaped like a lollipop on a stick, coated in
gingerbread spices, with green and black olives

La cassolette d'escargots de la Drôme, façon provençale
Provençal stew with escargots from the Drôme

Le médaillon de veau rôti parfume au romarin et huile de truffe
Roasted medallion of veal with rosemary and truffle oil

Les fromages d'ici et d'ailleurs
Cheeses from here and elsewhere

Le millefeuille moelleux café amandes, glace au caramel
Thousand-layer warm chocolate cake with coffee
coated almonds and caramel ice cream

ᕲᕱ

Le Poème de Grignan

It's already noon but nothing can stop me from racing from our villa in Vaison-la-Romaine to far-off Grignan in time for lunch. I know where we're going to eat: the attractive restaurant in the medieval village with the small courtyard garden and blue shutters. This is the restaurant that keeps eluding me. Every time I've been in Grignan I've tried to eat there, but something always prevent it.

"*Déjeuner à 2:00?*" the proprietress sniffed on our last attempt, "*C'est impossible!*" In France lunch is only served from noon until about 1:30. Today, though, I'm determined to make it.

We speed through the chilly countryside with lunch on our minds, barely noticing the beautiful towns we pass through on our route. Taking a "shortcut" through Vinsobres only adds extra minutes to the trip. We have to hurry, it's already 1:00!

We reach Grignan and run up the narrow passageway to the restaurant. *"Fermeture jusqu'a fev. 10"* reads the hand-lettered sign on the door. Closed for holidays. It takes a moment for that to filter through: does it mean it's closed for lunch? Of course it does. Not again!

I need another Plan B, but in shock from the madcap drive, the dash up the street, and the disappointment at seeing the sign, I stagger back a step... and run into the wall behind me. Slowly I turn around and find, posted on the wall, the menu for restaurant *Le Poème de Grignan*. The restaurant whose door is right now in front of me. Mark and I nod at each other and enter.

A petite, shy woman greets us. She notices that we're a bit haggard and, with few words exchanged, guides us deep into the restaurant, far away from the cold. At this point I'm relieved to be in any restaurant, but *Le Poème* is calm and inviting. The room is tastefully decorated in beige and white with paintings and drawings on the wall. Under the soft lighting I begin to relax. She takes our coats and presents the menu.

The commune of Grignan lies just inside the border of the department of the Drôme. It's famous for a magnificent château, but perhaps even more famous for the 17th-century Marquise de Sévigné, often called the greatest letter writer in Europe. Over the course of thirty years the Marquise wrote 1500 letters to her daughter, whose husband was *Comte de Grignan*, recounting life in Paris at the court of Louis XIV. The Marquise de Sévigné died in Grignan in 1696, and it has been a place of pilgrimage for students of literature ever since.

Madame delivers steaming hot soup to our table. For Mark, *raviolis aux escargots*, three large dumplings filled with *escargot*, something I haven't seen before, served in a heady broth of beef stock, vegetables and parsley, and topped with slivers of truffle. I start with *soupe de potimarron et quenelle de mascarpone*, a creamy pumpkin soup with egg-shaped quenelles of mascarpone, also topped with truffle. These two soups, worlds apart in ingredients and preparation, yet equally delicious, are alone worth the long drive. I feel every muscle unwind; long winter lunches in Provence really are the best remedy for the cold.

Nearby, a trio of businessmen quietly enjoy their meal. They are discussing the wine, avidly, but in the low-volume voice you find among French diners. I envy their ability to have lunches like this on a Wednesday afternoon.

For the main course a filet of *dorade*, pan-fried fish with a crispy skin, is served on a bed of spinach. Mark chooses *aiguillette de canard poêlées*, accompanied by mushrooms and *cardons*. *Aiguillettes* are the most tender parts of a duck breast, here they are perfectly pan-fried and soft enough to cut with a fork. In these dishes the chef again demonstrates his ability to handle two very different meals, with a solid understanding of each dish. A local *Coteaux de Tricastin* from Domaine des Rosier is perfect for both the meal and the region.

In between courses we chat with our server about the restaurant. It is owned by her and her husband; Hervé behind the stove while Valérie serves. She speaks in a soft whisper, so we lean in close to hear that the restaurant has been open for two years and they are happy with the business and the town. Chef Hervé comes out of the kitchen to greet us and we find him to be equally unassuming and soft spoken. I compliment him on his wonderful restaurant and tell him I think his food is star-worthy.

Dessert is another triumph for the chef. Mark is served a *soufflé chaud au Grand Marnier,* puffy and glorious and everything a *soufflé* should be. Meanwhile, on my side of the table there is a presentation of three quenelles of *mousse au chocolat,* layered with a Florentine cookie; with a scoop of vanilla ice cream, topped by caramelized sugar and finely chopped almonds.

Valérie brings the bill and surprises us with two glasses of Champagne to thank us for our patronage. The low winter sun is setting as we leave the restaurant. Plan B has come through once again. We will return to Grignan a number of times, but we never make it to the restaurant with the blue shutters.

Soupe de potiron au mascarpone
Pumpkin soup with mascarpone

Escargot raviolis dans un bouillon
Escargot ravioli in broth

Dorade poêlée aux épinards
Pan-fried dorade with spinach

Aiguillettes poêlé aux champignons et cardons
Pan-fried duck with mushrooms and *cardons*

Grand Marnier souffle
Mousse au chocolat
Domaine des Rosier, *Coteaux de Tricastin*

Pavé de Saumon Grillé
HIGH-BROILED SALMON

This recipe was inspired by Provençal chef Lydie Marshall and her wonderful cookbook, *Passion for My Provence*, a book I return to often. Though this is a simple recipe, the results are spectacular, a beautiful crusty skin with perfectly cooked flesh. It's important to use a heavy pan for this recipe and a cast-iron skillet is best.

1 2-lb salmon filet, skin on	Lightly coat the skillet with olive oil. Pre-heat the broiler on the highest setting. Adjust the oven rack to about 5 inches from the broiler.
1 T extra-virgin olive oil	
1 T lemon juice	When the broiler is hot, place the skillet (without the salmon) under the broiler and let it heat up for 10 minutes.

Without removing the skillet from the broiler, place the salmon in the pan, skin side up. (The pan will be extremely hot, so use caution.) The fish begins to cook immediately. Broil until the skin is charred and caramelized, about 10 minutes. It's important that your broiler stay hot, and that the flame or element is lit while the salmon is cooking.

Remove from the broiler (remember, the skillet is very, very hot), squeeze on some lemon juice, and serve immediately.

Pommes de Terre Rôtis au Four aux Pistaches
OVEN ROASTED POTATOES WITH PISTACHIOS

In the markets of Provence it's easy to find pistachios that have already been shelled and when I'm there, I use them in a variety of ways. Here I've added a handful to roasting potatoes for unexpected flavour and crunchiness.

3 lbs yellow potatoes

2 T extra-virgin olive oil

1 T *Herbes de Provence*

½ tsp   sea salt

2 shallots

2 T lemon juice

½ cup green pistachios, shelled

splash of extra-virgin olive oil

Preheat oven to 420° F.

Scrub the potatoes, peel them, cut them into quarters and place them in a baking dish. Coat with the olive oil and toss. Crush the *Herbes de Provence* in your fingers and sprinkle over the potatoes. Add the sea salt to taste and toss again. Put the pan into the preheated oven.

Peel and medium-chop the shallots. In a small bowl, toss the shallots and pistachios with the lemon juice and a splash of olive oil. Set aside.

After the potatoes have been cooking for 20 minutes add the shallots and pistachios mixture to the potato pan and toss together. Return the pan to the oven for another 20 to 30 minutes, for a total baking time of 40 to 50 minutes. Cooking time will vary depending on the potatoes; look for golden brown potatoes that are soft to a fork test. Serve immediately. Serves 4 to 8.

Chou-fleur Gratiné
CAULIFLOWER GRATIN

Whenever we eat at *St Hubert* in Entrechaux we are sure to be served delicious *cardon du pays*. *Cardon* is a hard vegetable to come by in other parts of the world, but gratin made with cauliflower is another classic at Provencal tables, and is often served at *gros souper*, the traditional vegetarian Christmas Eve dinner.

2 lbs cauliflower
2+ T butter
2 T flour
1 cup milk or chicken stock
4 ounces *Gruyère* cheese, grated
1/3 cup heavy cream
1 lemon, juiced
sea salt and freshly ground pepper
a pinch ground nutmeg

Preheat oven to 425° F.

Wash the cauliflower cut it into small florets. Put it into a steamer to cook for about 5 minutes. Drain the cauliflower and dry the pieces in a kitchen towel.

Melt the butter in a saucepan, add the flour, and cook for 2 minutes, whisking constantly. Don't let it burn. Slowly add the milk or stock, and keep stirring. Bring to a boil, then reduce to simmer for a few minutes until it thickens, stirring constantly. Season with salt and pepper, and fold in the cream and most of the grated cheese. (Save a bit of the cheese for the top of the gratin.) I like to add a couple of dashes of nutmeg.

Place the steamed cauliflower in the bottom of a shallow baking dish, cover with the sauce and toss. Scatter the extra cheese on top with a few dots of butter. Bake uncovered until it is well browned and bubbling hot, about 15 to 20 minutes. Serve 4 to 6.

PAIN DES
AMIS

Un pain tout en croûte,
légèrement fumé,
comme cuit au bois.. !

250g / 500g
2,1€ / 4,2€

OF BREAD AND IDEAS

Imagine if you had to have your holiday time approved by the police. Or imagine studying for seven years so you could work from four in the morning until nine at night, *six* days a week.

This is the life of a *boulanger*. In France, you can't simply take a baking course and call yourself a baker. It takes the same amount of study as a doctor to belong to the order of French *Boulangers* who follow a rigid code that dates back to the time of Napoleon. (Doesn't every code in France?)

I want to find out more about the workings of a *boulangerie* so I've arranged to visit a long-time baker on location. Making use of the GPS system on my iPod (the only way I can find my way around), I find the bakery on Rue de Richelieu, wedged between a laundromat and a tiny hotel. Claude Esnault has agreed to meet me at eleven, just after the morning rush, at his aptly named *Au Richelieu Boulangerie* in the 1st Arrondissement. A solid man in his sixties, his hands look like the dough that he has kneaded for fifty years. He grabs both my hands in a sturdy shake.

He takes me past the cash register through the kitchen where the *pâtisserie* is made, and then down a sloping ramp to the battered kitchen of his *boulangerie*. "This has been a bakery for two hundred years! Of course, I wasn't baking then" he jokes, "but I've been here a very long time." Claude enjoys his role as an experienced artisan and this shows as he banters, gesticulates and pantomimes. Bread is his life. "Where do you think we store the flour?" he asks. I look around and don't see any large sacks of anything. He points to the large pipes overhead. "These pump the flour from the delivery truck to our storage bin; no need for hauling heavy sacks of flour, the pipes do the work." Through other pipes, he explains, the flour is pumped into the mixing bowls, keeping the workroom neat and tidy.

By the age of ten Claude knew what he wanted to be: not a priest, not a rock star, but part of the fraternity of flour. His parents had different ideas and insisted that he stay and work the farm, but, at fourteen years old, he left for Paris to follow his dream.

A baker's apprenticeship takes seven full years. For two years Claude would spend two weeks at school, alternated with two weeks of work in a bakery. Then, for the next three years, he worked full time as a baker's assistant, often with fifteen-hour days. Finally, he was an associate baker under the direction of a master *boulanger* for another two years before becoming a full-fledged *boulanger.*

Claude has been handling dough for over fifty years, and has been a *boulanger* for forty. Now that he's retired, he doesn't come in until 7:30 in the morning and is able to leave with the last customer at 8:30 at night. But, for him, it's a passion. He loves his customers and he loves helping his daughter to take over the family business.

Before 1945 (*"Avant la guerre,"* he says), when there was a shortage of electricity in France, mixing and kneading were done by hand. As a result, baguettes from that era had a different texture and weight. Now giant mixers do most of the work, combining the ingredients and kneading the dough. He reminds me that good bread needs only four ingredients; flour, water, yeast and salt.

He takes a batch of kneaded dough and puts it into a cutting machine that divides it into eight equal pieces. He drops each piece into another machine to shape it. The dough that comes out now has the familiar flute shape of a baguette and is then hand rolled and placed into a special baking tray with eight cradles shaped like baguettes. Once he fills the tray, Claude pops it into the proofing oven, and takes out another tray to make space. Grabbing a razor blade, he slits the proofed baguettes with eight diagonal cuts, *"Exactement huit!"* and puts them on the baking trolley and walks them into a large electric oven. Claude has worked with gas ovens, wood-fired ovens, but finds that electric ovens work the best. He shows me the steam valve that releases the moisture that will help to make a crisp and brown crust.

Every element in the making of baguettes is controlled: the air temperature, the temperature of the water, the precise number of cuts in the top of each baguette.

"Every day, except Wednesdays when we get a day of rest, we bake 400 baguettes, 200 croissants, and 150 *pain au chocolat,* plus the pastries." Claude lets me know that the pastries are made by a pastry chef, not the baker. "Back in the old days, everyone ate more bread. Maybe three baguettes a day! Those were the days. Now, away from the farm and in the city, people eat less than one." But the good news, he tells me, is that croissant sales are up. Once only enjoyed on Sundays and holidays they are now a daily staple for Parisians.

Since Napoleonic times the *préfectures,* or local governments, have monitored the vacation times of the *boulangeries* in their district. A *boulangerie* cannot be closed for annual holiday without the approval of the local *préfecture.* This is to ensure that each neighbourhood or village has a *boulangerie* open at all times. Imagine a neighbourhood without a source of daily fresh bread!

The use of the word *boulangerie* is also monitored by law. "To say '*boulangerie*' on my sign means that the bread is baked here on the premises," he pats the work table for emphasis. Then he leans closer and lowers his voice, "You know the bakery chain called *Paul?* Next time you pass one, notice they do not have the word *boulangerie* in its name, because their bread is baked at a central facility, a *factory.*" Also, Claude says, if he happens to sell out of baguettes, he cannot borrow a dozen or so from a fellow *boulanger.* "*C'est interdit,*" he declares.

The baguettes are now ready to come out of the oven. He beckons me to view them and also to hear them. And, sure enough, they are crackling and frizzling. Just as Jean-Marc Larrue taught me in Avignon, you also cook with your ears.

I ask him what qualities make a good baguette. He lumbers to the tray of baguettes, picks one up and holds it close to the fluorescent light. "Colour and texture, *bien sur,* a crispy crust of a golden colour," he says. But, the real way to judge a baguette is to hold it up to a light. "*Si la lumière traverse, c'est bon.*" If the light passes through, it's good. "Of course I don't do that with all my baguettes," he laughs.

After the morning rush he likes to take a freshly baked baguette into his office and, in silence, enjoy his own breakfast. "After all these years, I still look forward to my baguette in the morning."

It's time to make croissants. "We use the same recipe, the same four basic ingredients, with one important addition: sugar. We make the dough fresh daily, hand knead it, and then leave it to rest." He demonstrates how the dough is rolled out and folded again and again with butter. "It was Marie Antoinette who brought the croissant from Austria. But it was the French who perfected it," he laughs.

"If a croissant is straight, like this one, it's made with butter. The croissants that are curved are made only with margarine," he lets me in on another secret. Croissants called *"nature"* are actually made with margarine!

"You want to make *pain au chocolat*? It's easy." He grabs another piece of croissant dough. "Instead of rolling, you fold it into a square and put in a special piece of chocolate, available only to bakers. This chocolate has a high cocoa content and doesn't instantly melt into a puddle, but stays firm yet soft inside the dough as it is baked."

Does he still love his job after all these years? "I see *mes clients* come in first thing in the morning, they are sad, tired, depressed. And then they take their first bite of my croissant or baguette and zing, they smile. Dentists can't say the same."

ಲಾ

Du Pain et des Idées

When I met with Christophe Vasseur, one of the most renowned bakers in Paris, he was shovelling snow off the sidewalk in front of his shop, *Du Pain et des Idées*. A rugged, handsome man, he stopped to greet each passer-by. After chatting with his customers, he welcomed me inside his picture-perfect *boulangerie*.

Christophe is a calm, serious man, and spoke about his work and career in a thoughtful manner.

"I have always loved beautiful things. Ever since I was a child I wanted to become a baker. But my parents are doctors, so this was just not possible. I started to work in fashion, and it took years for me to transform my life.

"By the time I was thirty I had decided to leave fashion to become a baker. It was unheard of - most bakers start when they are fourteen or fifteen years old. I had to beg to apprentice with Jean-Paul Mathon, a master *boulanger* I admired greatly. I asked him twenty or thirty times before he agreed.

"Finally, there I was on my first day of work, at three a.m. I think Jean-Paul was surprised that I showed up. My first job was to cut the brioche dough. As soon as I started I had a smile as big as a banana! I was so happy. I knew I had golden hands, I knew I had a special talent."

Christophe opened his bakery in 2002 and in 2008 he received the coveted *Gault Millau* award as the best *boulangerie* in Paris. His sense of fashion is apparent. Every inch of the shop is beautiful and carefully considered. Assistants move quietly as they top up and rearrange the displays.

Christophe points to his *chausson aux pomme*. "I don't use any sugar or jam, just apples and pastry. This way you taste each ingredient and don't hide behind sugar."

"When I first saw this location, I knew I had to have it. It is authentic, turn of the century. The last owners went out of business because it was not a good location. But look at the details, the classic architecture."

"Here's the bread that put me on the map, *pain des amis.*" He points to a huge display of rustic bread, "I used to make this bread only for friends on the weekend and they would say, why not make this for the bakery? So I did. Our customers tried it and wanted more. This bread is now served by Alain Ducasse at *Plaza Athénée.*

"The dough takes two days to make and an hour and fifteen minutes to bake. I wanted to create a bread that tasted like it just came out of a wood fire with a smoky taste.

"Through hands and heart and mind - that is how I express myself."

When I asked him if the life of a baker is hard, he shrugged. "I have arranged it works for me I woke up this morning at 7:30 with my kids,

I live just down the street, but my bakers come in early and start the bread. Most of my staff are women, they are more reliable. We only work Monday to Friday.

"My job is to maintain standards, so I am always here looking, tasting, talking to customers. I tried to open another location but it just didn't worked. Here, I can control it all."

As I was about to leave, an enthusiastic customer told me, "I live in the Marais, and I always come here for my bread. I would travel even further if I had to."

The Lifespan of a Baguette

It's shorter than you may think! The baguette has a six-hour lifespan making it shorter than the lifespan of a butterfly. The baguette bought for breakfast is dead by mid-afternoon and will need to be replenished by dinner time.

Scones au Citron Parisienne
PARISIAN LEMON SCONES

It was Paris during Christmas and we had been walking for hours. We finally stopped at a *salon de thé* in the 6th Arrondissement where we enjoyed a plateful of lemon scones served with cherry *confiture* and mascarpone cheese. Here's my version of the flaky lemony scones that we ate that winter day.

2 cups unbleached
　　white flour
½ tsp sea salt
¼ cup unrefined sugar
1 T baking powder
¼ cup butter, chilled
½ cup plain yogurt
2 egg yolks
½ lemon, zested and
　　juiced
3 T cream

Preheat oven to 425° F.

In a medium size mix together the flour, salt, sugar and baking powder. Cut in the butter with forks or your fingertips until the flour and butter mixture have a consistency of coarse breadcrumbs.

In another bowl mix together the yogurt, eggs yolks, lemon zest, lemon juice and cream. Add this to the flour mixture and mix lightly together. On a wooden board knead 3 to 4 times, but be careful not to over handle.

Pat the dough into an 8-inch round about ¾-inch thick. Using a round cookie cutter, cut into separate shapes. Carefully transfer the cut scones to a cookie sheet lined with parchment paper. Sprinkle with sugar and bake 12 to 15 minutes until golden brown.

Sometimes when I make these scones I add a lemon glaze made by mixing together the juice from ½ lemon with 3 tablespoons of sugar. Once cooled slightly, drizzle over the warm scones.

Serve with cherry preserves and mascarpone cheese.

Boule
FRENCH RUSTIC BREAD

As I learned from a Parisian *boulanger*, good bread needs only four ingredients: water, salt, yeast and flour. When I'm not in France and I find myself pining for the rustic breads found in every *boulangerie*, I turn to this amazing recipe for fast, no-knead bread. I adapted this recipe from *Artisan Bread in Five Minutes a Day*. This streamlined method produces lovely, crusty bread and because it's so easy to make, it's possible to bake fresh daily loaves.

To steam or not to steam? Much has been written about adding steam to the oven to help make a crunchier loaf. But after much experimenting, I discovered my bread is crunchy, with a holey, soft interior, without steaming. So, I now skip this step; just one less thing to do.

1½ T yeast, dry active
1½ T coarse sea salt, (it must be coarse!)
3 cups lukewarm water
6½ cups unbleached flour

Thirty minutes before baking, place a pizza stone in the oven and heat to 450° F.

Two hours before baking, in a large mixing bowl, add the water, yeast and salt and stir briefly. Then stir in the flour using a rubber spatula to integrate the flour into the water, salt, yeast mixture. Make sure the cups of flour are scant and not brimming over the top.

Mix until all the flour is incorporated, this step should take just about two minutes. If the mixture is bone dry, add a tablespoon of water to the bottom of the bowl and stir in, repeat if necessary. The mixture should be fairly wet.

Loosely cover the bowl with plastic wrap and set aside for two hours (or more.) After two hours, the dough will have risen considerably. Have some extra flour nearby and with your hands, grab a handful of dough about the size of a melon. Cut off this portion of dough with a sharp knife.

With flour on your hands, form the dough into a ball, pulling it smooth towards the bottom. Tighten it by pinching the seam underneath. Make sure the dough is not sticking to your hands, so use as much flour to dust your hands as you need. The *boule* shaping step should take about 30 to 60 seconds.

On a bread peel (or a cutting board) sprinkle a handful of corn meal so the bread doesn't stick. Place the formed dough onto the peel or board. If the dough has already been at room temperature for two hours, you are ready to bake. With a sharp knife or blade, cut about ½ inch deep slashes diagonally across the top of the dough (3 slashes are plenty): this helps to form the artisan crust. Now sprinkle extra flour on top and put into the oven. With a firm jerk, the dough will move from the peel and onto the stone. Set the timer for 30 minutes.

The bread will pop up into a lovely *boule* shape within minutes. When the crust is a deep golden brown it is ready to take out. Let the bread cool for at least 30 minutes before you eat. If you can wait!

This recipe makes medium-size 3 medium *boules* or 4 small *boules*. If you're not planning to bake them all, simply put the covered dough into the fridge. It's good for two weeks.

When using dough straight from the fridge, shape into *boules*, and let rest covered for about an hour before baking. This recipe can also be used for pizza dough.

THE CHEESE SHOP OF BELLEVILLE

"WEEeeeiii" I yell as I zoom toward the centre of Paris. I'm on longest slide in the city and Alexandre is right behind me. He throws his hands into the air as he flows like mercury toward Earth.

Parc de Belleville is forest boughs, grassy patches and wildflowers. It's the type of park you don't see in the centre of Paris; untamed, modern and breathtaking. There are no gendarmes keeping order. You can run through the grass and dangle your feet in the fountain without fear of reprimand.

It's big park. A long cascading pool cuts through the middle, leading downhill to a small vineyard growing *pinot meunier* and *chardonnay*. The highest park in the city, it affords the best view of Paris. On the slide it feels like you're heading right into the Eiffel Tower, seven kilometers away.

And the playground! It's a modernist interpretation of a child's dream with a curved climbing-wall that resembles the bottom of an ocean liner, complete with megaphones and tunnels. There's a rope-slung lookout platform and the zoomy slide that Alexandre can't get enough of.

We're on our way to take a behind-the-scenes look at life in an artisan cheese shop.

The *quartier* of Belleville is all zigs and zags, ups and downs, narrow streets winding through the neighbourhood. The place is buzzing with activity: cars, buses, people, construction. It feels like an older version of Paris, like a pop-up city from a children's book.

Belleville is Paris without Haussmann. In fact, many people who were forced out of their homes in the centre of Paris by Haussmann's ambitious rebuilding projects moved to this area. In the 19th century it was nothing but shanties, fields, windmills, taverns, and a gypsum quarry that is now the site of the park.

This was Edith Piaf's neighbourhood, a place for the working class and immigrants. Now, I've heard, Belleville is becoming trendy and celebrities like Audrey Tatou are choosing to live here. I could live here, too; it's alive, real, and vibrant.

The cheese shop is shuttered when we arrive at the lunch hour. It's hard to imagine there's anything interesting behind the steel rolling door. A head peeks out from the courtyard door next to the shop. "I'll unlock the door."

A minute later the door rumbles up to reveal the store, done in warm, cheesy, inviting colours; the sign above the windows proclaims it to be *Fromagerie Beillevaire.* "Welcome to the shop," says the head again, this time attached to a body. It's Jérôme the owner, apron on, sleeves rolled up.

I'm fully charmed by the small store. Dozens and dozens of cheeses are laid out on shelves of simple wooden slats. Cheese colours range from white to grey to dirty brown to bright orange. My nose twitches at the blend of aromas. Alexandre, for his part, takes a quick look around then pulls out his DS player and hunkers down in a corner.

"This is your shop?" I ask.

"Yes, I own it with Pascal Beillevaire," says Jérôme. "He is a friend of my father and so, now, I am his partner. Pascal has fourteen cheese shops found in all parts of Paris, but he still lives very near to the dairy farm he was born on."

Pascal Beillevaire, Jérôme explains, has been a cheese maker all his life. He makes and ages a variety of cheeses such as *Dôme St. Estephe, Charollais, Cathare, Couronne,* and *Trois Laits.* His dairy farm is near Machecoul in the Loire Valley where his family has deep roots. Today he not only makes cheeses, he searches for new cheeses and promotes unpasteurized dairy products from all parts of France.

"At first," Jérôme continues, "we sold only products made at his own dairy. But Pascal decided to expand to include *affinage*, the aging of cheeses. Now we also sell cheeses from small farms, *fermier* producers, who send their young cheeses to be aged in Pascal's caves."

By working with small dairy farms, Pascal is helping to keep the artisan trade alive. Two hundred producers send more than four hundred cheeses to his caves; cheeses that are sold all over France and even exported to the US.

"Cheese is very important to us in France. Fifty years ago there were perhaps four hundred varieties; now there are over one thousand! But only fifty-six cheeses are classified with *dénomination*. *Camembert, Brie de Meaux, Roquefort, Epoisses, Chèvre*, and *Tomme de Savoie* are just a few."

In my mind I can see French fourth graders memorizing the names of the fifty-six AOC cheeses.

Jérôme is one of those guys you wish your daughter would bring home for dinner. Smart, earnest, a bit of a mischievous smile and the cutest little cheese hat you've ever seen.

His display of cheeses is impressive. There are large round flat discs, big balls of various sizes, Hershey Kisses shapes, hockey pucks in wrinkled dark grey, little round pyramids with ash and dried spices on the outside, and rounds as big as a bistro table. Jérôme shows me one that looks like a moon rock and another that looks distinctly like the dust bunnies you find under the bed.

An amoeba-shaped, orange cheese in a round wooden box is *Mojette*, a *fromage maison* (that is, made by the Beillevaire dairy), shaped like and named after a bean traditionally grown in the Loire. The crusty moon rock is a *Mimolette*: a melon-shaped, neon orange cheese that gets its deep orange colour from annatto, a tropical dye, and its unusual pock-mocked exterior from cheese mites that are introduced during the aging process to give the cheese its distinctive flavour. With other cheeses, bacteria and molds perform a similar function.

"All of our yogurt, *crème fraîche*, butter and the *fromage maison* are made using raw milk," Jérôme explains. "At the dairy, fresh milk arrives twice each day from local farms. When it arrives, the milk is still warm from the cow, at the perfect temperature to make cheese."

Hearing about all the details reminds me how much goes into the production and *affinage* of cheese: artistry and science, tradition and technology. I taste cheeses from the Loire Valley, Provence, Auvergne, Normandy and Aquitaine. Alexandre declines.

Jérôme holds up little gray log, which he tells me is a *Saint Maure de Touraine*. "This is called the Masterpiece of Touraine. See how it is rolled in black wood ash with its blotchy rind. It happens like this with age. This cheese is famous for the long piece of straw in its middle. No it's not for drinking milkshakes. The straw makes the handling easier. Let's taste." Saint Maure is a goat cheese with a lovely, musty, citrus flavour.

The wrinkled hockey puck shape is a Rocamadour from the Lot, a department in southwestern France. "Like many French cheeses, it is named from the town. Rocamadour comes from a very young goat's milk. It can be eaten after just 14 days of ageing. Like this, fresh and young, it is very good on *tartines* and salads."

I'm surprised by the variation of these cheeses from different regions, where the animals feed on local grasses and grains. I swear I can taste the *goût de terroir*, the flavor of the place.

I've seen, tasted and learned much today, but now my visit to *Fromagerie Beillevaire* is coming to an end. Alexandre comes up for air from his game player and I tell him it's time for us to go.

"Yes, it is the best place in Paris!" Jérôme exclaims when I mention to him how much I like Belleville. "Everything is here: the shops, the parks. And there are many beautiful buildings. Come, I will show you."

With that he grabs his keys, shutters the shop, and takes us through the neighbouring double doors. I'm flabbergasted by what I find inside. Half a dozen four-storey buildings from the 19th century surround a massive cobblestone courtyard with large trees in the middle. It was probably originally a nursing college or a nun's residence, but I'm amazed that this magnificent space is here on this narrow, twisty street. Jérôme leads us around the corner to another courtyard door where we find a similar stupefying *manoir*.

We say our goodbyes and thanks to Jérôme, and then Alexandre and I head off, hand in hand, to Parc de Belleville, to take one more ride down Paris' longest slide.

FRENCH BUTTER

Butter is the not-so-secret ingredient of French cooking. The biggest difference between French butter and most others is its higher butterfat content. Yes, that's right, French butter has more fat and that's why it tastes better! And, of course, butter in France has an AOC, *Appellation d'Origine Contrôlée*. Two of them.

Perhaps the most famous AOC butter is from Isigny-sur-Mer on the northwest coast of France, at the D-Day beaches. (Isigny is also famous for its Mimolette and Camembert cheeses.) According to the *Isigny Sainte-Mère* Dairy Co-operative, producer of the butter, "It is yellow like buttercups, with a faint taste of hazelnuts. Our *terroir* has the advantage of a mild, damp climate, is near to the sea and enjoys the benefits of the Bessin and Cotentin marshes. The cows which graze there feed on grass rich in iodine, beta carotene and trace elements. It is impossible to confuse with any other butter." This is what I love, poetry and produce.

Butter made from fresh or cultured unpasteurized milk is called *beurre cru*, raw cream butter. *Beurre cru* has a clean, creamy flavour and it's what Jérôme sells at *Fromagerie Beillevaire.*

At eight kilograms per person, the French are, hands down, the biggest butter eaters in the world. On a trip to a French supermarket you might find a dozen brands with varieties including unsalted, lightly salted, fully salted; *beurre pasteurisé*, made with pasteurized cream; and artisan butter made on the dairy farm from raw cream. For bakeries there's *beurre pâtissier*, with an even higher fat content, 99.8% ! It's no wonder French croissants taste so good.

VIVE LE CHEESE!

When De Gaulle uttered his famous remark about cheese and the governing of France I think he was trying to say, "Cheese is what defines us as a nation, it's what sets us apart from the rest of the world."

I don't know why it took me so long to figure out how important cheese is to French life. I've been to France many, many times, but I didn't feel the full force of *fromage français* until recently.

When I asked Brigitte, a Parisian friend, if she eats cheese daily, she looked at me. With suspicion. She eats *fromage* not once, she told me, but at least twice every day. That night we ate at her apartment. It was just the two of us, but when she brought out the cheese course I thought maybe she had invited another dozen friends. It was huge!

But it took a visit to a cheese expert in Paris and her intensive cheese brain training for me to start to understand the history, background, variety and tastes of French cheese.

Gerri is a walking Google Search of French cheese who has spent several years studying this food group. She now leads a cheese tasting course called *Paris on Your Plate*. When I arrived at Gerri's apartment I found eight other participants with shining faces sitting around a table filled with grapes and baguettes. In front of each guest was a plate with eighteen different cheeses. And in front of the plates with eighteen cheeses there were four glasses, each with a different kind of wine.

It's clear that Gerri is a professor. She speaks well and takes her students through a fascinating presentation *while* sipping wine and tasting the cheeses herself. That day in Paris she lead us on a civilized trip around the French cheese world beginning with soft, goat milk cheese and made her way to aged *Comté* and, finally, blue cheese. Along the way, Gerri taught us how cheeses are made, when the traditions began in each region of France, and where to buy the best cheese in Paris (including how to ask the *fromager* to wrap the cheese for bringing home in your suitcase).

Gerri insists that anyone can learn the ways of French cheese, and her course demystifies the complexity. The French have been making cheese for centuries and, over the years, their techniques for production, aging and serving have been elevated into an art form.

The best French cheeses, of course, are almost always made from raw milk and this is a huge difference between us and them. In Canada and the USA using raw milk is treated like devil worship, strictly forbidden! But in France, they know that to make the best cheese you have to start with raw milk.

My tasting tour around the world of French cheese finally helped me to grasp the absolute importance of cheese to *les français*. So much so that I would say it is cheese that separates them from us.

Bifteck au Échalotes
STEAK WITH SHALLOT SAUCE

We had spent the better part of a morning in *Musée Carnavelet*, filling ourselves with the history of Paris, and found ourselves in the Marais for lunch. I noticed *bifteck au échalotes* on the menu of the first bistro we came to and thought again about how the French cook steak in a thousand different ways. In this version shallots, wine and butter elevate the simple steak into a culinary masterpiece.

1 or 2 rib-eye steaks
½ tsp *Fleur de Sel*
1 tsp black peppercorns
1 tsp thyme, dried
¼ cup shallots
2 T butter
½ cup good red wine

Remove the steaks from the fridge and bring to room temperature about 1 hour before cooking. In a mortar and pestle, crush the black peppercorns. Mince the shallots.

On a plate, mix together crushed peppercorns, *Fleur de Sel* and thyme.

Trim the steaks of an excess fat, pat dry, and press them into the seasoning on both sides. Heat a heavy skillet over medium-high heat. Add a tablespoon of butter. When it is sizzling hot, sear the steaks, turning once for 3 to 4 minutes per side, depending on the thickness of the steak and your preference. Transfer to a warm platter and cover loosely with foil while you finish the sauce.

Return the skillet to medium heat, melt the remaining tablespoon of butter and add the shallots. Sauté for about 2 minutes, constantly stirring and then add the wine and deglaze the pan. Continue to cook until the wine is reduced by half and the sauce has thickened, about another 3 minutes. Add the steaks back in the pan and thoroughly coat with the shallot mixture. Serve immediately.

Glacée au Crème Fraîche et Amandes Grillés
TOASTED ALMOND & CREME FRAICHE ICE CREAM

Ice cream without a machine is my kind of ice cream. This refreshing version is made with *crème fraîche* making it extra tangy. If you can't find *crème fraîche*, you can substitute heavy cream. Toast the almonds until almost burnt for a deep nutty flavour.

1½ cups *crème fraîche*

3 eggs

½ cup sugar

¼ cup butter

½ cup slivered almonds

¼ cup candied orange or lemon peels

¼ cup crystallized ginger

Place a medium size mixing bowl, the *crème fraîche* (in its container), and a whisk in the freezer for one hour.

In a separate medium bowl, whisk the eggs and sugar until well combined. Put the mixture in a small saucepan and cook over moderate heat, stirring with a wooden spoon until it has a slight custard-like texture. This step is very delicate, do not stop stirring. Once it has the consistency of lemon curd, turn off heat and let it cool for a few minutes.

Toast the slivered almonds in a small skillet until dark brown, almost burnt. Cut the candied fruit and ginger into very small pieces.

Take the *crème fraîche*, bowl and whisk out of the freezer. Beat the *crème fraîche* in the bowl and beat until it is frothy.

Add the cut fruit and almonds to the cooled egg mixture. Then add the whipped *crème fraîche* and stir carefully, do not over mix. Line a freezer-proof dish or ramekins with plastic wrap, leaving enough hanging over the edge to later cover the bowl. Pour some of the batter in each ramekin, or into the dish, and cover with the remaining plastic wrap and put in the freezer. Freeze for several hours before serving.

Remove the nougat from the freezer. Take off the plastic wrap and place into a small bowl. Serve with a generous serving of strawberry or raspberry *coulis*.

THE PRINCE OF CÔTES DU RHÔNE

The leaves on the vines are big and green and grinning at the sun, the grapes hanging below. The car windows are wide open and, as we skirt around the big brother of all those small Provençal hilltop villages, Châteauneuf-du-Pape, we see above us the remains of the castle it is named for, only one huge wall still standing. It's a glorious summer day in Provence, one of those days that makes you want to get out your paints and easel. Today we are in the heart of one of the best wine regions of France for a day of cooking.

On the other side of Châteauneuf-du-Pape we take the route to Roquemaure, passing through more fields of vines. A few gentle curves later we reach the courtyard of restaurant and hotel *La Sommellerie*. It's a lovely 17th-century building, all blue shutters and vines.

The owner couldn't be any more excited to welcome us if we were Gerard Depardieu and Catherine Deneuve. He hurries down the steps to shake our hands and ushers us inside. "Welcome," he says, "welcome to my hotel." He flourishes a handful of colourful, bound booklets and tells us, "Today you will help Chef prepare the lunch menu. Here is what we propose," he opens a page and reads to us, *"Escalope de foie gras pannée au pain d'épices. Canon d'agneau aux aubergines servi en croûte de pain aux olives."*

He hands each of us a booklet and I see they contain the *carte du jour* and recipes in both French and English. The selections showcase the flavours of Provence: *foie gras*, black olives, lamb, truffles. The booklets were created especially for us and start with a very nice greeting in English.

Dear Mrs. Shaskin and M. Craft. We are pleased to welcome you. Be sure that we will do out best to give you entire satisfaction. Our Chef is going to introduce you his recipes, courses you will be able to reproduce at home. We wish you a nice cooking class.

"Now come," he leads us forward, "I will show you the dining room and the kitchen." On the way he introduces us to the hotel's young concierge Sophie who will be working in the kitchen with us today, to translate and to learn more about the food of Provence.

The kitchen is modern, stainless-steel and gleaming. Sophie speaks excellent English and introduces us to *Chef de Cuisine* Mathieu Frigo. I am surprised at how young he is, to be in charge of a hotel kitchen. While we get suited up in our chef outfits, I take a minute to look more closely at the menu: pan fried *foie gras* coated in ginger breadcrumbs; filet of lamb with eggplant in an olive bread crust; sponge cake with chocolate mousse. The recipes look a bit complicated.

We work side-by-side with the chef and Sophie on a stainless steel table in the middle of the tidy kitchen. Chef Mathieu gets things going by showing us how to make the sponge cake. I separate a dozen eggs and froth up the whites in a KitchenAid mixer. Mathieu adds sugar to the egg whites and folds in just a bit of flour, along with almond powder, to create a thick, light batter. He spreads this onto a large baking sheet lined with parchment paper. His hand and wrist movements are like those of a master badminton player.

Ten minutes later the sponge cake is out of the oven, a lovely golden brown. Mathieu lets it cool on a rack, then peels off the parchment paper and lays it on a clean towel.

It's taken the better part of an hour for a team of four to complete three of the cake components and we still need to make the mousse, another key ingredient. We haven't even started preparing the other complex courses. It occurs to me that this is *not* something I'll be doing at home, but I'm having fun. Mathieu is a model of calm efficiency, each step smoothly flowing into the next. To gather the fresh ingredients he takes me for a tour of the gardens where herbs are grown year round.

During the garden tour I learn that, at 23 years old, Chef Mathieu Frigo, (yes, he tells me, that's "fridge" in French) has already invested six years of education toward his future as a chef.

Back in the kitchen it's time to learn about the art of bone baking, how to make ratatouille, and gingerbread coating. Chef Mathieu starts us on the main course, the filet of lamb with olive bread crust. The first step is to make a simple dough with flour, water, baking powder and Provençal black olives (without the pits, naturally). Then he shows us how to slice an aubergine thinly, using a *mandoline*, and how to pan fry them gently in olive oil.

While I sauté the aubergine, Mathieu skillfully debones a shoulder of lamb, leaving only the saddle. He then wraps the eggplant slices around the slender piece of lamb, neatly tying it with several cords of string. Chef Mathieu produces a beautifully wrapped parcel. When I tie up my piece of lamb, though, it looks like a six-year old has been tearing at a present trying to get it open. But the chef only looks at my lamb and nods.

A lot happens in the next forty minutes. We prepare oyster mushrooms for the fricassee that will accompany the *foie gras* course. The aubergine-wrapped lamb pieces are browned in olive oil, drained, sliced into segments, and then wrapped in the bread dough to form giant dumplings that will be finished in the oven. I'm sent outside to gather more fresh herbs. The baked lamb bones are brought to the stovetop and cooked further, along with coarsely chopped carrots, onions and tomato; olive oil, fresh bay leaves and rosemary.

Mathieu retrieves the chilled mousse from the *frigo* and calls me over to finish the assembly of the sponge cake. I spoon the mousse onto half of the flat cake and carefully began folding from that end. Perhaps remembering what I did to the lamb, Mathieu takes over to show me how to make the fold slightly tighter, and then spreads the filling over the balance, completing the folding as he goes. The completed cake is put back into the refrigerator for final chilling.

A half hour before lunch we begin preparing what is my favourite dish, gingerbread-coated *foie gras*. When Mathieu pulls the tray of *foie gras* out of the cooler, I almost weep with joy. Giant rosy-hued loaves of golden *foie gras*, cut into thick slices.

Coating the *foie gras* is an easy task, just like preparing fried chicken. I take the giant lobes, dip them in egg and roll them in the gingerbread crumbs. Then I sauté them in a hot pan for just a few brief minutes. In a saucepan Mathieu reduces a sweet Rasteau wine for the sauce.

Mathieu places one of the pieces of *foie gras* onto a white dinner plate next to a small bowl of salad greens, picked fresh from the garden. Fricasséed mushrooms are artfully spooned on to create dividing line between the two. A light drizzle of the reduced wine turns the plate into a piece of art. And then, to my amazement, thin slices of truffle are strewn on top. And this is just the starter!

Our cooking class is over and it's time for lunch,. The owner leads us back into the dining room where a table is set. While the courses of the meal are served by the spiky-haired *maître d'* the owner tells us the story of his recent purchase of the inn and his plans for its future.

Over dessert he leans in close to me and whispers, "There is someone very special here today," he nods to a table of men across the room. "I will see if he will meet you." He makes a respectful approach to one of the men and, after a few moments, brings him back to our table.

As if introducing royalty, the owner bows his head to us and says, "It is my pleasure to introduce Monsieur Marc Perrin, of the Perrin winemakers." Of course we know the name, we have been drinking the Perrin family wines for years. We exchange pleasantries and he says now that we have met we should stop by the winery for a visit. We know we never will, but it was an honour to meet Rhône royalty.

Quiche Lorraine
AUTHENTIC FRENCH QUICHE

One summer we stayed in a villa close to Beaumes-de-Venise where I'd visit both of the town bakeries. At the big bakery on the square I would buy *boules, baguettes* and *gâteaux*, but I would always visit the smaller bakery in the *haut ville* for their delectable individual quiche.

When I asked the owner why her quiche were so delicious, she surprised me with her answer, "Authentic quiche has no cheese."

"You must," she added, "boil the cream first, it will make the custard *plus moelleux*, creamier." And she was right! Bacon and cream are the stars of this recipe and you'll find you don't miss the cheese at all.

½ lb bacon

2 cups cream

3 eggs

pinch sea salt

freshly ground black
  pepper

pastry (see separate recipe)

Preheat oven to 375° F. Smear a bit of butter into each muffin mold.

Use thick-cut, high-quality bacon and fry it until it's almost crisp. Drain the bacon on paper towels, and then cut it into small bite-size pieces and set aside.

In a small, heavy-bottom pot bring the cream to a boil. Turn down the heat, and continue to simmer for about 2 minutes until the cream has thickened. Remove from the heat and let it cool for about 10 minutes.

In a medium bowl beat the 3 eggs with a fork or whisk. When the cream has cooled, add the eggs and beat together. Add salt and pepper to taste.

Roll out the pastry and cut rounds to fit into the prepared muffin tins. In each muffin mold, gently press a piece dough round into place to form a cup. Make sure there's extra dough to fold over the top edge slightly. Place the muffin tin on a baking tray before you fill them for easy transport to the oven.

Divide the cooked bacon into two parts. One half will be sprinkled directly on top of the dough in the molds. Set aside the remaining half of the bacon for later use.

Using a soup ladle, pour the creamy egg mixture into each mold, filling almost to the top. Bake for 20 minutes and then sprinkle the remaining bacon on top. Return to the oven and cook for an additional 10 to15 minutes. The crust should be golden brown and the custard slightly springy.

Let the quiche cool in the muffin tin for a few minutes, then transfer to a wire rack. These can be served warm or cold.

Pâte Brisée
PASTRY DOUGH

In France this pastry dough is called *pâte brisée* (pronounced "pat breezay"), and it really is a breeze to make! It can be used immediately or frozen for later use.

1 cup unbleached flour

¼ cup butter

½ tsp sea salt (if butter is unsalted)

3 T cold water, heavy cream or milk

Measure the flour and cut the butter into tiny cubes. In a large mixing bowl, add the flour and, using a food process or your fingertips, mix the butter into the flour.

The dough should have the texture of coarse cornmeal. Add one tablespoon of the liquid at a time and pulse the food processor, or use a fork to push the dough into the centre of the bowl as you stir. As soon as the dough sticks to itself, stop adding liquid. Weather factors, such as humidity, will affect the amount of liquid needed.

Turn the dough out onto a well-floured board and lightly knead the dough then form it into a ball. Wrap the ball of dough in plastic wrap and let it rest in the fridge for at least 1 hour before using.

Let the dough warm up for about 10 minutes before rolling it out. On a well-floured board flatten the dough with your hands into a circle shape. Then, using your rolling pin (a marble pin works best), gently roll out it into a round of about 1/8-inch thick.

There's enough dough for one 9-inch quiche or 6 individual quiches. Be sure to use a fork to prick the dough when it's in the muffin tins or tart pan to prevent it from puffing up.

Gâteau au Grand Marnier
GRAND MARNIER CAKE

5 eggs

1½ cups butter

1+ cup Demerara sugar

2 oranges, grated & juiced

1 cup plain yogurt

2 tsp baking powder

2 tsp baking soda

½ tsp sea salt

2½ cups unbleached flour

½ cup whole wheat pastry flour

⅓ cup Grand Marnier

¼ cup white sugar

½ lemon, juiced

Preheat oven to 350° F.

Separate the eggs and let them come to room temperature.

In a food processor cream together the butter and Demerara. Add the egg yolks and the grated rind. Blend. Add the yogurt and juice from one of the oranges. Blend.

Sift together the dry ingredients. Add the mixture to the food processor and blend. If the mixture seems too dry, add an additional 1/4 cup of yogurt. Transfer mixture to a large mixing bowl.

In another bowl beat the egg whites until they are stiff. Fold by hand into the cake mixture.

Thoroughly butter and flour a bundt pan. Using a spatula, transfer the mixture into the pan. Bake about 60 minutes, until golden and the sides pull away from the pan. Cool on a rack and then remove the cake from the bundt pan onto a rimmed plate.

Once the cake has cooled, and just before serving, prepare the syrup by mixing together the juice from the second orange, the lemon juice, the Grand Marnier and the white sugar. Heat in a saucepan and simmer for 4 minutes. Pour over the cake, slice and serve.

La Femme Chocolat

"Ви українською?"

I turn around, puzzled; it's a woman with a big smile on her face. She says it again, this time louder and slower. I finally understand what she's saying, "Are you Ukrainian?"

It's an odd question to be asked in the middle of the St. Germain *quartier,* but it's just another one of the small adventures of Paris. I am on way to the best *chocolatiers* of the city, congregated in this part of the 6th Arrondissement. I'm early for my first visit so I take a break in a little park at the corner of Rue des Saints-Pères and Boulevard St. Germain; a small peaceful square with a playground, trees, and benches in this very busy neighbourhood. I notice the bust of a familiar figure. I cross the park to have a closer look. Three women sitting on one of those ubiquitous green park benches watch me closely. They look vaguely familiar, as if I've seen them before.

I can hardly believe my eyes, the bust is of the Ukraine's greatest poet, Taras Shevchenko, who is considered almost sacred in most Ukrainian families, including my own. When my grandmother left the Ukraine in 1944 she took with her a handful of soil from her orchard and a framed picture of Shevchenko. And when she arrived in Canada in 1950 she brought with her a large wash tub with corrugated sides, some US army blankets, and the picture of Shevchenko that now hangs in my office.

The name of the church is Saint Volodymyr, the plaque at the gate declares the square to be Taras Shevchenko Park. It's a bit of the Ukraine in Paris, and these women are my people! She is asking me if I am Ukrainian. I nod my head and murmur the few Ukrainian words I can dredge from my subconscious. With thoughts of *babushkas* and the ancestral homeland swirling in my brain, I excuse myself and cross the street to the oldest *chocolatiers* in Paris, *Debauve & Gallais.*

Chocolate in France is an art form, a national obsession, and there are artisan chocolate shops throughout the city. I've heard that there are two hundred *fromageries* in Paris, and there are probably as many *chocolatiers*. But *Debauve & Gallais* is the godfather.

The storefront is nothing but class. It's got history, you can tell just by looking at the impressive sign and elegant window displays. This historical chocolate establishment was around long before the Eiffel Tower existed, long before Baron Haussmann wrenched Paris into its modern shape. In fact, Napoleon had just seized power when Monsieur Sulplice Debauve began selling chocolate in 1800. But that was only after he had already been creating medicinal chocolates for Marie Antoinette! Until she lost her head, of course.

In 1818, the year Taras Shevchenko turned four years old, Monsieur Debauve moved his shop to a brand new building at 26 Rue des Saints-Pères. He was appointed royal chocolate supplier to Napoleon's successors: Louis XVIII, Charles X and finally Louis Philippe. D&G was the company that put chocolate on the map. They're the French Willy Wonka, inventing among other things the first instant cold chocolate, which they claimed "is good for women, children and people of weak constitution, whose delicate palate can appreciate the sweet flavour of caraway mixed with sugar, vanilla and almond milk."

It's not surprising that the shop carries on with an apothecary theme. Through the window I can see, behind the stylish chocolate displays, antique silver canisters of loose teas sold in bulk.

In the store, on blankets of blue silk, it's all about order and perfection. Every piece of chocolate is either wrapped in a colourful foil wrapper, a piece of ribbon, or stamped with the company's seal in gold-coloured embossing. Some of the chocolates have their name stamped on top: *Palet Argent* with silver letters and *Palet Or* with gold lettering. There are playful items like perfect replicas of golf balls, in chocolate, and mushroom-shaped creations filled with *nougatine* and caramel.

I choose a short round cylinder of chocolate with *Thé Earl Grey* stamped on top. The sign tells me it's *Palet au Thé, Ganache Earl Grey*; it's a miraculous, luscious blend of 60% rich dark chocolate and a distinct, but not overpowering, essence of bergamot. Next I try a *Châtaigne* filled with a pâte of chestnut (*châtaigne*) and rum; and what a combination it is.

At the 1900 Paris World Fair, which introduced the Gare de Lyon, the Gare d'Orsay (now the Musée d'Orsay), the Pont Alexandre III, the Grand Palais, the Petit Palais and the first line of the Metro, *Debauve & Gallais* received another gold medal, their third. The Eiffel Tower was just eleven years old and Taras Shevchenko had been laid to rest forty years before in the Ukraine by the River Dniper.

A Short Guide to the World of Chocolate

Praline – roasted almonds and hazelnuts cooked in
caramelized sugar and ground as fine as desired.
Ganache – a mixture of chocolate with cream, butter or milk.
Nougatine – a roasted almonds cooked in caramelized sugar.
Caramel – a mixture of milk, sugar and butter.
Pâte d'amandes (almond paste) – trimmed
almonds ground with sugar.
Gianduja – an Italian specialty of ground
roasted hazelnuts and chocolate.
Nougat – beaten egg whites mixed with
honey, sugar, almonds and pistachios.

It's only a few short blocks from the 18th-century granddaddy of chocolate to a prize-winning newcomer, but it's a walk through the history of Paris. As recently as the 12th century there were open fields here, outside the walls of Paris. The modern name of the neighbourhood reflects this: *St Germain des Prés*, St Germain of the Fields.

The roots of the place goes back to Clovis I, the first king of all the Franks, whose son Childebert built an abbey in these fields in about the year 500. This was in the days when French rulers had all the great names. None of that *Nicolas* or *Jacques* or *Francois*, but kingly monikers like *Chlothar the Old, Chlodio the Longhair,* and *Clovis the Lazy.*

As I pass by the two most celebrated cafés in Paris, perhaps in the world, I think how just a few centuries later this area became the haunt of Jean-Paul and Simone and Ernest and Pablo. At the sidewalk tables outside *Les Deux Magots* and *Café de Flore* is the usual eclectic mix of French and foreigner, young and old, wine and *Coca*.

The abbey is long gone, replaced by the church of the same name. On this beautiful summer day the sidewalk next to the church is lined with two dozen white peaked tents where vendors are hawking everything from colourful straw hats, to scarves, jewellery, printed fabric from India, wind chimes and reed flutes.

I wend my way through people carrying bags from the chic shops across the street: *Stephane Délian, Jean-Baptiste Rautureau, Yves Saint Laurent Rive Gauche*; young couples holding hands, families with small children, tourists with puffy white running shoes, staggeringly thin women wearing jeans that would fit nine-year-old Alexandre, pickpockets and priests; all in the promenade.

Giant chocolate elephants stand majestically in the windows of the shop of *Patrick Roger*. They seem almost barbaric compared to the graceful *Debauve & Gallais* shop. But Patrick Roger, though a relative newcomer to the world of chocolate, is today considered one of the best in Paris. He's outspoken, brash and a great marketer. We step inside.

"Maybe one day 'flavour' will come in boxes," Patrick's promo piece reads, "completely sanitized and devoid of all scent. Maybe flavour simply won't exist anymore." The giant chocolate elephants are symbolic defenders of the "principle of flavour." Like I said, he's a good marketer.

He's also the recipient of the prestigious award for the best chocolate maker in France, *Meilleur Ouvrier de France Chocolatier*. The *Meilleur Ouvrier* system honouring the best craftsmen of France was created in 1924 and today includes awards in 162 categories including pastry chefs, hairdressers, butchers, jewellers, and even taxidermists! When I lived near St Placide my butcher had a banner proclaiming "Best Head Cheese of France 1997."

Everything is displayed in boxes: flat tin boxes, robin-egg blue boxes. There are acres of chocolate. Chocolates with pistachios on top. Space-age lime-green balls looking like huge shiny marbles.

I settle on an *Amazone*, a bold combination of caramel and lime from Brazil, and a *Savage, ganache* with verbena and yuzu (a Japanese citrus).

These unusual flavours work beautifully with the dark chocolate. Patrick works with chocolate like *parfumiers* work with scent.

❧

Large martini glasses line the shop window, each one filled with a jewel-toned jelly and garnished with a single macaron, balancing on the lip of the glass. This shop is all about cool elegance and *macarons*.

In case, like me, you've been living in a culinary desert: Paris is in the midst of *macaron* mania. Not macaroons, but *macarons*. *Macarons* are the new cupcake, the new black.

I'm at the chocolate establishment of Pierre Marcolini. Stepping into this shop is like stepping into a chic haberdashery. A single, long glass case faces the windows. Shelves on the wall neatly display boxed chocolate, all in a neutral palette: black, white, grey, brown.

Pierre's trademark is the cocoa bean and its image appears everywhere: on the shop sign, on all the wrappers and boxes, at the home page on his website. Like Patrick Roger, this is chocolate as fashion. Every year a brand new line of luxury chocolates is released. This season it's *macarons*, essentially cookie sandwiches (think Oreos in heaven), crunchy on the outside with a creamy filling inside, in a palette of jewel tone colours that Pierre calls *macaron* cocktails; *limoncello, mojita, vodka melon*. I choose a variety of them, enough to fill up one of the elegant and oh-so-perfectly-designed black boxes that proclaim on the top, *Macarons by Marcolini* in silver letters printed over two large letters X in orange.

This Belgian *chocolatier* is known for travelling the world in search of the raw materials for his chocolates; he calls himself a "chocolate gringo." His global explorations are evident in his shop here on Rue de Seine, which he opened in 2003. Boxed chocolates made from cocoa beans he has personally sourced line the shelves: *Fleur de Cacao* from Venezuela and Ghasa; *Tabasco-Mexique; Orient-Cuba; Los Rios-Équator*. I feel like I'm on a Chocolate Grand Tour.

I turn from the boxed chocolates to the display case to sample a few of Marcolini's individual praline chocolates. There's a *Caraïbe Grand Cru*, a bitter chocolate made with vanilla pods from Madagascar and Tahiti; *Mangue*, milk chocolate cream mixed with Brazilian mango *confiture*; and, my favourite, *Cassis*, which contains a mixture of blackcurrant cream and blackcurrant jelly. Around the world without a passport!

Before I leave the shop I'm also tempted by Marconlini's offering of *confitures*: There's *Passion*, from passion fruit, and *Orange* and even *Confit Chocolat Au Lait*, a milk chocolate sauce. But I resist and step out onto Rue de Seine laden with my purchases.

Profiteroles à la Fleur de Sel Sauce au Chocolat
PROFITEROLES WITH CHOCOLATE SAUCE

Some things in life you just don't forget. It was a chilly fall day in Paris when I first had real profiteroles. With one hand, the waiter placed before me a plate of three luscious puff pastries, each filled with vanilla ice cream. In his other hand was a silver jug, from which he poured a generous amount of hot chocolate sauce, which went to work immediately melting the ice cream.

In this version I've used a luscious chocolate sauce with *fleur de sel*.

2 ounces dark chocolate
⅓ cup heavy cream
pinch *Fleur de Sel*
2 *pâte a choux* per serving
(see separate recipe)
2 small scoops vanilla ice-cream

Break the chocolate into small pieces and melt slowly in a small pot or double boiler. Stir in the heavy cream until well blended. Stir in the *Fleur de Sel*. Transfer the hot sauce into an attractive pouring dish and set it on the table.

Place 2 *pâte a choux* in each serving bowl. Cut them in half crosswise, almost, but not all the way, through. Add a small scoop of ice cream in the centre, the ice cream should not overwhelm the pastry, so go easy.

Set a serving before each guest and then pour the hot *Fleur de Sel* chocolate sauce directly on top of the profiteroles for a dazzling dessert.

Truffes au Chocolat
CHOCOLATE TRUFFLES

At our first multi-course tasting extravaganza in the summer dining room of *Hôtel Bristol* the meal concluded with a selection of chocolate truffles. It's those kind of little things that are long remembered. Now at home, I often offer a plateful of truffles of at the end of a special meal.

¼ cup heavy cream
2 T *Grand Marnier*
9 ounces dark chocolate
4 T butter
1/8 tsp *Fleur de Sel*

In a small heavy-bottom pan, bring the cream to a boil and reduce to about 2 tablespoons. Remove from the heat and stir in the *Grand Marnier* and 6 ounces of the chocolate pieces, save the remaining 3 ounces for tempering. Return the pan to low heat until the chocolate melts, stirring continuously.

Whisk in the butter. When the mixture is smooth, pour it into a shallow bowl and refrigerate until it's firm, about 1 hour.

Scoop out chocolate with a spoon or a small melon baller and shape each piece into a 1-inch balls. They shouldn't be too perfect! Place the truffles on a baking sheet lined with parchment paper and return to the refrigerator for another hour.

Now the truffles are ready to be dipped into the tempered chocolate sauce.

How to Temper Chocolate

Tempering is a method of heating and cooling chocolate for coating or dipping. Once tempered the chocolate will have a glossy finish and won't instantly melt in your hands.

Grate or chop the remaining 3 ounces of chocolate. Place two ounces of the chocolate in the top pan of a double boiler. Melt it over hot, but not boiling, water, stirring constantly, until the chocolate reaches 115° F. Remove the top pan with the melted chocolate from the heat and place it on a towel.

Let it cool to 100° F, then add the remaining 1 ounce of grated chocolate to it, stirring until melted. The chocolate is now ready to be used for dipping.

Place each cooled truffle into the tempered chocolate. With a fork, quickly turn it over until the truffle is coated. Remove and place it back on the baking tray lined with parchment paper.

When all the truffles have been dipped, garnish each one with a pinch of lemon zest, a few granules of *Fleur de Sel*, or a shelled pistachio. Makes 2 dozen truffles.

A Day in Champagne

Louis grimaces and slowly shakes his head, indicating that he is clearly in the presence of *idiotes*.

"What!" I ask him. "What's wrong?"

He hesitates for a second, seemingly reluctant to bring up the issue. Then he shrugs and says, "That eez not how you cut *foie gras*."

We are having lunch at a small restaurant in Reims, in the middle of a day of touring the Champagne country, with Louis as our guide. During the morning we already established that Louis is a *foie gras* expert, but cutting it the wrong way?

Now that he has started, there is no stopping him. "To do it properly, you must hold the knife and fork like this, and cut down, from the top to the bottom of the *tranche*. You must have, in each bite, the *gélatine*, a sliver of the top part, which is oxidized and then a slice of the middle, which is not, as well as the lower level, that is quite delicious too.

"And, please, do not eat it with *that*," he points to the small pieces of toasted bread on the plate. "Here," he says, handing me a slice, "eat it with a piece of baguette if you must."

It is irritating, but Louis is absolutely right

The day hadn't started out well. Louis was late. Very late. Our friends Russ and Mary-Lynn were standing in the cold, dark street outside their apartment waiting and we had no way to reach them; no cell phones, no homing pigeons. After picking up our friends in the 6th Arrondissement, the van was supposed to swing by our apartment in the 16th.

Finally, at 8:20, we telephone and leave a message for the driver. Minutes later, Louis calls back to say that the van needs brake work, and that he is waiting for the dealership to open. "What can I do?" he says. "I must fix the brakes, *non*?"

I suspect Louis has slept in and is now enjoying a *croissant* and *café crème* while he is lying to me about the brakes. Couldn't he have taken care of it yesterday? Couldn't he have called at 7:30 so we could have warned our friends? I am fuming!

It is quarter to ten when the van pulls up in front of our apartment and we jump in. The atmosphere in the van is frosty but Louis tries out his Gallic charm. "Ah, we will have a nice drive to Champagne, *non?*"

As we leave Paris, the terrain becomes slightly more rolling and the sky bluer. Louis tells us the itinerary as we get closer to Reims, home of some of the finest Champagne houses.

"Today we will visit two houses; very old, very famous houses. One is still owned by the family and the other is owned by a luxury group. But then, afterward, as a special reward, we will visit a very small producer, *Philippe Martin*. I take very few people there." I suppose it's his way of apologizing to us. How can I stay angry as we drive towards the place of my dreams? Champagne.

Our first lesson of the day from Louis is how to pronounce the name of our destination. For no apparent reason, Reims, Louis tells us, doesn't rhyme with, say, "rhymes", but with "France", like "rance". Once in Reims, we drive to the house of *Taittinger*. The main building is new, but as Louis points out, most of Reims was destroyed in the First World War and now it is, "a sad little town, except for the Champagne."

The modern reception of *Taittinger* is like any high-end accountancy office; a display of commemorative Champagne bottles lines the ecru walls and a blue door is the only punctuation of colour. A pleasant woman welcomes us. She looks like a hostess from Air France; every pearl is in place, her pumps are sensible, yet sexy. She tells us to wait and that the tour will start shortly.

It is 11:00 and we haven't had breakfast yet so I send Louis on a mission to find food to absorb the bubbles we are about to receive. He returns with flaky pastry rolls, still warm, filled with spicy sausage. Louis explains, at length, that these are a specialty of the Champagne region. He is proud as only a Frenchman can be.

We have barely brushed the crumbs from our chins when another perfectly-coiffed woman enters the room and beckons us beyond the blue door. Our tour is about to begin. As we walk through a long corridor and down several flights of spiralling staircase, I notice how our guide expertly manoeuvres the irregular stairs in her heels.

We have left the sad modern town of Reims and have entered a world of ancient chalk caves that reaches back three thousand years. The essence of Champagne lies underground. When the Romans arrived in Gaul they extended the existing chalk caves and since then the caves have been expanded by slaves, monks, and Champagne makers.

The town and the caves have seen much over the centuries. Several cathedrals have been built above this site. Some of the cathedrals have burnt down, others were bombed, and generations of French have spent time living in the safety of these caves during tumultuous times. During WWI whole villages camped in these caves, building schools, medical treatment centres, and cooking facilities. It was the only safe place when their world above was the centre of bloody trench warfare and daily bombing.

Our guide takes us through every aspect of the making of Champagne. She relates the familiar legend of monk Dom Pérignon and his accidental discovery of sparkling wine. During World War I, she said, each French soldier was allotted one bottle of Champagne daily to brighten his day. She shows us cave after cave filled with vintage Champagnes lightly covered with dust. The chalk caves naturally provide a steady temperature and a dark environment perfectly suited for aging wine.

We are filled with Champagne history and lore. Now it is time to return to ground level and fill ourselves with the product. The tasting room is over-lit and mundane but even the beige walls can't detract from the bubbles. We sample a *brut*, a *rosé*, a vintage and a *demi-sec* and leave *Taittinger* on a soft cloud.

◦◦

It is during the drive from the *Taittinger* château to our lunch in Reims that we learn that Louis has a serious hobby. He is a *foie gras* expert, *un grand connaisseur en foie gras*, who makes authentic *foie gras* with his family. Louis' uncle has a contact with a producer from the Dordogne who supplies them with fresh goose livers. "We make enough to last our entire family, and most of our neighbours in our apartment building, for a season."

Louis becomes serious when he talks about *foie gras* and shares the secrets for selecting the appropriate goose livers. "You must inspect it with all your senses. You see the colour, is it a bright rosy hue or is it a dull, beige thing?" his nose wrinkles. "Does it smell like the woman you love? Or does it offer no complexity? It could be past its prime, *beh oui?*" He demonstrates how to smell the liver, cupping both hands to his nose as we speed along at 130 km per hour.

Louis was born in a hospital in Paris but quickly returned to the only home he has ever known: an apartment building in the Marais, in the 4th Arrondissement. As the years passed, his family acquired other apartments in the building as they came for sale. In fact, both his mother and brother live in the same building, one above and one below.

"I know every brick, every stone in my Arrondissement. I cannot imagine living anywhere else." When I ask him about his favourite restaurants in Paris, he replies it depends on the dish.

"If I want the best *rognons*, I head to a secret restaurant in the sixth; if it's *steak frites*, then only a particular restaurant in the seventeenth will do, but other than that I rarely venture out beyond the fourth. For *foie gras*, I eat that only at home."

ॐ

Now it is time for lunch. Louis herds us up the main street of Reims, as charmless as the prairie towns I grew up in. We are, he assures us, about to sample the finest food found in Reims. Taped to the glass door of the restaurant is a faded, dog-eared copy of an article published in *"Champagne Today"*, with the owners smiling into the lens. The owner comes outside to greet us, chats with Louis, and motions us inside. He leads us to the back, down a hall, turns left, turns right and finally arrives in a little dining room.

I order *foie gras*. Louis shrugs and insists that, here, I must try the specialty of the region: a massive amount of ham sausages and hocks in a slow simmered sauerkraut. I am still burping up the tasty sausage snack from the morning, but what can I do? Louis takes charge of the wine and he orders Champagne to start followed by a red Burgundy to complement the ham platter.

The *foie gras* arrives. Louis glances at it. But, when I make the first cut he grimaces and gives me his lecture.

Louis whistles and makes a pained expression when he sees the bread that accompanies the *foie gras*. *"Jamais, jamais le* white toast!" He explains that the white toast often served with *foie gras* is a threat to civilization, an insult to all Frenchmen, and the absolute worst thing that can ever happen to a person. "Always, if you must, use the baguette, but a true *foie gras* lover uses nothing. *Rien."* He explains that the sugars in white bread destroy the delicate flavours of *foie gras*.

Now I, too, am shocked, having final grasped the gravity of the situation. I shun the white toast and reach for the baguette. I offer Louis a forkful of my *foie gras*; he eyes it, he sniffs it, he turns his ear to it and finally he takes a mouthful.

"Pas mal," he mutters. Not bad at all.

～∽

After heaps of ham hocks and Burgundy, we set out for our second destination: *Moët & Chandon*. It is, Louis explains, owned by LVMH, a luxury products group that also owns Louis Vuitton, Hennessy, and Kenzo, among other high-end brands.

I ask Louis what he thinks about *Moët* compared to other Champagne. "It's just a product," he shrugs. *Moët & Chandon*, it seems, is barely worthy of his consideration.

We enter a beautiful showroom filled with everything a *Champagnephile* needs, displays of 500-Euro vintage Champagne, monogrammed tote bags, bejewelled Champagne bottles. A bank of TV screens display glamorous images of the life of luxury. Compared to *Taittinger*, this is like being in Louis Vuitton's flagship store, perhaps not surprisingly.

We are introduced to our guide; Josie is in her late 40s, her thin frame and tight suit gives her a classic appearance. Her tour is much more efficient: no chalk caves from Roman times, no meticulous explanation of the making of Champagne. She focuses on numbers and the prestigious history of the house. Do we know who their biggest client is? Lebanon, where jeroboams are shipped by the thousands. Every decent disco in Tehran is serving *Moët & Chandon*. Did we know that *Moët* was founded in 1743 by Jean-Rèmy Moët, a friend of Napoleon, who often visited the very château we are standing in?

We end the tour in a lovely room where Napoleon would feel at home. After all the numbers and self-promotion, it is an unexpected pleasure to end on such a civilized note. Josie takes her time as she serves us glass after glass of various Champagnes. The view of the garden makes the Champagnes taste even better.

We learn that Josie actually lives in Aix-en-Provence and, although she has a small apartment in Épernay, she catches the TGV to Aix on weekends and holidays. She finds life in Épernay very different from southern France, "here they drink Champagne like it is water. They find every reason, daily, to drink Champagne." I feel much better about *Moët & Chandon* and I notice the day now has a wonderful glow about it.

Louis called *Moët* merely a product, but to me it is a link to a nobler time. We don't dare buy a bottle, knowing Louis will not approve. Dusk is now falling. We wait in the van for Louis, who appears, carrying a bottle from the sales room! I look at him and he knows what I am thinking. He shrugs, again, and says, "This is a special *cuvée*, quite good."

Louis drives us to nearby Hautvillers where legend relates Dom Pérignon said, "I am drinking stars." The view from the ridge above the valley is gorgeous: the river Marne and rolling fields where the battles of WWI were fought.

We continue on to find *Philippe Martin*. Louis is lost, he knows it is close, but he can't quite remember where it is. Clearly he doesn't take many people here. After a few checks on his map, he drives through the gates of the 18th century complex and across the crunchy gravel courtyard where there are three modest buildings close to the river Marne. He parks, avoiding children's toys and bicycles.

Louis goes to find Monsieur Martin. He returns with a small, lean man eager to greet us. M. Martin, it seems is in Paris attending to political business, but this is his right hand man, Alexandre Duprés. He shouts to the main house that there are visitors.

M. Duprés seems slightly bemused, though clearly pleased to have visitors. He welcomes us into the winemaking building and takes us step-by-step through the process of making Champagne, from pressing the grapes to the final re-corking. We are shown the method of processing the wine before it is turned into Champagne. He insists we taste barrel samples from the steel vats. This is a rare privilege and something I have never experienced before. Even Louis, who has seen many Champagne houses, is excited and asks to see their cellar. M. Duprés gives us a tour of the dark, cobwebbed chambers, a far cry from the chalk caves, but authentic, wonderful, and thrilling.

Although M. Duprés does not speak English, he looks me straight in the eye and describes each phase of the process as if I understand every word.

The tasting room is also the office and is outfitted with a secretary's desk, typewriter, shag carpet and adding machines. It is here that the serious business of tasting Champagne begins. M. Duprés treats us like rich Arab buyers; we first try a pink Champagne that is redolent of fresh, wild strawberries. I want to purchase every case he has in stock. We then move onto their *Brut*: crisp, clear bubbles with a hint of almonds. We also taste a vintage Champagne from 1999 that has the colour of honey and the taste of sunshine.

Through Louis, we explain that we are from Canada and shipping and duties will greatly increase the cost of his Champagne. Mary-Lynn, though, fights the good fight, prepared to pay the improbable cost to get some *Philippe Martin* into her cellar. But, then she discovers that a 14-Euro bottle would cost over eighty dollars by the time it arrives in Victoria. Like the armies of the Marne, she finally admits defeat.

But we are still in Paris for another week, so we leave with a case of *Philippe Martin*, glowing and happy with the knowledge that we have learned much that day about the lies of Frenchmen, the truth of chalk caves, the horrors of war, and the sweetness of good, honest Champagne.

On the way back to Paris, tired and in an effort to stay awake, I ask Louis every question about France that I have been storing since middle school.

How do you feel about the Italians?

We love their soccer team, their coffee and their women.

What's your biggest regret about France?

Losing the world cup in 2006.

Do you have a girlfriend?

Of course, she is also living in my building.

Can we try your *foie gras*?

I'll drop some by tomorrow.

We don't believe him, but the next day Louis delivers a terrine of *foie gras* to Russ and Mary-Lynn. We eat it with some baguette, slice it vertically from top to bottom, and toast Louis with *Philippe Martin rosé.*

CHAMPAGNE TASTING NOTES

Nothing says celebration more than toasting with a glass of real French Champagne. And although we usually think of it as an aperitif, with its high level of acidity and low sugar content, it's also a great wine to serve with appetizers, main courses and after dessert.

Champagne loves salty, fatty foods, think potato chips and calamari. Of course it's wonderful served with oysters, shellfish and tiny *canapés*. But also try lightly smoked fish like salmon and tuna, and hard mature cheeses like *Parmigiano-Reggiano*, cheddar and *Pecorino*. And if you're so lucky enough to have them, try Champagne with *foie gras*, caviar and truffle dishes, such as a truffle omelet.

Champagne can even handle spicy dishes, some claim it is great with Indian curry. I wouldn't go that far but I would serve it with mild Thai curries and even with sushi. Just make sure there's only a hint of wasabi, otherwise the heat will destroy the gentle notes of the bubbly.

The toasted nuts, yeast, and straw flavours of Champagne are also great with lobster, roast chicken and duck.

Ignore all those who claim that Champagne with strawberries and chocolate are a good match. I would never waste a good glass of Champagne with dessert. The sweetness of desserts overpower the low sugar content of Champagne and destroy its flavour. Save it for after dessert as a lovely, bubbly way to end a meal.

Sole Meunière
THE MOST FAMOUS FRENCH FISH DISH

At one time, this was the signature dish at *Le Bon Accueil* (before the restaurant changed hands) and I longed to recreate it at home. I finally got it right when I realized that this recipe is all about the butter. Burn the butter and it's ruined, you will have to start over. Undercook the butter and it's not *sole meunière*. Also essential is a heavy-bottomed skillet that can take the entire filet.

It's best served simply: on a plate with a light dash of freshly chopped parsley, a garnish of the nut brown butter sauce and a ramekin full of garlic mashed potatoes. Once you've mastered the butter the rest is a breeze. The secret is to cook the butter until it's golden brown, with the fragrance of hazelnuts.

1 large or 2 small sole filets

6 T butter

1 cup unbleached white flour

½ tsp salt

½ tsp ground pepper

Warm a couple of plates in the oven or warming oven.

Put the flour on a large plate and mix in some sea salt and ground black pepper. Dredge the sole in the flour mixture to coat both sides and lightly shake off any excess flour. Set aside.

Heat a large, heavy skillet to medium. Melt the butter, making sure that the pan is not too hot. The butter should be nicely bubbling, but not burning. This may take a bit of trial and error.

When the butter is bubbling (this should take only a matter of seconds) put the sole into the skillet.

Cook the sole until you can see the edges browning nicely, being careful to control the temperature so the butter doesn't burn. Gently lift a corner of the filet with a spatula to check that the first side is golden brown. This should take 3 to 5 minutes.

Flip the sole by carefully lifting up a corner of the filet so you can slip a spatula under it without scraping off the coating. Be careful that the filet doesn't break while you're turning it. Cook the other side the same way, for another 3 to 5 minutes.

Transfer the sole to the heated plates.

The butter should be a nutty, golden brown colour. If it isn't, continue to cook it in the pan for a few moments after the fish has been removed. Spoon the butter over the filet and serve immediately with a slice of lemon and a glass of Champagne. Serves 2.

Purée à l'Ail
GARLIC MASHED POTATOES

Lunch at *Cafe Marché* on Rue Cler always includes a ramekin filled with the creamiest mashed potatoes. *Ever.* Here's my version with a nice bit of garlic flavour added.

For years I searched for the perfect potato masher. This one was too small, that one was too quirky, the other one had sharp edges. Finally I found what I was looking for : a long wooden handle (16 inches) attached to a large, solid, traditional, potato-masher head. It's one of my favourite kitchen tools.

Using chicken stock and butter instead of milk gives the potatoes a delicious, creamy lightness. Serve these potatoes alongside any dish but it's especially good next to *sole meunière*.

3 large yellow potatoes, preferably Yukon Gold
½ tsp sea salt
5 garlic cloves, peeled
¼ cup butter
¼ cup chicken stock
sea salt
freshly ground black pepper

Peel the potatoes and cut each one into 6 chunks. Put the potatoes in a large pot, cover with water, add ½ tsp of salt, and bring to a boil. After six minutes, add the garlic cloves to the boiling water. Cook the potatoes until a fork easily penetrates them, about 12 to 15 minutes in total.

You can prepare the potatoes and boil them up to a half hour in advance, shutting off the heat just before you think they are done. Leave the potatoes and garlic in the water until you are ready to mash and serve.

Drain the potatoes and garlic and return to the pot for mashing. Add the butter and, using a traditional potato masher, mash it together with the potatoes. Add chicken stock, a bit at a time, and mash until it has the consistency you want. Salt and pepper to taste and mash one last time.

You can keep the mashed potatoes warm until serving time by leaving them in the pot, covered, and placing over a low heat. Serves 2 to 4.

Sunday Lunch in the Country

Sunlight dusts the tops of naked vines and distant hills, creating long shadows even though it is only midday. As we turn into the country lane, we pass *the tree* that marks the way to Françoise and Laurent's house. It's a tall cypress in the shape of a perfect fan and is, in fact, an ideal landmark; the lady pump-jockey was right. Flanking the lane are fruit orchards, olive trees, a swimming pool and the house of Françoise and Laurent's neighbours, our hosts Louise and Didier.

It's the first Sunday of the new year, when *La Saison des Fêtes*, the holiday season, is still in full swing and meals are even more festive. Today we've been invited to lunch in the country.

Louise and Didier are outside to greet us in the gravelled courtyard of their Provençal villa. A large wooden table sits under an oak tree in front of a stone building that houses an outdoor kitchen. The bright winter sun paints an exaggerated version of the table on the gravel, pointing to the entry of the main house, on the opposite side of the courtyard and up a few steps.

Didier leads the way into a formal sitting room, overlooking the pool and the cherry orchard, furnished with antiques and a harpsichord. Here we meet his friends, Pierre and Sandrine, and introduce Joe, Mark's childhood friend from Detroit. The introductions are barely complete when Didier offers us an aperitif and passes around small bowls of olives and pistachios.

Although Pierre speaks English perfectly, his mindset is distinctly Gallic and he seems intent on telling us every bit of knowledge he has gleaned during his lifetime. As he launches into a history of the French Revolution, Didier winks at me, as if to let me know he shares my observation.

Didier and Louise were born and raised in France but their attitude is cosmopolitan. Didier was an international banker and his job took the family around the world; their five children learned English in British boarding schools, French in Paris *lycées*. Now their grown children and grandchildren are scattered around the world and make frequent visits to the family home in Provence.

Just as the revolutionaries are storming the Bastille, Françoise and Laurent arrive and the mood lightens. Close to 80 years old, Françoise loves being with people, and her interest in others is evident. She sits on the edge of her chair, listening to the conversations, smiling with pleasure. Laurent's shiny silver hair is kept a little longer in the front, so he occasionally runs his hands through it to move it back. They are the most delightful couple I've ever known, and even Didier, who has that certain French reserve about him, later confides to me that he thinks Françoise and Laurent are special people, and that their ten children are as well.

The older couple each take a tiny aperitif and appear overjoyed to see us. Joe has brought them a photograph of a sailboat near Key West. They beam with pleasure and are clearly happy to see Joe again. On Joe's first trip to Provence we took him to meet him Françoise and Laurent. It was June, when towns and villages throughout France celebrate the summer solstice with a *Fête de la Musique*. As soon as Françoise found out that Joe was a musician and had brought along his sax, she swung into action. Twenty-four hours later Joe was playing live on the *place* of Puyméras in front of the whole village. It was Joe's first trip outside of his native country, and he already had French groupies.

Pierre gestures Joe over to the sofa next to him and begins to hold forth on French accomplishments. "I see you brought a photograph. Did you know that a Frenchman, Nicéphore Niépce, took the very first photograph?" He then switches to French to explain this to Françoise and Laurent.

Joe is lucky; he doesn't speak a word of French. He doesn't have to pretend to know what's being said or stumble around conjugating verbs. He's tremendously appreciative of French life and is a good guest. Didier is pleased when Joe gives him a photo of a Michigan autumn scene and is also impressed that Joe works as a photographer for the Detroit electric utility company. Little does Didier know that Joe hates his job. The only thing that keeps Joe alive is his passion for music and his photography.

He might not pack many clothes, but he always travels with a tripod and a saxophone.

Louise interrupts the hit parade of French history and asks us to follow her, as dinner is served. She is one of those French women we think about when we think about French women. In her early sixties she always looks great; her hair casually coiffed in a swingy bob, perfect make-up, cashmere twin-set, with just a strand of pearls finishing the look. Today she not only looks good, she is also quite relaxed about serving dinner to a mixed group of nine.

As we sit down at a big table Louise serves us two appetizers: a tapenade with toast points, and a grated carrot salad with capers. The spicy green tapenade is rich and smooth, a perfect contrast to the crunchy, slightly sweet salad. Didier pours the wine, filling each glass barely halfway.

Louise brings out the *plat,* the main course: a tender, rosemary-scented lamb with golden roasted potatoes. She serves each person a few slices of lamb and two potatoes. Much has been written on why the French are slim, but perhaps here is a clue. Didier pours us each another half glass of wine.

Next she serves a salad on the same plates as the main course, without comment or apology. There is none of the clatter and disruption of changing plates and cutlery. A little thing, but it makes the meal seem effortless while the conversation flows smoothly.

The conversation, in two languages, ranges from politics, both American and French, to history, travel, real estate in Provence, the impact of the conversion from francs to Euros, and the best ways to cook lamb. Because Joe is an American, the men often ask his opinion about political and economic topics. Joe would be much more interested in discussing photography or jazz, but he holds up his end of the conversation with lots of shrugs (very French), *ouis* and *bien surs*.

I ask Sandrine about her life and her children. She seems a bit surprised at the nature of my questions. I have forgotten that in France it's not considered polite to ask personal questions. Not because the French are rude, they simply have a different opinion on what constitutes well-mannered dinner conversation. I suppose I would react similarly if she were to ask me about my bra size. Nonetheless, Sandrine answers my questions in her delightfully accented English.

The cheese course follows and Laurent tells a story about a blunder on my part the previous year when we invited him and Françoise for lunch. I found it nerve wracking to prepare lunch while trying to keep the conversation going with my poor French, and I forgot to plan for a cheese course. When I tried to serve dessert, Laurent's jaw dropped. The cheese must come before the dessert! Somewhat ruffled, I scavenged in the refrigerator for some cheese to serve.

The table breaks into peals of laughter at the story of my enormous gaffe. Didier then carefully explains the characteristics of each of the cheeses he is serving as if we were adopting a puppy: "this one has spirit, this one has good bite". I choose a few pieces, careful not to take too much, uncertain if I am expected to finish what I put on my plate.

I comment on the ease with which Louise has served the meal. "I cannot believe how many cookbooks American women buy," she says. "French women do not have them. We are taught by our mothers how to cook; we don't consult a recipe book on how to roast lamb or how to make tapenade. It's all here," she points to her head. "French women are not expected to turn out an elaborate meal every day. In all honesty, we eat simply and pleasurably. I find American and English women more willing to spend hours in the kitchen. That's just not my cup of tea." I find her observations insightful, it's like seeing inside a French woman's head.

The conversation turns to a discussion of cookbook authors. Sandrine mentions that she went to a presentation in Paris given by a famous expatriate American food author. "Her accent was terrible," is her only comment on the lecture.

For dessert Louise presents the *galette du roi*, a buttery, flakey cake of pastry layers filled with *frangipane*, an almond cream paste, and which is only available in the *boulangeries* during *La Saison des Fêtes*. Each *galette* comes with a gold paper crown that is awarded to the person who finds the hidden ceramic figurine, called a *fève*, or bean, in their piece of the cake. That person becomes the king or queen for the day.

Didier and Pierre begin an argument about the origins of the *galette*. Pierre is convinced that the cake and the bean have religious meaning. I prefer Didier's explanation that the *galette* represents the fertile soil and the *fève* is like a seed planted to produce fruitful harvests in the year to come, bringing good fortune for all.

Whatever explanation is correct, I feel a special connection to these people who cherish their stories, and to a country with centuries behind each tradition.

We move back into the sitting room time for *digestifs*. The bold green Chartreuse is a delightful way to end the meal. Joe is still wearing the crown he won.

The last light of the sun delicately illuminates the courtyard as we make our farewells. I know now why Sunday lunch is such a honoured tradition in France. It gives the day a feeling of luxurious, structured relaxation. From the precise sequence of the courses – *apéritifs, entrée, plat, salade, fromage, dessert, digestif* – to the intellectual stimulation of conversation with friends and new acquaintances. And it occurs to me that I am no longer a tourist, but part of Provençal life.

Tomates Confites
SLOW ROASTED TOMATOES

This dish will revolutionize the way you think about tomatoes. It may seem like a lot of work, but the job is really done by the slow roasting. As with any fresh tomato dish, try to find big, ripe, juicy tomatoes. But, given that these are roasted long and slow, you can often get away with less-than-perfect tomatoes.

It's a great feeling when planning dinner to open the refrigerator and find a jar of *tomates confites*! Once you learn to peel and seed tomatoes this way, you'll apply the technique to all kinds of tomato dishes, such as pizzas and pasta sauces.

8 large ripe tomatoes
8 cloves garlic, peeled
extra-virgin olive oil
Herbes de Provence
fresh herbs, optional
sea salt
sugar

Preheat the oven to 200° F.

Peel and core the tomatoes by dropping them in boiling water for 20 seconds and then plunging them into a bowl of cold water. While the tomatoes cool in the water, prepare a ceramic baking dish by brushing it lightly with some olive oil.

Cut each garlic clove into 2 or 3 slices lengthwise and lay them in the baking dish, along with any shredded fresh herbs you may have, such as basil, rosemary or thyme.

Prepare the tomatoes: slice off the tops, remove the skin, cut in half, and remove the seeds and cores. Place the tomato halves in the dish, covering the garlic and fresh herbs. Sprinkle the tomatoes with some *Herbes de Provence*, sea salt, and a pinch of sugar. Generously drizzle olive oil on top.

Roast for 1 hour and then turn the tomatoes. Roast for an additional 1½ hours or more. To store, spoon the tomatoes, olive oil, garlic and seasoning into a glass jar. It will keep in the refrigerator for a week or more, but I doubt it will last that long! It's too delicious.

Use the tomatoes on pizza, for bruschetta, on sandwiches or fresh homemade pasta.

Pâtes Fraîches Maison
FRESH HOMEMADE PASTA

Although not French, pasta has become more popular in France and especially in Provence where the Italian food influence is felt.

Traditionally, homemade pasta is mixed by hand (literally with your hands) and kneaded on a wooden board for ten minutes or more. This makes delicious pasta, but the amount of kneading, plus the cleanup, were barriers to making it very often. But now, with this easier method, the hand kneading time is reduced to about two minutes, yet makes the same delicious pasta. Extra bonus, the cleanup is much easier, too! A large KitchenAid type mixer is ideal but you can get by with a good food processor fitted with a plastic dough blade.

Using a hand-cranked pasta machine makes the process easier and produces better pasta, as the rollers of the pasta machine provide additional kneading. Once you taste your own homemade pasta, you'll know it was worth the investment! It's amazing that only two simple ingredients are used to create this amazing dish.

Fresh homemade pasta and dried pasta are two different foods. Homemade pastas don't need complicated sauces; even butter and parmesan cheese will do. Even though we make our own pasta, we still keep high-quality dried pasta in our pantry, because we love them both.

3 large eggs
3 cups unbleached
   white flour

Using the beater or whisk attachment on a countertop mixer, beat the eggs until they are thoroughly blended.

Change to the dough hook, add 2 cups of the flour to the eggs, and mix on low speed until the dough clings to the dough hook. (On the Kitchen Aid use speed 2, out of 10.) If the dough seems sticky to the touch sprinkle on more flour while mixing; if it's too dry, add another egg or a half teaspoon of water.

Mix at low speed for another 5 minutes to knead the dough. Turn the dough out onto a floured wooden board and knead by hand - push the dough out with the heels of your hands, fold it in on itself, and knead some more. Two minutes will probably do it. On the wooden board cut the dough into 6 pieces. Flatten a piece with your hand. Now comes the fun part. Set the pasta maker to 1, the widest setting. Roll the piece of flattened dough through the machine. Fold into thirds and roll again. Repeat this 6 times.

Lay the rolled dough out on the wooden board. Repeat with the remaining 5 pieces of dough. Dust with the remaining flour frequently during the rolling process.

Change the pasta machine setting to 2, and roll all the pieces just once more. Repeat for setting 3 and, finally, for setting 4. Lay each piece on a clean cloth as you finish it. Cut each piece of flattened dough in the wide cutter of the machine - about fettuccini size.

You may need to pinch the feed-end of the dough to flatten it. As the cut pasta comes out of the machine, catch it with your arm or the handle of a large wooden spoon. Lay out the cut pasta on clean tea towels lightly sprinkle with flour (A sifter works well for this) and repeat for each piece of dough. You can prepare this an hour or two ahead of time and cook the pasta when you are ready. Use the largest stock pot you have, filled with water. (Pasta needs a lot of water to cook properly.)

When the water is boiling strongly, add salt and the pasta. Cook until "toothy", around 8 minutes. Drain and serve immediately. This makes enough pasta for 4 to 6 people.

A Glass of Wine in Paris

One of the joys of being in Paris is the extensive selection of affordable French wines. In Canada, wine is treated the same as dangerous explosives and is monitored and taxed by puritanical committees that even ban its sale in grocery stores. Heaven forbid that you'd eat food while drinking wine! So, when we were planning our four-month stay in Paris, we looked forward to keeping our apartment well stocked with our favourites, particularly two wines that are not available back home. However, initial visits to nearby wine sellers were not encouraging.

"*Muscat de Beaumes-de-Venise? Bien sur,*" one wine shop owner after the next said, producing a bottle from the Beaumes-de-Venise cooperative. "*Mais, Domaine de Durban? Non.*"

No *muscat* from *Domaine de Durban?* Surely, though, given the extensive Champagne selection and the sheer number of wine stores, I would find *Philippe Martin?*

"*Non. Je suis désolé.*"

"*Je suis désolé, monsieur.*"

"*Pas de Philippe Martin. Désolé.*"

Surprised, but undaunted, I set out to solve the problem. First, *Domaine de Durban*. From the Durban website I discover there are two, and only two, wine stores in Paris that sell their *Muscat de Beaumes-de-Venise*.

I find the first store, *Caves du Marais,* on Rue François Miron in the Marais. It's a small shop with an attractive store front: ochre coloured, windows piled high with wooden wine crates. But it's closed. The next day I try again, it's still closed. How can a wine store in Paris, given the high rents, never be open? Just another mystery of Paris. My next stop, then, is *Lavinia* on Boulevard de la Madeleine.

Lavinia was founded in Barcelona, but it's the three-storey wine extravaganza in Paris that is the company flagship. Although it is the largest such store in Europe, with thousands of wines in stock, it is not among my favourite Parisian wine sellers. I'm not interested in a wide selection of wines from Portugal, Argentina or Austria. Paris, to me, is about drinking the best French wines I can afford.

They do have the *Domaine de Durban muscat* and, on my first visit, I learn about their free delivery service. This sounds much better than hauling a case of wine in the shopping trolley, so I select a few dozen bottles (including plenty of *Durban*) and head home, happy in the knowledge that the apartment will soon be stocked with enough *Beaumes-de-Venise* to last months, if not days.

Forty-eight hours later, our wine cellar still bare, I call *Lavinia*. "Sorry, it is not possible. *Ce n'est pas possible.* Our delivery service is halted and will resume on Friday." But with Tom and Jos coming for dinner, we'll need a certain quantity of *Côtes-du-Rhône* to make it through the evening. I argue half-heartedly, although I know it is hopeless. With a sigh, trolley in tow, I walk to the local *Nicolas* wine shop and purchase emergency supplies for the British troops.

It takes another week for our wine to arrive from *Lavinia*. It is, after all, a ten-minute drive.

I return to *Lavinia* from time to time, to pick up a bottle and to eat at their lunch-only restaurant on the second floor. Here I sit with businessmen and chic *Parisienne* shoppers, all smoking and talking, while I dine on a raft of marinated sardines, paired with a glass of sardine-appropriate wine.

With the *Beaumes-de-Venise* in our cellar (a wine box beneath Alexandre's bed), half the battle is over. Now for the Champagne. There is no webpage or other Internet presence for *Philippe Martin* but, finally, in a listing of members of a wine organization, I find the contact phone number for *Philippe Martin Champagne*. Using my shaky French I learn from the winery that there are no wine sellers in Paris stocking *Philippe Martin*! For a city virtually floating in the stuff, this is disturbing news.

But salvation is at hand, for, in only a few weeks, *Philippe Martin Champagne* will present at the annual Paris Wine Show. They will bring some Champagne for me and send free passes for the event, including one for Joe, who'll be visiting at the time. I eagerly accept their offer and set about to make up our order.

Let's see, we'll be in Paris for another eight weeks. How to determine our Champagne needs? How many times a week? How many glasses? Given that Russ, Mary-Lynn and Joe will be visiting for part of that period I finally decide on four cases, just to be safe. On second thought, though, I realize the only way I have to transport the Champagne from the wine show to our apartment is either to carry it or pull it in the shopping trolley. Reluctantly I place an order for only two cases; one of the Brut and one of the *Rosé*.

⤳

It's the day of the wine show and Joe has arrived in Paris. I've known Joe since we were twelve years old, when we lost every game in the Little League season, and I know he's a laid-back kind of guy. The kind of guy who spent most of the last two decades living on a 26-foot sailboat docked on the Detroit River, summer and winter; a gifted photographer and musician who easily fits in everywhere and sponges up the vibes (that is to say, atmosphere).

Just before we leave our apartment, I call Joe on his cell phone to synchronize the time and meeting place at the wine show. "Yeah, I'm just leaving the hotel, but, man, my battery's almost dead and I don't think I ..." Silence.

Diane and I catch Metro line 12 out to Paris Expo at the edge of the 15th Arrondissement where we wait outside the exhibition pavilion for Joe. And wait. I try his cell, but answer comes there none. Finally, long past the agreed time, we give up and enter the wine show.

At the show check-in counter, we are each given a tasting glass (not plastic) and our badges. We are now officially wine tasters at the biggest wine event in France! If this isn't being an insider I don't know what is.

Walking into the pavilion I suddenly feel light-headed. For here, before me, spreading to the distant horizon like the wine-dark sea, are the growers and the *négociantes en vin* (vintners, or wine sellers) and dozens and dozens of Châteaux from every corner of France. There are over 1200 booths. My eyes grow misty as I raise my arms to the skies and shout, "Yes! I've made it, I've finally made it. My whole life has been just a prelude to this moment." In reality, perhaps, I simply smile as I survey my new domain.

I want to go directly to *Philippe Martin,* while Diane wants to visit each and every booth and sample each and every wine from the twelve hundred growers. I point out that having a taste at only a fraction of the booths will be like drinking a bathtub full of wine. So we devise a strategic plan focusing on two regions: the Loire and the Rhône, especially the whites from Châteauneuf-du-Pape, which I find irresistible. At each booth the eager winemakers surreptitiously check our badges, hoping we might be an influential buyer from *Monoprix* or *Nicolas* or a large US importer. There are shoulder shrugs and sighs of disappointment when they read *"Philippe Martin"* on our lapels.

At the *Philippe Martin* booth, we practically throw our arms around M. Duprés, whom we met at their estate in Champagne. Then to the important business of tasting; they want to be sure we still love their Champagne. Once again I savour the wild strawberries of their Rosé and the white chalk and toasted almonds of their Brut. With due ceremony we cram the two cases into our shopping trolley, where they barely fit, and, handshakes all around, we shepherd our precious cargo out of the pavilion and toward the Metro.

It's hours past our meeting time and still no word from Joe. Halfway along the moving walkway that takes us from the wine pavilion to the building exit, we spot Joe coming the other way. "Hey, man," he says as he glides by, as if running into us in Paris is a completely unexpected surprise. "How's it going?" To catch up to us Joe travels all the way to the end of his moving walkway, changes over to our walkway, and meet us at the other end.

I ask where he's been and he says, "Why, what time is it?" Sensing my frustration vibes, he explains. "Yeah, like, ah, when I left my hotel it was cold outside, so I had to go back to change my coat and then I couldn't find where I put my wallet. And when I got outside again it was, like, raining, so I had to get my umbrella. Bummer, eh? What you got in the cart?"

Maneuvering the trolley through the Metro is like Sisyphus pushing his stone up, then down. The difference is that ours is a two-person job and it's lucky that Joe is with us. I want to head home but Diane insists on taking us to a restaurant she has discovered, *Le Dôme du Marais,* which means extra Metro transfers and a walk down cobblestone streets with the over-laden wheels of the trolley screeching in protest.

The *maître d'* at *Le Dôme*, impressed by our cargo, promises to keep it safe while we lunch. We are seated at a table beneath the magnificent, backlit glass dome that gives the restaurant its name. The oyster season has started in France and here at *Le Dôme* they are luscious. Afterward, we sit with Joe, drinking our coffee and soaking in the atmosphere. The experience is so pleasurable that, on impulse, we make advance reservations for New Year's Eve dinner.

The rest of our stay in Paris will be made even brighter by the two cases of Philippe Martin. We'll save a few bottles for *La Saison des Fêtes*, when we will spend another Noël in Provence, and toast friends as they arrive for the celebration.

ᘓᘖ

Ô Château

We arrived for the wine tasting fifteen minutes late and found the gate to the courtyard locked. I fumbled through my bag looking for the reservation information to see if I had a gate code while Mark tried random combinations of numbers. I was just starting to get frustrated when a voice calls, *"Cinq sept un quatre."*

I turned around and looked up at an old woman leaning out a window across the street, gesturing to the key pad. "Five seven one four," she said again. I felt like I was in an episode of *Lost*. Then a light dawned; this was the gate code. I entered the numbers and waved my thanks.

Cramming my stuff back into my bag we hurried across the courtyard; without her guidance, would we have ever have gotten in? We entered through a door discretely marked *Ô Château* and climbed a twisty staircase to the wine tasting studio. Four or five tables were filled with glasses, bottles, and trays of cheese, bread, and *charcuterie*. Oliver Magny sat on a stool at the front of the room, next to a map of French wine regions, warming up the audience of about a dozen Midwesterners who didn't know the difference between concord and sauvignon. Oliver was about to change that.

By twenty-four years of age Oliver Magny had already done a stint in California wine country and returned to his home in France to open a wine tasting salon to marry the two cultures. He knows what North Americans want to know about French wine, and he knows how to deliver it.

Now, several years later, I'm visiting Oliver's new location in the 1ˢᵗ Arrondissement, a wine cellar right in the thick of Paris tourist country. This time we're a bit early. I stand outside *Ô Château's* door on Rue de l'Arbre Sec, just steps from the high-end shops on Rue Saint-Honoré, waiting for a grandmother to cross our paths to give us the code, but this time, it's a handsome, lanky French man, wearing the *Ô Château* apron, who greets us.

"You are here for ze wine?" he asks in what I think is the cutest accent I have ever heard. He must be an actor trained for the role. Yes, I reply, explaining that we have arranged with Oliver to visit the new wine tasting cellar.

He leads us into a neighbouring courtyard, through heavy wooden doors and down ancient, curving stone steps. The whole set-up seems like something created on the back lot for a movie about wine tasting in Paris.

The new studio is an actual *cave*, a cellar beneath one of the older buildings in Paris. The room is a long arch, entirely built out of stone. Low-key halogen lights send shadows down the walls and illuminate the tables with pools of light. Other bulbs provide red and orange accents. The effect is perfect; it screams "wine cellar."

Every type of Paris tourist is here today; a couple from Alabama; a middle aged woman from Hollywood, who worked on the *Star Wars* movies, here with her glamorous daughter; a boastful chap from England who, in the first sentence he says to me, manages to include the phrase "my Jaguar" twice. People from Chicago and Texas sit on the other side of me.

Oliver, as it turns out, will not conduct the tasting today; it will be young Nicolas, who led us to the cellar. Though looking the part of a French wine expert, Nicolas is struggling with his English. He starts the show by pouring us all Champagne. We're not sure if we are supposed to drink now or wait for an explanation, or a blessing. I take the lead and have myself a good sip. Others follow. Finally, Nicolas speaks.

"What are you looking for?" asks Nicolas. Blank looks from around the table. "Here," he demonstrates, "You look, you smell, you taste. You are looking for clarity, sediment, crystals, colour."

Meanwhile, people are drinking and sampling randomly from trays of food. As before, there are cheeses, meats, and bread. Wait, I think, almost saying it out loud, there is an order to a wine tasting. There are rules! But Nicolas has a plan; he carries on, pouring one wine after another, explaining the grapes and regions, and exploring the flavours. It's all about enjoyment, he says, not rules.

If you drink a wine in France and like it, Nicolas tells his audience, there is almost no sense in trying to find another bottle of it elsewhere. "There are 600 wineries in New Zealand and 3000 in California, but in France we have 150,000 wineries!" This number seems extraordinarily high to me, but maybe that's why the average bottle of wine in France costs four Euros. (A fact I will later remember in my local wine store at home where the new *Bordeaux* cost over $100 a bottle.)

Nicolas waves his hand across a map of France. "France has the second largest amount of vineyards in the entire world and it is only the size of Texas," he pronounces with a nod to my neighbours.

France is divided not only into wine regions, but small areas called *appellations*. "In France we love the *appellations*," Nicolas proclaims. "Even fennel has an AOC." He goes on to talk about *Bordeaux*, where, he says, some of the best and some of the worst wines come from. "*Bordeaux*, the name, is very prestigious and any wine that says *Bordeaux* will sell. So, there are good and there are bad wines from Bordeaux. But I look for wine that comes from regions that are not so popular, that are not so prestigious, like Alsace and Languedoc. There I find good value."

Through the afternoon Nicolas leads us through a flight of wines: *Champagne Rosé* from *Eric Phelizon* at twenty-three Euros per bottle; a lovely and flirtatious *Sancerre* with classic citrus flavours; a white *Burgundy Chablis* from the appellation called *Côte Chalonnaise*, which Nicolas describes as "yummy with tamed minerality". The *Crozes-Hermitage* has all the pleasure of the Northern Rhone. And we finish with a *Bordeaux*, an *Haut Medoc* from *Château Lanessan*, 2003, at a mere twenty-five Euros per bottle.

The tasting comes to an end. I notice that the glamorous Californian has barely touched her wines. "I don't really drink wine," she giggles. "I prefer Diet Coke."

⁊

La Tartine

Through the smoky haze I see him. A wizened man, bent over his walking stick, dragging one foot behind as he shuffles into the room. Watching is agony, I can't imagine what it's like for him. He hobbles forward with painful steps until he comes to a corner of the room. Is he going to walk right into the wall? But he slowly reaches out his hand, inserts a key, and opens a hidden door, to reveal an ancient, twisting stairway, leading to the owner's living quarters on the upper floor, above the wine bar.

I'm at *La Tartine*, a wine bar on Rue de Rivoli in the Marais. *La Tartine* was built in 1926 and looks like it hasn't been cleaned since. I'm sitting in the No Smoking section in the back, but I discover that not smoking is purely optional. The large mirror above me is coated with yellow smoke, wearing it like a badge of honour. A huge crack has been repaired with yellowed tape. Everything has the patina of age and grime, including our waitress. Beneath the grime, though, are the original mosaics, decorations, chandeliers, and zinc counters. *La Tartine* won an award for the best wine bar in Paris in 1966. But more recently it was cited by one Paris publication as having *"les chiottes les plus dégueulasses du monde,"* the most disgusting toilet in the world.

It is like being in a Simenon novel set in the '30s: Parisians sipping their glasses of wine at the zinc bar, puffing their cigarettes, and talking about the things Parisians talk about. In other ways, too, *La Tartine* harks back to older times, when Paris was dotted with small bars featuring the wines of a specific region, usually the region the owner was born in.

I move to the bar, nearer the door that opens occasionally to let some of the fumes escape. The bar is perfect for resting my elbows while I sample the current vintage of Sancerre and eat a ham and cheese *tartine*, made before my eyes in what is possibly the world's first toaster oven.

Postscript: *Plus la meme chose, plus la change*, to flip the expression on its head. There is now a cleaner, newer version of *La Tartine*. The cracked mirrors have been replaced, the room painted, the tables replaced. The heirloom toaster oven has been retired.

Steak au Poivre
PEPPER STEAK

On a crisp, bluesky day in fall, we shared a delicious lunch at *La Boeuf sur la Toit*, a lovely original 1920s Art Deco brasserie, where I had the luck of ordering this completely decadent dish. When it's done right, you absolutely swoon.

I've added *Fleur de Sel* to the peppercorns to harmonize the seasoning. Don't be alarmed by the butter, cream and red meat, I've found that a small portion is plenty. We often share one 6-oz steak between the two of us.

This has become a regular at our house, and whenever I makes it I am transported back to Paris. This dish really shines when the steaks are cooked to just rare.

2 6-oz tenderloin steaks
1 T whole black peppercorns, coarsely crushed
1 T *Fleur de Sel*
1 T butter
1 T extra-virgin olive oil
¼ cup *Cognac*
½ cup heavy cream

Remove the steaks from the fridge and bring to room temperature about an hour before serving.

With a mortar and pestle, or broad side of a knife, coarsely crush the peppercorns, then add the *Fleur de Sel*, and give a few more turns with the pestle. Spread out the mixture on a large plate. Press the steaks directly onto the salt and pepper mixture on both sides.

In a heavy skillet, heat the butter and olive oil until sizzling hot. At a near high heat, cook the steaks on each size for 2 to 3 minutes depending on the thickness. Remove the steaks with a pair of tongs, as forks will puncture the meat.

Remove the pan from the heat and wait for about a minute to let it cool slightly. Add the *Cognac* and stand back! The *Cognac* will practically ignite and then quickly boil down. With the heat still off, add the cream and then bring back to a low heat until it boils and thickens, about 2 to 3 minutes.

Return the steaks to the skillet, completely coat it with the mixture and serve immediately. Serves 2.

Moelleux au Chocolate
WARM CHOCOLATE CAKES

At *Chez Clementine*, the *moelleux au chocolate* arrives to the table warm and with just a flick of a spoon, a soft puddle of warm chocolate is released. This is a particularly easy recipe to master and it's one I use time and time again.

½ cup white sugar

¼ cup brown sugar

½ cup unbleached flour

pinch salt

2 eggs

½ cup butter, softened

4 ounces semisweet
  chocolate

1 tsp vanilla extract

Preheat the oven to 325° F.

Line a muffin pan with paper baking cups or use any individual molds that you would have on hand - ramekins do nicely. If you're using ramekins prepare them by brushing the insides with melted butter.

In a large bowl, mix together the sugars, flour, salt and eggs and stir briskly until mixed. Put the butter and chocolate in a double boiler and melt, stirring frequently until melted. Let cool slightly and pour over the first mixture and beat until blended. Stir in the vanilla.

Spoon the batter into the prepared pans, filling half full. Bake for about 15 minutes, (don't over-bake). Remove from oven and turn out onto a cooling rack. Voila! Very chocolaty!

THE MARKETS OF PARIS

A Sunday in Puteaux

"Let's step on this ledge and try to climb over the wall."

It's Sunday morning and we are trapped behind walls of glass at the exit of La Défense, the westernmost stop of the Paris Metro, half way on the trip from our apartment to a market tour and cooking class in the neighbouring suburb of Puteaux. We try every ticket we have, but it's no good; the exit gates remain closed. I push on the glass, first here, then there. I feel like Marcel Marceau.

Luckily there's no one else around as we clamber over the top of the 7-foot glass wall and drop down on the other side. It's easy for me, but Diane has more trouble trying to manage her skirt and heels. Effecting our escape, we hurry to a nearby platform to catch Tram 2, and then spend the ride to Puteaux revelling in our newly-gained freedom.

Waiting for us at the train station is Rebekah, wearing a stylish trench coat and scarf and pulling one of those shopping trolleys that everyone in France uses. Hers is blue plaid. This is not a chance meeting at the side of the tracks, Rebekah is gong to show us the market at Puteaux. She greets us warmly, asks us questions about ourselves, and tells us a bit about herself: born in Hong Kong, she studied to be an architect in San Francisco where she lived for ten years. But food was always her first love, so she left for Paris and has been here for the past three years, teaching piano and leading cooking classes.

"Today," she says, "we will go to the Puteaux covered market and then head to the cooking school just a few blocks from there." As we walk down the quiet Sunday streets towards the market, Rebekah warns us that the market will be less active today because of the annual *vacances*. "Some of my favourite vendors will not be there, but we'll still find lots to choose from."

The life of the vendors in the travelling, weekly markets of Paris is not glamorous. Six or seven days a week they rise before dawn to drive to the city's distribution centres, where they pick up their goods, then travel to wherever the market is that day. Every day their booths have to be set up and displays created. While that would be a full day for many, the vendors then spend the rest of the day serving customers, before having to break down and clean up at the close of the market. And each day, a new location.

"But don't feel too sorry for them," Rebekah tells us. "It's hard work but they make a good living. If they didn't the markets couldn't exist."

Life is better for the vendors at the covered markets. Here, they have permanent booths, with display stands, coolers, and signs remaining in place. And there's no travelling since the covered markets are in the same spot every day. There are only a handful of covered markets still operating in the Paris region, and this one at Puteaux is a thriving example.

The scent of roasting chicken wafts towards us as we near the market. Among the scattering of outdoor stalls are the roasters found at every market in France, filled with a variety of large and small birds, pressed pork, and roasted potatoes.

As I start taking photos an unusual thing happens: the vendor stops what he's doing to tell me about his products. He seems genuinely interested in explaining how long it takes to roast a bird and how he has to recharge the oven throughout the day, so there are always freshly roasted birds available for his customers. He even smiles for the camera. Although Puteaux is a mere eight kilometres from Paris, it reminds me what France might have been like forty years ago. Vendors here are not used to seeing tourists at their market or hearing English being spoken, and they enjoy the attention.

Inside the market Rebekah stops at the cheese counter, "What are the four types of cheese?" she asks us. We guess more or less correctly: hard, soft, goat, and blue cheeses. She points out examples of each and explains their origins and launches into a detailed description of the *Appellation d'Origine Contrôlée* system (controlled designation of origin, or AOC).

"The system dates back to the 15th century," she tells us. *"Champagne* and *Roquefort* are two AOCs you probably recognize." The system, she says, was created to ensure the source and the method of production of various foods, including cheese, meat and wine. Even lentils have an AOC, the best coming from *Le Puy.* I have often read about the AOC but Rebekah makes the information come alive. I look around and see shoppers pointing, prodding, asking questions, conversing with the people who are selling the food. There is still a connection in the minds of the French between food and where it comes from.

Everyone at the market seems to know Rebekah. With her Hollywood good looks, genuine smile and perfect French, the vendors treat her as a special customer, pointing her to the best products and sharing a joke or two.

"Ah, we're in luck, my favourite produce stall is open." Rebekah greets the gregarious vendor. His displays are magnificent: stacks of apricots, rows of asparagus, heaps of tomatoes and best of all, friendly service with plenty of samples. His staff are all just like him, outgoing and upbeat, and are continually slicing fresh melons, mangoes and apricots for customers to sample. As they reach over to give us fruit to try, they tell us about its origin. Once they hear us speaking English with Rebekah the samples of fresh ripe fruit come even faster.

"Look at the signs," Rebekah points. "In France vendors identify where the produce is grown, not only the country but the region, and will rate the quality. *Extra* means best quality: no bruising, no spots, perfect. *Catégorie 1* means good quality with little bruising. *Catégorie 2* is everything else, still good product, but perhaps suitable for cooking or preserving. The fruit here is all *Extra* and *Catégorie 1.*"

Aha! The signs that I've usually ignored actually contain vital information about the source and quality: the apricots are from the Drôme, *haricots verts* from Kenya, the tomatoes from Bergerac. It's all about the *terroir.*

The good times continue at the *boucherie.* As I'm taking pictures the brawny butcher jokes with me. *"Notre boeuf est la meilleure en France."* Our beef is the best in France, he says as he slaps a side of beef. Rebekah smiles and tells us about the history of meat vendors in France: *volailleries, boucheries,* and *charcuteries.*

"Traditionally, poultry was sold only in *volailleries,* although, for some reason, rabbits are considered poultry too. *Boucheries* were the domain of beef while *charcuteries* sold pork products, including sausage. Nowadays, though, the lines are blurred and you see *boucheries* selling sausages and *charcuteries* selling beef pies."

The beef in the market looks different than what I'm used to. It's brighter in colour and I don't recognize any of the cuts. Rebekah tells me that French meat standards aren't the same as in North America and the cuts are entirely different. "French meat is brighter in colour because the butchers don't hang it, also it is aged only three to five days." And, she says, French beef is grass-fed with less marbling and fat.

I step across to the *volaillerie* to inspect the vast display of fresh poultry: *Bresse,* a highly-prized AOC chicken from Normandy; *pintade*s, guinea fowl; *coquelets,* young chickens; and their cousin *lapin,* rabbit. I've never seen this many chickens, row after row, each row two metres long. Beyond this multitude of birds is the *charcuterie* booth where bacon, ham, sausages, terrines and *pâtés* are displayed and sold.

My mind is overflowing with all this new information, but it's probably what every second grader in France knows from watching her mother shop the markets. My brain wants to rest, but Rebekah leads us on to the *poissonnerie.*

Stacks of freshly caught fish are piled high at the fishmonger's stall: blue fish, red fish, big fish, miniature fish and octopus. Some have heads, some are fileted, some are displayed with their mouths gaping open. I assume that the fish who know how to keep their mouths shut won't be here! Rebekah points out the signs, "This one is wild, caught in the north Atlantic, *péché en Atlantique nord-est.* This one is line caught, *de ligne.* This one is farmed, it says *élevée.* They even tell you what kind of vessel the fish were caught from." Small boats are preferred since the catch is smaller and fewer fish means less crushing. Another advantage is that the smaller boats return to dock more frequently, and the fish is fresher. The *poissonere* winks at Rebekah as he casually removes the innards from a stack of fish.

I'm filled with enough food knowledge to start my own primetime cooking show. As we leave the market and walk with Rebekah towards Marguerite's kitchen to cook our purchases, we discuss life in France, food in Paris, our histories and backgrounds. We're like old friends by the time we arrive at the cooking studio.

Rue Poncelot

At Parc Monceau Alexandre is spinning around and around on the carousel, his reward after another robust day in French school. He jumps down and runs to me, carrying a bag, "Mama, look how many chestnuts I collected. I can use them for conka-monka." He and his friends like to throw chestnuts at each other as they run around the park in a sophisticated game called conka-monka.

Parc Monceau, set in the iconic 8th Arrondissement, the right-bank home of the *Arc de Triomphe* and the Champs-Élysées, is a scene out of a Paris movie: nannies push their young charges in strollers; grandmothers wearing pearls and *Hermès* scarves walk with children dressed in blue sweaters and patent-leather shoes; the vendor in the park sells hot cocoa, fresh crepes and a collection of toys; gendarmes keep order by chasing young boys out of trees.

We wend our way along Boulevard de Courcelles, heading for our neighbourhood market street, Rue Poncelet. On the way we make a stop at *La Fromagerie,* one of the two hundred cheese shops in Paris, for *chèvre Bûchette de Banon,* an unripened goat cheese of Provence. Tonight Mark is making *sole meunière* and I am in charge of the cheese course.

Past the *Hediard* outlet we come to the Place des Ternes where, on an island in the middle of the traffic circle, three flower and plant shops flourish. Alexandre stops to smell the flowers. "Which one is your favourite?" he asks. "My favourites are the sunflowers. Smell this one." In December the *place* will be filled with Christmas trees, which Alexandre will inspect one by one.

Around the corner we call in at *Boulangerie Jean-Pierre Cohier* for our daily baguettes. Jean-Pierre has been baking at this spot for twenty years and won the award for the best baguette in Paris last year, which means that his are the official baguettes at *L'Élysée*, where the President of France lives. I always like to go with prize winners; if it's good enough for the President, it's good enough for me.

Reaching Rue Poncelet we pass street vendors offering pots and pans, scarves, and toys to the market shoppers. Alexandre stops to admire a wind-up bird in a cage while I walk across the pedestrian street to my favourite produce stall to pick up lettuce, tomatoes and fruit.

There's an etiquette at the markets. In general, you don't touch the food, you get the attention of the vendor. Sometimes if my fruit monger is busy with another customer, he'll hand me a bag and give a nod for me to choose what I want. Today he offers me a luscious cherry to taste and I order half a kilo. I should have known that cherries in October will be pricey and the total of twenty euros stops me in my tracks. I'm glad I know how to say, *"Désolé, c'est trop cher"*. While there are occasional expensive items — today I buy fresh *girolle* mushrooms, but pass on the wild woodland mushrooms — mostly there is plenty of wonderful, affordable food in our market.

Because the market is filled with locals, the vendors assume I can speak French. In this environment even *I* think I can speak French, and am always sad when such mangled vowels come out of my mouth. I'm sure I detect a look of disappointment on the vendors' faces, too.

Mark, Alexandre and I drift apart. I go to the flower shop to pick out a bouquet while Mark puzzles over the selection of Bordeaux at 4€ at the wine store. I don't worry where Alexandre is. The live lobsters and crabs at the seafood vendor's are an attraction to children in any language.

Alexandre's isn't the only seafood vendor, there's another one facing it. This is a fish lover's dream, a chance to compare selection, quality and price. There are beds of *crevettes*, usually in two sizes and often the subject of a price war. *Crevettes roses cuites de Madagascar. Super promotion!!* one vendor's sign will proclaim and within minutes the price will be matched by his neighbour.

The selection is mind-boggling and the quality is always top-notch. Open to the streets are large display tables, filled with ice, showing off *pavé de saumon, cabillaud, thon rouge, filet d'espadon, calmar.* Stepping around the tables into the store the selection continues with *filet de merlan, raie, tombe, dorade grise, mérou,* sea urchins, along with seafood salads, prepared dishes, and sauces. Here we often buy *escargot*, prepared with pesto and garlic and ready to put in the oven.

October is the start of the oyster season and today there are piles of them: Normandy oysters, *fines de claires.* But Mark limits himself to a couple of fresh sole filets, along with *crevettes,* of course, which he buys on every trip to Poncelet. Finally, we buy Alexandre half a roasted chicken and, as always, the seller hands him a lollypop.

The markets of Paris are living history, a link to a time when food shopping was a key aspect of daily life, when you knew all the vendors and spent time chatting and visiting. For now I am living that life, on Rue Poncelet, with my Parisian neighbours, shopping for dinner.

Asperges Rôties au Four
OVEN ROASTED ASPARAGUS

Once I discovered this method of cooking asparagus I gave up steaming, pan frying and baking. It works especially well with big, fat spears of asparagus fresh from the market.

1 lb asparagus

2 T extra-virgin olive oil

½ tsp *Fleur de Sel*

¼ cup Parmigiano-Reggiano (optional)

1 T lemon juice

Pre-heat oven to 450° F.

Cut the tough ends off the asparagus.

In a baking dish, arrange the asparagus in a single layer. Using your hands coat the spears with olive oil and sprinkle with salt. Roast for 10 to 15 minutes. The asparagus are done when the tips are turning golden brown.

Remove from the heat and squeeze on the lemon juice. Add the grated *Parmigiano-Reggiano* and serve. Serves 2 to 4.

Salade Maison
DIANE'S HOUSE SALAD

Susan Hermann Loomis, cookbook author and cooking teacher, is a salad perfectionist. From her I learned three of the most important rules to follow to make great salads: wash, spin and rehydrate. And she's right; a great salad should be crisp, fresh and perfectly dressed.

I love herb salad mix with its combination of arugula, *frisée*, red chard, dill, parsley and cilantro. Unless it's a main course salad, I like to serve salads in interesting dishes, like my Eiffel tower glasses, or small soup bowls. When the salad is made fresh, it will become a highlight of the meal.

5 ounces herb salad mix or fresh spring mix

1 carrot

¼ cup maple balsamic vinaigrette (see separate recipe)

Remove the greens from the package and place directly into the colander part of a salad spinner. Rinse well under the tap, using your hands to ensure that all the greens are washed. Spin several times to make sure the majority of water is removed. Water is the enemy of crisp salads!

Now for the important step, place the greens into the refrigerator for at least 15 minutes. This guarantees that they will become crisp. While the greens re-hydrate, make the vinaigrette. This can be made well ahead of time, but I usually make mine fresh.

Just before serving, in a large salad bowl, add the refreshed greens and, using a vegetable peeler, add long strips of carrot. Now it's time to toss. Drizzle the vinaigrette and, with salad tongs, toss until the greens are completely covered and all the vinaigrette is integrated. Serve immediately!

Serves 2 to 4.

CULINARY BOOT CAMP

"Ahh, it's closed." She makes that shoulder and head gesture. That French one. "I thought it would be open." She stands in front of the shuttered *boulangerie*, eight of us huddled around her like chicks around a mother hen.

"They were open the last class, but now it's shut for the holiday. I apologize. No, I don't need to apologize. Come!" And with that she marches down the street, leaving her polka-dot shopping trolley behind. I grab the trolley and follow with the rest of the befuddled members of the brood.

Suddenly she halts, and the rest of us skid to a stop behind her. "But be sure to watch for vehicles. This street is *semi-piéton*, although I don't know how it can be semi-pedestrian. What does that mean?" Shoulder and head gesture. She goes on, "I consider anything on two wheels to be a menace. These bicycles! I know it's not correctly environmental, but..." The gesture and an irritated shake of the head. "The mayor... It's a political issue. Pah."

The market on Rue Montorgueil. Paris. *Le Bon Gourmand* market tour and cooking school. Class is in session.

The first stop is the *poissonnerie*, the fish shop. The front of the stall is open to the street, like all fresh food market shops in Paris, with the fish displayed on great mounds of ice. It's only nine in the morning and the market stores are just getting rolling. The fishmongers are laying out the fish for today's shoppers.

"Come everyone, but please stay out of the way! This is their business. Fish is very important to the French but one must be very careful when purchasing. There is now all this cheap fish becoming popular in France: sardines, mackerel and whatnot," a dismissive wave of the hand. "What they serve in restaurants!" the shoulder and head gesture. By this time my own neck is getting tired from following her hand as she points first to one kind of fish and then to another.

"I adore the firm white fish. Look at this tuna. Very controversial. I really don't want to get into it now!" she declaims mysteriously. As she pokes and prods the fish she banters with the staff but, in the end, buys nothing.

Next, the neighbouring produce stall. We waddle behind her, looking particularly out of place, while our leader dashes ahead. "It's plum season, look at these divine *quetsche* from the Alsace. Look, over here. Cherries from Belgium. Pah! You must look carefully at the signs to find the origin. Apricots from the Drome, good; *Reine Claude* plums (you say greengage) from Moissac, that's French; tomatoes from Bergerac. Always you must try to buy French produce, it's the *terroir*, you know."

While speaking she scurries between the produce bins, choosing items for her basket, dashes around the corner of a display, zooms past the eggplants and garlic, and heads for the cash desk. The brood follows, wending our way between the produce bins and the other shoppers. "Does someone have the trolley?" I raise my hand. "Good. *Venez*. Come."

Our leader, Mathilde, native *parisienne* and owner of *Le Bon Gourmand*, chats with the cashier, asking about her *vacances* and telling her about her own upcoming departure to Morocco, all the while putting our purchases in the shopping trolley. Saying *adieu* she bustles out of the store, until the cashier politely calls out to ask if she could please pay. *"Bien!"* Back into the store to pay while the rest of the group stands at attention. Again, the polka-dot trolley is left behind, with one of the brood retrieving it.

With a flourish Mathilde leads us a few doors down to the *fromagerie*. "This place is my favourite," she drops her voice, "Look at the handsome young men who work here." She flicks her hair and gives a flirty look at the Tom Cruise of *fromagères*.

We spend a long time in the cheese shop while Mathilde banters, giggles, and teases the men behind the counter, buying almost nothing. However, I have plenty of time to admire the selection of cheeses. Then we're off again (I grab the trolley again) on the ten-minute walk to her apartment in the Marais.

Her apartment is found in a quiet courtyard and up one flight of stairs. By Paris standards it's impressive. A large entry gives way to a spacious kitchen containing a five-burner *La Cornue* stove. The kitchen is built around an island with seating for eight. Mathilde flings the groceries on the island, checks her watch, clucks and informs us we have to get a move on. Hands washed, we wrap on aprons and get a move on.

The first job is to use a *mandoline* to cut the onions. She demonstrates how the onion is to be held and manoeuvred against the sharp cutting blade. And then, ignoring every safety rule ever created by the French bureaucracy, she passes around the *mandoline* to give everyone a chance to cut off a finger tip. The onions are so strong that by the time Penny from Arkansas has a turn, her eyes are burning so badly that she has to apply eye drops. Gary, the only man in the class, does the manly duty of finishing the cutting of the onions.

We start out making a lamb *tian*. The sliced onions, with a little olive oil, are set to browning in a skillet on the stovetop. Meanwhile, we slice tomatoes and eggplants and line them up in a metal pan in alternating layers: tomato, eggplant, tomato, eggplant.

"Margery, we like pretty food. This is ugly! Please remove those tomatoes," our leader clucks. Margery from Toronto is not pleased at being admonished about her tomato slicing skills.

When cooked, the onions are removed from the skillet and placed at the bottom of the flat ceramic pot for which the dish is named. Next, the lamb is set to brown in the same skillet. "Diane, please get me the paper towels, and the vinegar is found in the drawer." Somehow I have been given the role of assistant, maybe because I kept track of the trolley. "Can anyone tell me what *confit* means? Diane, you don't answer since you have a food blog." We will, she says, *confit* the lamb *tian* by cooking it slowly until tender. This will take more than an hour.

When the lamb is browned to her satisfaction it's transferred to the *tian* pot on top of the onions. The sliced vegetables are moved from the metal pan to the *tian*, on top of the lamb, in the same alternating slices. Fresh thyme and rosemary are added, along with unpeeled garlic cloves, and the dish is sprinkled with olive oil. We stop to admire our creation before Mathilde pops it into the oven.

"The enemy of *tian* is water," Mathilde tells us a few minutes later. "As it bakes you must remove the excess." She demonstrates with a ladle, scooping moisture out of the bottom of the *tian* pot.

The Big Show is now about to begin: making the crust for the quiche. "I will show you a method that will change your life. When I told David Lebovitz about this he was so intrigued he came to my kitchen to see for himself. You know David Lebovitz? First you put water and butter into a bowl and put it into the oven until it boils."

Well, you could knock me over with a plume, as David said in his blog about her anarchistic pastry recipe.

Once the quiche is ready it's time for cheese tasting. It was the Berbers, Mathilde tells us, who introduced the goat to France in the 8th century. "The Loire River is the dividing line between north and south when it comes to cheese," she explains, gesturing to an invisible map. "There is no goat cheese north of the Loire."

She continues on to describe the flavours of various types of cheese and the order of how cheese tasting is to be done, from mild to strong. She demonstrates the proper way to cut cheese, so that each piece has part of the rind as well as the inside. By this time I am so famished I could eat a goat.

We begin with *Pouligny-Saint-Pierre*, a fresh goat cheese from Berry, and work our way up to the *Fourme d'Amberta*, a blue cow's cheese from the Loire and one of the heirloom cheeses of France. She warns us about the enemy of cheese: pasteurized milk. "Don't even bother with Brie or Camembert made outside of France," she sniffs. Natalie from Calgary tries to argue, "We have tons of great cheese makers around Calgary!" Mathilde is not convinced. "Where is this *Calgary*?"

She teaches us how to cut a baguette, "Not like that, Hannah! We're not barbarians!" The baguette, in case you're wondering, is to be cut as needed, never sliced the whole length at one time. Oxidation is the enemy, Mathilde warned us. There seem to be plenty of enemies in her kitchen. The enemy of chocolate soufflé is getting any bit of yolk in the whites. The enemy of caramelizing shallots is excess heat.

When it's time to make the chocolate soufflé, Mathilde expounds on the chocolate in France. "We do not have what you call *bittersweet* chocolate here, it's all described by cocoa percentages. *My* favourite chocolate is *Valrohna*, from the Rhône valley, here in France."

Natalie from Calgary pipes up again. "We have a wonderful and famous chocolate maker in Calgary! His name is Bernard Callebaut and he's won chocolate awards in France."

I can see that Natalie from Calgary is turning into an annoying mosquito for our leader. "This *Calgary*, it seems, has everything. Even chocolate makers. This man, Barnard whatever, I have not heard of him." She gives her hair a flick.

As the battle of Calgary vs. France rages, Penny from Arkansas is trying her best to fold egg whites into melted chocolate. "Penny stop! You are playing with your food like a child. I said fold! Surely you know what that means." The rest of us look on nervously, secretly glad that we aren't Penny.

A few minutes later, while Mathilde's husband is helping out, he accidentally breaks a cup. "You know how much I love those cups," Mathilde complains loudly in French, "that one is irreplaceable!" Even if the other guests didn't understand what she's saying, they understand the tone, and more nervous glances are exchanged, "Mommy and Daddy are fighting again."

I'm certainly getting an insider's view of Paris, but I'm not sure it's the inside I wanted to see.

෴

Margueriteville

As I leave the covered market in Puteaux, a suburb of Paris, laden with food purchases, I think about all this things I've learned about French food this morning from my guide and new friend Rebekah: produce classifications, AOCs, AOPs, type of cheeses, cuts of meat, the best fish to buy. It's as if I've entered a whole new food universe. But there's no time to ponder, it's time to cook what we bought at the market.

Rebekah leads us to the cooking studio of *Marguerite's Elegant Home Cooking*, located in Marguerite's house. The spacious dwelling contains a striking curved staircase at the rear that takes us up to the kitchen. Unlike most cooking class spaces, this one has four cooking stations and four sinks so that each participant can work in their own area and learn, hands-on, the techniques as they are presented.

We start with *poulet farci à la cardamome*, stuffed chicken with cardamom coating, using tiny birds called *coquelets*, a French version of Cornish game hens, though smaller and more tender. I chop onions and dice tomatoes for the sauce and then, while that simmers, coat the *coquelets* with ground cardamom, stuff them with spiced ground veal, and wrap each bird with slices of prosciutto.

Rebekah is a meticulous cook and every time I present her with my version of chopped onions or tomatoes she chops them even finer. As we work, Rebekah talks about the quality of French produce. "Tomatoes are not bred for long distance travel, but rather for flavour and a skin so fine that you don't need to peel them before cooking." Even the garlic is better; we cook with large firm, rosy-hued cloves.

Rebekah teaches me to heat the oil in a skillet so the tomatoes or *coquelets* sizzle when they hit the pan. As I place the wrapped *coquelets* in a hot pan and hear the prosciutto sizzle, I know this dish is going to be a winner. "These recipes are designed for the home cook," Rebekah emphasizes. "I want people to rush home and make this food for their friends."

While the birds cook we freeze some *crème fraîche*. This is the key ingredient in the *nougat glace* we are making for dessert. Once frozen, we beat the *crème fraîche* with a large whisk, adding chopped crystallized pineapple and ginger, and sliced almonds roasted until they are almost burnt. We beat eggs and sugar on the stovetop until they are thick and creamy and then blend them with the *crème fraîche*.

The *nougat glace* back in the freezer, we go on to complete the *coquelet* recipe by simmering the browned birds in the tomato sauce. Then we get ready for lunch.

The cloudy morning has changed into a hot August afternoon, and we set the table in the shade of the interior courtyard. As our conversation continues over lunch, we learn that Rebekah shares a past with us: Edmonton. She was married there, and so were we. Edmonton, Alberta is about as far removed from Paris as you can get. Located on the northern Canadian Prairies, it's famous for its long, cold winters, flat landscape, and perogies. It's astounding that, a decade after our weddings, we are here in Puteaux sharing stories, laughing and enjoying a fine day of cooking.

༄

Susan

It's a warm September evening and the Seine is a delicious inky black, reflecting lights from the *bateaux mouches*. I arrive at Rue Jacob, thrilled to be entering the Left Bank cooking studio of Patricia Wells, tonight lent to Susan Herrmann Loomis. Susan is a pillar of the French cooking class establishment and a prolific cookbook author. I can't believe I'm finally going to meet her.

The studio is divided into three spaces: an entry, a dining and sitting area, and the large kitchen. I recognize the mighty *La Cornue* gas stove that Patricia Wells describes in her writing.

I have only seen photos of Susan and they don't do her justice. In person she is strikingly good-looking: statuesque, with toned arms, and exuding confidence. Her experience shows as she welcomes me and the other participants and brings us to order. It's a good thing, since we are a rag-tag collection of what you would expect; middle-aged North Americans with adoring eyes for Susan.

Susan firmly starts the class by standing in the power centre of the kitchen and passing around tiny bowls. She is about to educate us in salt. I love how she starts the class on this note, a microanalysis of a single ingredient. Susan explains how important sea salt is to cooking and how we must seek out the finest *Fleur de Sel*.

"There are two kinds of salt," explains Susan. "Salt for cooking and salt to finish a dish." She indicates which of the tiny bowls we should taste. One salt is very grey in colour and almost damp, the other is finer with a whiter hue and softer granules.

"Never waste *Fleur de Sel* to cook with, this wonderful salt is used to finish a dish, just before you serve it." The biggest sin, she tells us, is to under-salt your dishes.

Salt! Who knew there were so many different types and so many specific uses?

"What's more important than salt?" Susan asks next. Chocolate! Tiny chunks of chocolate are passed around for tasting. Susan explains what the percentages of chocolate mean and where the best dark chocolate can be found in Paris.

"Taste with your tongue, not your teeth," she warns us, "let the chocolate melt on your tongue." As we savour each little chunk of chocolate, Susan talks about the flavours we're tasting: flinty, astringent, smoky, woodsy, fruity or spicy.

Following salt and chocolate we move on to toasted nut oils. Susan shows us a collection of bottles from a company named *Huilerie J. Leblanc* that specializes in toasted nut oils: almond, pine nut, pistachio, hazelnut and walnut. The flavours are incredibly intense. My favourite is *huile de pistache*, which is also, of course, the most expensive. Susan explains that these oils are used only as a condiment in cooking. "We'll only need a dash of the toasted almond oil to heighten the flavours of the salad."

This simple tasting of sea salt, chocolate and toasted nut oils grounds the group and gets us prepared for the class. Susan is an organized leader and divides us into teams: one to prepare the salad, one for duck duty and one for the dessert.

Everyone wants Susan's attention, and she's very good at keeping people happy and keeping the momentum going. She's a pro at getting all of us involved in cooking the meal, instead of just watching what she's doing.

I am on salad duty and Susan is a perfectionist. She shows me how to wash lettuce: first she washes the leaves under the tap and then lets them soak for a few minutes in cold water. She asks me to inspect each leaf carefully before spin drying them.

"There is no bigger crime than dirt on a salad," she tells me. But she's not done yet. Once the leaves are squeaky clean, they're put back in the fridge to refresh and spring to attention. Lettuce leaves, Susan firmly states, are to be torn into bite-size pieces. They must never be cut!

Susan points out that most people do not know how to toss salad correctly. "They just don't toss enough!" Susan demonstrates how to toss the leaves with just a bit of vinaigrette toss, for longer than you think, until the leaves feel heavy. That's the signal that each leaf has been completely covered with vinaigrette. "There should no pooling of vinaigrette on the bottom of the bowl," she warns.

When the other groups finish their cooking, dinner is served. I am a little disconcerted to be in Paris surrounded by a group of boisterous Americans. As we eat, wine is poured and the talk and laughter become louder. At one point Susan tells the group sternly, "Please, you mustn't laugh so loud. There are other tenants in the building." I like that. Susan reminds us that while we are in France we should do as the French do: mind our manners!

Like the best instructors anywhere, Susan inspires with new ideas. Good classes like this are memorable, I take away a lot of new food knowledge.

When I leave I notice the shop of *Huilerie J. Leblanc*, the source of the nut oils I tasted at the class. The little store, only six feet wide, is closed now, but I know I'll be back.

Cardamome Poulet
CARDAMOM CHICKEN

Rebekah was right, I rushed home to make this dish. But, my neighbourhood grocery store in Canada being short of *coquelets*, I made this version with chicken breasts. Rubbing the chicken with cardamom and then wrapping it in prosciutto adds layers of flavours.

1 lb fresh, ripe tomatoes

2 cloves garlic cloves, minced

1 small onion, chopped

2 whole chicken breasts, with bone and skin

1 tablespoon cardamom, ground

6 thin slices of prosciutto

1 tablespoon butter

2 T extra-virgin olive oil

Prepare the tomatoes by washing, coring and chopping into small pieces and setting aside. Finely chop the garlic and onions set aside.

Pat dry the chicken breasts. Rub the chicken with the ground cardamom making sure to fully cover the breasts. Wrap each breast with 2 to 3 pieces of proscuitto and set aside. I like to secure the proscuitto to the breast with cooking string.

In a large skillet, on medium-high heat, melt the butter with 1 tablespoon of the olive oil. When you add the proscuitto wrapped chicken to the skillet, it should sizzle!

Brown well on all sides. Remove the chicken from the skillet and set aside. In the same skillet, add the remaining tablespoon of oil and immediately add the chopped onions and garlic. Sauté until they are golden brown. Now add the tomatoes. Stir and bring to a boil, then reduce the heat to low, cover and simmer for another 20 minutes.

Now it's time to add the chicken back to the skillet, covering with the tomato sauce. If the sauce is too thick, add some water. Cover and simmer for another 20 to 30 minutes. Taste before serving, adjusting with sea salt and pepper. I like to serve the chicken over a bed of freshly made basmati rice.

COOKIN' AT THE RITZ

I felt like I was on "Cooking with the Stars", but as one of the paparazzi. There I was, standing in the last place Princess Diana was seen alive, huddled in rainy weather outside the service doors of the most famous hotel in the world.

But that was a generation ago and today the well-dressed and perfectly groomed staff of the Ritz Hotel Paris had other things on their mind: like grabbing a cigarette between serving guests.

As for me, I was there for a cooking lesson in the kitchens of the Ritz. I went down stairs and along an extended corridor, noticing the activity taking place in rooms to the left and right of me in the rabbit warren of side kitchens and teaching facilities.

Men and women in chef's costumes bustled about, keeping the empire going. In one of the teaching kitchens was the fabulous Chef David Goulaze, master chef and our instructor for the day. With a grin as big as Liberace's, Chef David invited us into his classroom. But this classroom had a giant gas burning stove, a bank of ovens, an overhead mirror, and a large work table crowded with ingredients. In a side room staff stood ready beside sinks and dishwashers.

This was a lunchtime lesson and, with no time for formal introductions or overview, Chef David got us cooking within five minutes flat. "Who wants to take the heads off these puppies?" asked Chef, holding up a bowl of giant shrimp. "Save the heads, though, we're putting them into the cardinal sauce. Know why it's called cardinal sauce? Who cares?" Chef gestures to student who has the risotto moving at a brisk pace, "Just keep stirring.

"Now, we're going to chop, chop, chop. *Stop! In the Name of Love,*" Chef broke out into song. In between giggles, guffaws and show tunes, Chef David coaxed out of us a lunch worthy of royalty.

With his techniques, shortcuts and expertise, in a mere hour we hammered out a meal that stunned even me, the jaded food critic: *gambas, parmesan tuiles,* and risotto.

After plating our meals we moved to the Ritz's basement library where a table has been set for us. As we devoured our creation, I asked David, "What's your favourite restaurant in Paris?"

"Le Ritz."

"Where's your favourite place to buy chocolate?"

"Le Ritz."

"Where's your favourite place to be in Paris?"

"Le Ritz."

"No, really, David, the microphone isn't on. Stop! In the name of love!"

∾

Cooking for Friends at Cordon Bleu

Eight in the morning seems a bit early for the first glass of wine, but I am at *Le Cordon Bleu* in Paris and, as a visitor, I want to be polite. We are on another food adventure, along with Mary-Lynn and Russ, two friends who are always up for any crazy scheme I suggest, from touring the Champagne region with Louis, to cooking classes in Florence and even renting a castle with us in Tuscany. But getting up at seven on a Sunday morning to catch a long Metro ride to a cooking class may be the nuttiest plan so far.

As I sip my wine in the reception room, assistant chef Ben, a Jamie Oliver doppelganger, tells us about the day ahead in the *Cooking for Friends* class. "Although it's called an amateur class, we will make the same dishes the professional students tackle." There is a ripple through the crowd.

"Today you are going to make *magret de canard rôti aux raisins frais, navets longs, pommes de terre et pleurotes cuisinés au gras de canard.* Don't worry, folks, these are just fancy French words for roasted duck breast, potatoes and oyster mushrooms cooked in duck fat. Oh, did I mention the hand-peeled grapes, roasted in Muscat?"

And that's not all. "Just to be sure that your friends will be happy when you graduate from this class, we're also going to learn how to pan-fry scallops, make homemade pasta, and fig and banana *clafouti.*" It seems intimidating, but Ben says not to worry, by lunchtime we'll be ready and eager to hit the kitchens.

After this motivational speech Ben ushers us into the theatre kitchen, where we'll start the day with a cooking demonstration by Chef Patrick, one of the pillars of *Le Cordon Bleu.* Ben stands at attention to one side of a massive *piano,* what French chefs call their cooking station, ready to translate the chef's rapid-fire monologue (and inject a few jokes of his own). At the other end of the counter two Japanese apprentice cooks wait for their orders. In between these sentinels is Chef Patrick, attired in chef's whites and the familiar tall toque, the star of the show. With the splendour of a celebrity chef, he stations himself behind a huge cook top and a battery of pans, bowls and utensils. He addresses his audience.

"Chef says he'd like everyone to stand up and give him a round of applause," Ben translates. Just kidding, says Ben, Chef says he is happy to have you here with us today at *Le Cordon Bleu.*

Chef Patrick starts the class. "To create a memorable meal you must begin with the best ingredients you can find," translates Ben. "After the ingredients are looked after, the only job of the chef is to use the appropriate techniques to make the most of them. Chef says, above all, you must have a plan before you begin; review the recipe, pre-measure, ensure you have everything you'll need."

Ben pauses, waiting for Chef Patrick to finish, "And, of course, the most important ingredient is passion. A passionate cook, Chef says, will always create a superior dish".

Ben adds, "Chef says don't use macaroni and cheese for your pasta course." Ben laughs at his own joke.

He begins with the fresh pasta: large amounts of flour are mixed, kneaded, and rolled out into long sheets of dough using an enormous hand-cranked pasta machine. As he cranks he addresses us with a twinkle in his eye.

"Chef says that although pasta is an Italian invention, it's the French who have elevated it into *haute cuisine.* Of course, we know he's joking. Right?"

In France, Ben tells us, a chef is a very respected professional and has the same prestige as a CEO, judge or doctor. This is apparent in the approach of Chef Patrick; he knows he is the leader and instructs us with ease and professionalism. Master Chef Patrick Terrien has worked in some of the best kitchens of Paris and owned a Michelin-starred restaurant in Tours before joining *Le Cordon Bleu* in 1989.

Chef Patrick's focus on detail is impressive. While pouring olive oil into the blender for the pesto he bends over the machine, head at the same level as the bottle, carefully monitoring his work.

"A trained chef brings all his attention and focus to the matter at hand." This total focus helps Chef to create a better dish, keeps him free of distractions and prevents kitchen accidents. "Plus he looks super cool, doesn't he?" adds Ben.

It is a busy morning. After the fresh pasta and pesto are made, Chef moves onto the duck breast. He demonstrates how to trim off just enough fat to keep it juicy without being greasy. Next he scores the duck breasts with a knife, lightly salts and pan-cooks them with the fat side down. Chef checks for doneness by pressing his thumb onto the cooking duck and then turns it over for just a brief minute.

While the duck is cooking he expertly carves potatoes and turnips into three-inch ovals. The turnips are slowly steamed with a sheet of parchment paper on top while the potatoes sauté in duck fat. His assistants take over the duck, potatoes and turnips and peeling some grapes. "You didn't think Chef was going to peel grapes, did you?" quips Ben.

Chef turns his attention to dessert. A *clafouti* is a simple fruit flan, made with eggs, sugar, milk and a dash of flour, traditionally with whole cherries. Cherries aren't in season so Chef Patrick makes an inventive substitution with bananas and figs.

The cooking is complete and chef prepares the food for serving. The duck breast is carved into thin slices and spread, fan-like, on plates with the perfectly carved potatoes and turnips lain beside. The peeled grapes have been gently sautéed to release their juices. A few grapes are placed on each plate and the *jus*, reduced from the pan drippings of the duck, strained, thickened with flour and wine, is artfully dribbled over top.

The class breaks into applause at the artistry. Chef says it is time to taste.

The support team serves the dishes while Chef Patrick makes jokes at their expense. I get the idea that to be a chef in training means developing a thick skin for the Chef's bantering. Wine is opened to accompany the sample meals.

The formality of the class breaks down and I turn and chat to other students. I assumed all the students are tourists but discover that Isabelle, sitting next to me, lives in Paris. Although she is British and has lived in Paris for ten years with her French husband, she still revels in the joy of living *la vie Française*; simply walking across Pont Neuf on her way home from work gives her a daily thrill. Ben, Chef Patrick's assistant, tells me about teaching his five-year old to cook, reasoning that if you don't teach your kids, they will never know how to feed themselves.

After lunch, it's time to stretch our legs and have a break. On the steps outside of *Le Cordon Bleu* student chefs lounge on the sidewalks, smoking and talking. It is a bright spring day. The sun shines on the colourful storefronts creating brilliant splashes of colour. Mary-Lynn and I wander among the local shops and discover a *boulangerie* called, *Toute Beurre*, "Everything Butter." As we step inside the scent of baking with butter is unmistakable. We look at each other and break into laughter. Somehow, this all-butter experience is another of those Paris moments. Mark and Russ do the masculine thing and go to a wine shop where Mark helps Russ pick out a corkscrew.

We return to *Le Cordon Bleu* and follow Ben upstairs to the teaching kitchens where we will recreate the same menu. Chef Patrick made it look effortless this morning, but I can't remember the last time I carved a potato into a perfect oval, three inches long, or peeled a grape. And my turnip carving skills are woefully lacking. Strangely enough, I find myself wanting to please Chef Patrick and I am secretly thrilled when he passes by and says *"bon"* as he inspects one of my carved potatoes.

Russ isn't doing so well. He's butchered his *magret* by cutting off too much fat, and gets a raised eyebrow from Chef Patrick. Meanwhile, Mark is enjoying draining the duck fat juices and adding it to the potato ovals to watch them sizzle. He learns that if you want good fried potatoes, you need duck fat.

Mary-Lynn may be the first person to fail this class. *Ever.* She cuts her finger badly with the knife and burns herself while cooking the duck. Danger, it seems, is everywhere. The accidents don't faze the assistants and I assume their first-aid kit is often cracked open. Mary-Lynn's wounds are cleansed and wrapped with all the finesse of a trussed goose.

This is a class for amateurs, but I can see how demanding and rigorous a chef's training is. After eight hours I am exhausted, but at least I can rest the next day, unlike the young trainees who will be back in the training kitchens early in the morning. Food is important in France and Chef Patrick takes his role seriously. He is the leader, the chief, and, even though we are amateurs, he never drops his professional role or diminishes the importance of what we are learning.

Russ and Mary-Lynn, with their band-aids, treatment ointments and mangled *magret*, are glad the day is ending. As a reward (or punishment) we all leave with the *magret* we have cooked that day. But after eight hours, the duck looks as tired as I feel. I will be happy to resume my career from the other side of the restaurant, as a diner.

Magret de Canard aux Sauce de Cerises
DUCK MAGRET WITH CHERRY SAUCE

It was Chef Patrick at *Le Cordon Bleu* who taught me how to work with duck *magret*, the breasts from ducks raised for *foie gras*. I watched him closely as he used a sharp paring knife to score the fat in a crisscross pattern, without cutting into the meat.

As you might expect if you've ever eaten *foie gras*, the *magret* breasts have a thick layer of fat that you will render (melt off). In my version, I first brown the breasts in a skillet and then finish them in the oven. Make sure to save the melted fat for making duck-fat fried potatoes.

The sweet cherry sauce is spiked with tart vinegar and brandy to complement the dark flavours of the duck. In traditional versions of reduction sauces, the juice of the meat is used, here I've simplified the process so it can be easily prepared before cooking the duck and set aside. cherry sauce (see separate recipe)

2 *magret* duck breasts
sea salt
freshly ground pepper

Preheat oven to 400° F.

First, make the cherry sauce and set aside.

Place the duck skin side down on a cutting board and trim off any fat that extends beyond the edges of the meat.

Turn the breast over and, using a sharp knife, score the fatty side, cutting about 1/8-inch into the skin and fat in a crisscross pattern. Be careful not to cut into the meat. Season the duck breasts on both sides with sea salt and freshly ground black pepper.

Place the duck breasts, now skin-side down, in a large skillet and cook over a low heat to render most of the fat. Pour off the excess fat one or two times. (Save the fat in a container in the refrigerator for future use.) The fat from the duck will take 10 or 15 minutes to melt down.

Drain off the last of the duck fat, then cook the breast over medium-high heat for only a minute or two until the skin is crispy. Turn the breasts over and cook the flesh side for one minute (if needed, add a splash of olive oil).

Move the breast to a baking dish, skin side up, and roast in the oven for 8 minutes for a nice medium-cooked duck with a bit of red inside. Test by pressing your thumb into the cooking meat. It should be slightly springy.

When ready, rest the duck on a warm plate for a few minutes. Slice the duck breasts thickly on the diagonal and fan out over the plate. Spoon over the cherry reduction sauce. Serve immediately.

Sauce aux Cerises
CHERRY REDUCTION SAUCE

1 T butter
1 T extra-virgin olive oil
¼ cup shallots, minced
¼ cup cherry preserves
3 T sherry or red wine
  vinegar
¼ cup brandy
sea salt
freshly ground black
  pepper

In a medium-size skillet, heat the butter and oil until they are sizzling. Add the minced shallots and sauté until they are just brown and almost caramelized. Remove to a plate and set aside.

In the same pan turn down the heat to medium and add the cherry preserves, the vinegar and the brandy. Stir them thoroughly and gently simmer for about 5 minutes.

Return the cooked shallots to the pan and stir them into the cherry blend until they are completely reheated. Spoon directly on top of the prepared duck breast. Serves 4.

Polenta Poêlé
PAN-FRIED POLENTA

What's long, yellow, crispy and delicious? These tasty polenta treats perfectly accompany meat dishes like Duck Magret and *Steak au Poivre*. You can make your own thick polenta from scratch, but I usually use the pre-cooked tubes of polenta you can find in most grocery stores. It's fast and easy.

1 tube pre-cooked
  polenta
2 T butter, for cooking
1 tsp extra-virgin olive
  oil
Parmigiano-Reggiano,
  grated
Fleur de Sel
freshly ground black
  pepper

Trim the rounded, long edges off the polenta tub to make a rectangle. Cut this into pieces to create fingers about 1 inch by 1 inch by 3 inches long.

Melt the butter in a heated skilled, adding a dash of olive oil. Brown the polenta fingers in the oil, turning to cook all four sides. Total cooking time is about 15 minutes.

Transfer the cooked polenta fingers to a towel to drain, grate on some *Parmigiano-Reggiano*, pepper to taste, and finish with *Fleur de Sel.*

RÉVEILLON

Mark bursts into the kitchen. "Grab the shopping baskets! It's a frenzy out there."

I jump up, a bit startled. I'm preparing for our last breakfast of the year and the gang is beginning to drift into the kitchen. Joe is on coffee duty, my sister Rana is setting the table. All that's missing are the morning croissants. Mark is in charge of the morning baking and he's been out to the *boulangerie*.

Catching his breath, Mark reports on the flurry of shoppers in the street. "I forgot that all the stores are going to be closed this afternoon and New Year's Day. Even the *patisseries* and *boulangeries!*" He gesticulates to indicate the seriousness of the situation.

In France the *Réveillon de la Saint Sylvestre*, or New Year's Eve, is celebrated with friends and food. Most restaurants offer multi-course *Réveillon* menus, but this year we have decided to spend the evening at home, taking advantage of the fabulous foods of Provence to create our own feast.

"We'd better go now, it'll be gone soon!" There's nothing worse than food panic. December 31; it's now or never.

Reluctantly we abandon the breakfast croissants, grab our coats and shopping baskets and join the crowds. Soon we too are caught in the excitement of hunting for just the right ingredients for *Saint Sylvestre*.

It seems like all the citizens of Nyons are out on the streets: jostling, greeting each other, crowding into the stores, although in the French civilized manner. This is serious shopping. The shopkeepers have piled their fresh merchandise high, knowing the crowds will clean them out before lunch.

My favourite vendor, the butcher, a happy, round fellow, attracts a large crowd on any day. On New Year's Eve it is madness. We split into teams: my sister and I join the line-up for a roast chicken, while Mark and Joe head for the organic bakery.

Standing in line, I overhear the friendly butcher explain to a customer how to roast a lamb so it won't dry out; how to add the rosemary toward the end of the baking to get the best flavour from the herb; and how best to serve the resulting tender, fragrant roast. In the midst of the pandemonium he remains calm and has time to spend with each of his customers. When it is my turn, we exchange *bonnes fêtes*, and I make my reservation for *un poulet rôti*, telling him I will return to pick it up. *"Bonne année,"* he calls out as I leave.

Rana and I next stop at the outdoor flower market to buy sunflowers and holly to decorate our table. From the market stalls that crowd the *places* of Nyons we fill our baskets with big, fat scallops; pink *crevettes*; local but still expensive *foie gras*; the famous *Nyonsais* black olives; and finish with a stop at our corner *pâtisserie* where we pick out three luscious tarts. One *poire*, one *abricot*, and one *noix*.

Mark and Joe show up with their basket loaded with the best-looking loaves of bread I have ever seen. *Ever.* Walnut bread, a sesame baguette, and *fougasse au lardon,* the traditional Provençal bread studded with bacon. I'm sure we have forgotten something, so, just in case, I rush to the grocery store to fill up another bag with extra sausage and cheese.

By the time I pick up my roasted chicken it is just past noon on New Year's Eve, shopping is over, the stores are closing and everyone is returning home.

Everyone, that is, except for tourists like us who haven't yet settled into the civilized Provençal tradition of an extended lunch. During our time in Nyons we have developed the routine of taking a daily drive through the countryside, each day discovering new villages and landscapes. And so, loaded with our baguette sandwiches and bottled water, we set off over the iconic Roman bridge with cloudy skies above us. We decide to head to the blue band we see on the horizon; due south.

We traverse curvy roads where the land and people seem to be in hibernation. There are flickers of light in the windows of the farmhouses we pass, but we have only the vineyards to keep us company. The route to the sun takes us in the direction of the *Dentelles de Montmirail,* the short, steep mountains that sport dramatically jagged peaks of exposed limestone.

Forty minutes later we are at the foot of the *Dentelles*. Our first stop is the village of Séguret, one of a handful of places designated *les plus beaux villages de France*, the most beautiful villages of France. As we park at the base of the ancient village, warm sun breaks through the clouds.

A medieval fortress town, Séguret winds up a steep hillside and offers a breathtaking view from the top of the village. I can almost hear the hooves of knights' horses clattering on the cobblestones as we climb the narrow, winding streets.

Although crowded in the summer months, today only a few people wander the narrow streets and explore the minute shops. At the top of the village we come to the church that has been on this spot since the 10th century. I'm surprised to find the door open. The caretaker motions me in and begins asking questions: who am I, where am I from. He tells me the story of the church and how it has transformed through centuries of fires, revolutions and renovations. I look at a display of drawings and sepia photos of Provençal celebrations through the ages – weddings, youth groups, pageants – reminding me that people have lived here for centuries; Séguret is not just a quaint tourist destination. The palpable antiquity of the place, combined with the closeness of the church, makes me light headed. It's time for fresh air. I thank Monsieur for the tour and step outside.

Our journey then takes us through the nearby town of Gigondas and up into the limestone ridges of the *Dentelles*. Driving on narrow rutted paths through the high vineyards that produce the famous Gigondas wines, we see fields covered in fist-sized white rocks. Just beneath the peaks we stop the car and hike high up to a vantage point where we look out over the vines as the sun begins to set. In the dimming light it looks like the aftermath of a hailstorm from a medieval tale of giants and dragons. White rocks, craggy vines, silhouetted trees, and the pink sky of sunset above the Rhone Valley. How better to end a year?

Back home in Nyons we begin putting our New Years' Eve *fête* together. Mark is chef, Rana and I are *sous* chefs, and Joe is in charge of opening the wine. We settle into a comfortable work pattern and the kitchen is all the cozier with the sounds of our meal preparation, mixed with the occasional bells from the church tower across the street.

Our conversation meanders and crisscrosses like the roads we have just explored.

We dine like the French: each course served separately, relishing each flavour while we talk about our day and how lucky we are to be in Provence at this time of year.

We begin with the giant *crevettes*, sautéed in butter, and served with a Dijon mayonnaise sauce. Next comes the *foie gras* from the market, with toasted walnut bread.

When midnight arrives, Joe hauls out his sax and blows in the New Year with *Misty*. I learn that the acoustics of a stone house are not ideal for a honking saxophone.

It has been a memorable New Year's Eve. We will sleep well tonight. We call goodnight to each other from floor to floor to floor. Outside there is a light drizzle, but we are cozy in our villa on Rue de la Liberté in Nyons.

Crevettes sauteéd in butter, with Dijon mustard sauce

Foie gras with organic walnut bread

Stuffed mushroom caps

Coquille St. Jacques

Roast chicken from the butcher, with rosemary and lemon

Mashed potatoes with roasted garlic

Mixed greens with fennel, pear, walnuts,
bacon and fresh lemon dressing

Cheese course, featuring three local *chèvres*

Dessert course: pecan tart, walnut tart, and apricot tart

Assorted fresh chocolates with a glass of
Muscat de Beaumes-de-Venise.

January 2, Vaison-la-Romaine

The year started in Vaison-la-Romaine with market day. It was overcast but warm and by nine o'clock it almost felt like a spring day.

It's been quiet in the market during the last days of the *Saison des Fêtes*, and today was no exception, there were far fewer booths than normal. I bought some souvenirs of the region: Provençal tablecloths, watercolours, a pocket knife; and shopped for groceries for tonight's dinner: *pavé de saumon*, garlic-stuffed *escargots*, potatoes, *chèvre*.

While we were having our *croissants* and *café crème* at *Au Pain Romain* the clouds began to break and sunlight poured onto the streets and we moved outside to eat. During the Christmas weeks, the counters at *Au Pain* have been heaped with special orders for the holidays. Everyone knows that to have a happy holiday you need plenty of cakes, bread and *bûches de Noël*. But today the pile was much smaller as the holidays draw to a close.

By noon it had turned into a beautiful day, so we hiked up to the 13-century château above the *haute ville*. Relaxing on the top, we compared the North American lifestyle with the *joie de vivre* of France. The essential difference, we decided, was food. Is it the quality of the ingredients? Is it the way it's prepared? Or is it the leisurely pace at which it's enjoyed? Food in France, I concluded not for the first time, is more than just fuel, it's a pleasurable part of life. As we talked, we revelled in the view of the town of Vaison spread out below us, with French voices in the background and church bells ringing in the distance.

Since the light was still good I suggested we drive over up to Villedieu. The road to Villedieu is magical with a panoramic view of the valley below. We walked around the ramparts and ended our visit at the *Bar au Centre* for a glass of, you guessed it, *Muscat de Beaumes-de-Venise*. A sweet little girl, about four years old, sat at the bar with her papa, dangling her feet off the stool. She was stylishly dressed with a beautiful pink scarf wrapped around her neck.

We drove home among gentle hills and setting sun, ready for dinner. What a splendid start to the New Year.

LAVENDER, OLIVES AND HONEY

The narrow road to Nyons curves its way through olive groves, apricot orchards and villages. It's an ancient route, people have travelled this way for thousands of years, and there's a palpable connection to the history of the place. This is one of the few remaining olive growing areas in France, and the road leads to a place that celebrates the best of the history and the land.

Vignolis, the store operated by the *Coopérative Agricole du Nyonsais*, is filled with products made from the region's bounty. The foothills of *haute Provence* with its mild winters and endless sunshine favour fruit, olives, grapes, honey, lavender, walnuts. It's here, at the *Coopérative*, where I stock up on the Provençal classics: organic Nyonsais black olives, extra-virgin olive oil, *Herbes de Provence*, lavender-scented olive oil soap, walnut honey, tapenades from olive and artichokes, and my favourite, apricot *confiture*. And I never leave without picking up a bottle of *Crème de Cassis*, the local variety that inspired me to make *Kir Royales* at home.

The Nyons cooperative was formed in 1923 and now has one thousand members, the majority of the olive-growers and wine producers in the region. Their *tanche* olives are small, jet black, shiny with a mild, salty flavour and the oil they yield is smooth and buttery with a mild aroma of herbs and toasted almonds.

Boxed wine and *quality* don't often appear in the same sentence, but here you can find good local wines in boxes, in bottles, or from a pump. There's a casual feel to the place where wines, olive oils and olives are sampled at the tasting bar and throughout the store.

I always leave Nyons feeling invigorated, the trunk of the car stuffed with everything good about Provence, and a 5-litre box of *Coteaux des Baronnies Rouge* on my lap.

Thon au Poivre
PEPPER AHI TUNA

Red ahi tuna is a favourite in Provence and can be found in abundance in the markets. Choose the freshest tuna you can find, in steaks about 1-inch thick. For me, the shallot sauce is the crowning touch to this dish. Buy some Madeira for this recipe, you won't be sorry. Any leftover Madeira certainly won't go to waste! To preserve the buttery, meaty flavour sear the tuna quickly on the outside and leave it rare in the inside.

2 T black peppercorns
1 tsp *Fleur de Sel*
2 shallots, finely chopped
Ahi tuna steak
1 T extra-virgin olive oil
1 T butter
¾ cup chicken broth
⅓ cup Madeira

Warm a plate in the oven at 200° F.

Coarsely crush the black pepper with a mortar and spread it on a plate. Sprinkle on the salt. Coat the tuna by pressing into the mixture, on both sides.

Peel and finely chop the shallots.

Heat a non-stick pan on high until it is hot. Turn the heat down to medium hot and add the olive oil to coat the bottom. Sear the tuna from 60 to 90 seconds on each side, depending on the thickness. Don't overcook, you want to leave the middle of the steak rare.

Remove the tuna from the pan and place it on the plate in the oven.

Pour out most of the olive oil from the cooking pan. Add the butter and the shallots. Cook on medium heat until the shallots have softened, 3 or 4 minutes. This is my favourite part of the process, watching the shallots bubbling in the butter!

Add the chicken broth and Madeira and continue cooking, uncovered, until the sauce has thickened.

Cut the tuna in half to reveal the pink inside and place each piece on a dinner plate. Sprinkle with a pinch of *Fleur de Sel*. Spoon on the shallot sauce and serve immediately. Serves 2.

Macarons Noix de Coco
COCONUT MACAROONS

I came to baking late in life and macaroons were my first baby step. It was a good place to start, since macaroons are delicious and make a lovely light dessert. I like to serve them with a scoop of coconut ice cream or melon sorbet. This version uses the whole egg instead of egg whites, giving them a cakier, firmer texture. It's important to use parchment paper on your baking sheet, otherwise the macaroons will stick to the pan.

1 1/3 cups coconut, grated and unsweetened

1/3 cup sugar

2 eggs

1 T butter, melted

tempered chocolate (see separate recipe)

Preheat the oven to 350° F.

In a mixing bowl combine the grated coconut and sugar and blend together with a fork. Beat the eggs and measure out 1/2 cup, discarding the excess. Combine the eggs and butter into the coconut mixture until blended.

Line a baking sheet with parchment paper. Using a teaspoon or a tablespoon (depending on whether you want big or small macaroons), scoop out little mounds of the mixture, spacing them 2 inches apart.

Bake on the middle shelf of the oven for 15 to 20 minutes, until lightly brown on top.

Gently pry them loose and set aside to cool on a wire rack. Once cooled they are ready to be dipped into chocolate, if you wish. Use the recipe for tempered chocolate, found with the chocolate truffle recipe.

Partially coat each macaroon with the tempered chocolate, either by dipping in one side or by simply placing the bottom of each macaroon in the chocolate. Once dipped, place on a clean sheet of parchment paper on a plate to cool at room temperature.

Makes 8 to 16 depending on the size.

TRUFFLES. TO DIE FOR.

"Truffle Grower Imprisoned" reads the front page headline in the *Vaucluse Matin*. It's murder in Provence and the motive is truffles. A young truffle grower shot and killed an intruder who was stealing his precious crop. The shocking story fills the entire front page and continues on page four and page twenty-nine. It's big news in truffle country, the *département* of Vaucluse in the south of France.

It's an odd coincidence that I am reading about this on our way to visit one of the most important producers in the region. We're going to a truffle plantation just outside of Carpentras, home to the largest wholesale truffle market in the world.

The sign on the roadside is unassuming: honey, olive oil, but no mention of truffles. We drive up a gravel path to a shack where the products are sold, including truffles. Clearly you need to know where you're going to find this place.

Inside, an elderly man greets us. He's right out of central casting for *A Year in Provence*: cap, vest, gentle voice. It's the *grand-père* of the family. "It's my son you are waiting for," he tells us. A few minutes later J arrives (we've protected his identity). He seems surprised to find us in his shack, as if he's forgotten he has an appointment with us this morning.

But the soft-spoken *truffliteur*, truffle producer, recovers quickly and welcomes us. Before he begins to tell us about his work and products, the talk is all about the increasing problem of truffle theft and how one producer took the law into his own hands. Everyone, we learn, is sympathetic.

There are rings of professional truffle thieves who come at night and raid private truffle orchards. The frequency of the raids has increased with the price of truffles. Given the work involved to produce even a single truffle it's no wonder the producers are up in arms.

Once the sensational news has been adequately discussed, J begins on the history of truffles. Truffles are no longer mainly hunted in the forest, they are grown in plantations under oak trees tended to exacting conditions. Human *in vitro* fertilization seems easy compared to growing a truffle. Only 30% of J's oak trees will yield truffles among their roots, and that's a good result for truffle production. And for the oak trees that do provide truffles the productive life is only about four to five years. After that it's just a tree.

But to start at the beginning: before the oak tree is planted, when it's just a young sapling in the greenhouse, various species of truffle spores are grafted to the root. Eventually it is planted in a truffle orchard where it is carefully tended with the hope that in about five years it will produce baby truffles.

The real study and cultivation of truffles began only about forty years ago. Truffles had been harvested in the wild for centuries, of course, but as the clearing of forests increased, the truffle harvest dwindled until, by the 1970s, there were hardly any truffles to be found in France. Truffles are actually the result of the activities of humans. Truffles require the specific conditions of an oak forest bordering on meadowland, with a delicate balance of humidity, sunlight, and soil conditions. No one knows why the truffle grows only under certain species of oak trees.

In the 1970s truffles began to be studied by agricultural scientists with a view towards restoring the harvest. What they discovered is surprising and complicated. The oak trees need to be planted between five and seven metres apart. The soil needs to be aerated and then covered with mulch. Trees need to be pruned regularly. It's a matter of trying to slow the growth of the oak so that the roots can support the fungus.

J's detailed explanation is interrupted when a couple enters. J asks if they have an appointment. "No," they say, looking down at the floor, "They told us at the truffle market to come to see you."

He disappears into the back room and emerges a moment later with a tiny sack of three or four jet black truffles. Weighing them on a kitchen scale he says, *"200 grams, 180 Euros, s'il vous plait."* At 900 Euros per kilogram he's giving them the wholesale price. In a gourmet shop they might fetch two or three times that.

After the customers leave it's time to visit the oak grove and hunt for truffles. The mistral arrived last night and now, at 11 o'clock, the cold wind is biting. My scarf and hair are flapping in the wind as *grand-père* drives off to get Lisette, one of the three truffle dogs they have working for them.

When we arrive at the grove Lisette barrels out from the back of the small truck and begins circling and yelping in excitement. *Grand-père* yells instructions for Lisette, *"Allez, allez, cherches-la."* The strong wind makes picking up the scent difficult for Lisette, but she perseveres and, in seconds, begins digging up the soil near one of the trees. *Grand-père* shoulders her aside and, using a two-pronged digging tool, extracts a black nugget from the ground. Lisette is rewarded with a treat from *Grandpère's* pocket. Two and three times more Lisette picks up a scent and finds the prize.

Grand-père puts the little nuggets in my hand: four truffles, a handful. "It's only second-grade," shrugs J. "You can keep them."

J'AIME PROVENCE

To be in Provence is to be surrounded by vineyards, hilltop villages, markets and olive groves.

I love the food, the wine, the sky, the rosemary-scented breeze, the cypress growing wild, the country roads rambling through acres of vineyards, and the scattering of ancient fortresses. I love the celebration of life, food and wine.

Two thousand years ago the Romans embraced the good life in southern France and put up a mighty fight before they were pushed out by the Visigoths, and the Visigoths by the Franks.

Today Provence belongs to everyone lucky enough to be there. Well, actually it belongs to the French, but they are generally willing to share it. It isn't paradise, but you can almost see it from there, especially if you climb to the summit of the Dentelles, the jagged limestone range that dominates the region.

The very first time I visited Provence I felt at home. I love being in a place where good food and wine are an important part of everyday life. A place where people, when they are not eating, are either planning their next meal or talking about their last.

I like the small, human scale of streets, towns, farms and cars. From Vaison-la-Romaine you can bicycle, almost walk, to nearby towns and villages. Every five or ten or fifteen kilometres you come to another lovely town with a charming square and working fountain. Sablet and Séguret to the south; Faucon and Puyméras to the east; and, to the north, Villedieu with its lovely shaded *place* surrounded by the distinctive stone walls, the *Mairie*, and the *Bar au Centre*. I've passed many warm afternoons sitting beneath the plane trees of Villedieu, listening to the fountain gurgle while drinking a *Ricard*. This is the Provence that I have loved and known for almost *quinze années*.

Champignons à la Crème
MUSHROOM PASTA SAUCE

While you can use a variety of specialty mushrooms to make this sauce, it's equally delicious using plain white mushrooms. Simmer it slowly to release all the flavour.

At one time I was afraid to rinse the mushrooms with water, but it's really the best thing to do. Simply put them in a bowl of water and use a mushroom brush or a soft, clean cloth to wash off any dirt. Drain and dry with a clean towel.

And if you're lucky enough, you can add a few shavings of real truffle on top!

1 lb fresh, white mushrooms, thinly sliced
2 T extra-virgin olive oil
1 T garlic cloves, finely minced
½ cup shallots, finely chopped
½ cup white wine
1 T butter
½ cup heavy cream
freshly ground black pepper
sea salt
2 T fresh parsley, chopped
Parmigiano-Reggiano

Rinse the mushrooms in water, making sure to get all the dirt off. After you dry them, slice them thinly lengthwise. In a large skillet heat the olive oil and add the garlic, shallots and stir occasionally until soft but not browned.

Now add all the mushrooms and salt to taste. Turn the heat down to medium low and cook for 10 minutes or more until the mushroom's liquid has simmered away. Add the wine and cook down for another five minutes or so. Then add the butter, cream and lots of freshly ground pepper. Raise the heat to high and reduce the cream to half its volume, stirring often. Finally, add the parsley.

When the pasta is cooked and drained, toss it with immediately in a warm serving bowl with the mushroom sauce. Add grated *Parmigiano-Reggiano* to taste, toss to coat the pasta thoroughly and serve at once.

L'Omelette Parfaite
THE PERFECT OMELET

I'm not too certain about most things in life but I can guarantee this is the best omelet recipe in the world. Once you master the technique your breakfast and brunch guests will be amazed and delighted when you turn out puffy, light and tender omelets. The secret ingredient is... air.

2 eggs
pinch of sea salt
2 grinds of freshly
   ground pepper
1 T butter

Crack the two eggs into a small bowl. Add the salt and pepper. Beat the eggs with a fork or whisk for about a minute so the eggs are frothy with air.

Heat an 8"-inch small skillet at medium heat, then add the butter. The pan should be hot enough so that when the butter hits the pan it sizzles, but doesn't burn. A little browning is okay, but if the butter burns, start over.

Beat the eggs a few more strokes and pour the mixture into the sizzling butter. Now here's the part that separates this recipe from the rest. Do not shake, lift or move the eggs! Just let them cook to your taste. If you like your omelets a bit runny, fold it over while the middle is still quite uncooked. In any case, don't let the eggs get completely cooked, they will continue cooking after you've folded the omelet.

To fold, using a spatula, lift one side of the omelet and fold it over on itself; the omelet will look like a half circle. Here's the other secret to the puffiest omelet you'll ever see: turn off the heat immediately and place a lid over the omelet. If you have an electric stove, remove the pan from the heat.

Busy yourself with setting the table and pouring yourself a nice glass of something and about one minute later, the omelet will be ready.

It will be puffy, tender and delicious. If you're fortunate enough to have a nugget of truffle laying about, shave a few slivers on top. If you like fillings in your omelet, add them while the omelet is cooking, just before you fold it. Do not try to make an omelet with more than two eggs. It's best to just make an additional omelet for those with hearty appetites.

CLOSE ENCOUNTERS OF THE PARISIAN KIND

There is tapping on the window beside me. I turn to look at a man outside, on Rue de Monttessuy. With one hand he is pointing upwards, with the other he is gesturing me to come outside, then making picture-taking motions. *Come, come, come, snap, snap snap*, he signals, while *look, look, look* goes his other hand.

I take a sip of the *Château de Cardaillan Graves*. *Tap, tap, tap.* With a sigh I excuse myself, grab my camera, and go outside to see what this is about.

The tapper isn't alone. A small group is looking up, over my shoulder. I turn and there, looming over us like some massive alien craft, is the Eiffel Tower; I almost can reach out my hand and grab it. Blue and white lights run sparkling up and down the tower, while the interior grid is bathed in a warm yellow light. On top, the beacon that turns around and around is now sending out two narrow laser-like shafts of blue. The Tower is showing off its brand new light show, and it is spectacular. A shining example of how in Paris, when they get it right, they really get it right.

Tonight, at a restaurant in the 7th Arrondissement, on a street that, visually at least, runs right into the Eiffel Tower, the light show isn't all that is new. We are also talking with new friends, a Parisian couple sitting at the next table. Contrary to the enduring myth that Parisians are aloof and hard to meet, we've had many friendly encounters with strangers, often in restaurants.

For me, dining in a Paris restaurant is a near-transcendent experience. My senses are heightened, I'm more aware of both detail and the overall ambience: the shape of a wine glass, the presentation of the *plat*, the flavours and aromas, the gentle murmuring of the diners. The background noise of the French spoken in a Parisian restaurant is calming, like the burbling of a brook in the forest. Whatever the reason, it's a place I find solace, and perhaps that is perceived by others nearby.

Of course, practice helps as well. After years of experience we know the rhythm, the protocol, of Parisian restaurants. There's a structure, a certainty, but within that structure there are large variations. Each good restaurant has its own character, its own details, its own ambience; and I revel in the discovery.

It also helps that Diane's French is very much better than mine. In fact, to say "my French" is somewhat of an oxymoron. In one hotel I asked where I could buy a postage stamp, and they handed me an umbrella. That's *timbre* versus *parapluie*.

On this warm spring evening, the menu includes the best of the season: fat white asparagus, *potage parmentier* with baby leeks and potatoes, and desserts featuring the fresh *gariguette* strawberries you find in France only in late spring.

After hearing Diane order from the menu in French, our neighbour turns and asks in the same language if we are from Quebec. (Diane says that she always thought her accent was just bad French, she didn't know it had regionality to it!) As we converse, pooling our French skills, we learn that our neighbours are a professional couple from the *quartier*, in their 40s with no children. They love to travel, but have never visited Canada. They are interested to know what we think of their country, of their city, their president. The conversation is fluid and friendly, but when our plates arrive they wish us *bon appétit* and let us enjoy the meal, only continuing our conversation between courses.

Every hour on the hour, the Eiffel Tower struts its light show, and I take a break between courses to stroll outside and watch it. Through the windows I can see Diane continue her chat with our neighbours. At the end of the evening Paul and Sylvie give us their phone number and invite us to get together for dinner when we next come to Paris.

Asperges blanches a la Grecque
White asparagus, Greek style

Potage Parmentier et Petite croûtons dorés
Potato and leek soup with toasted croutons

Canette de barbarie rôtie et poires pochées au vin chaud
Roasted duckling and poached pears in a hot wine sauce

Sole de ligne meunière au beurre de Champagne
Line-caught sole meunière with Champagne butter

Nage de fraises gariguettes rafraîchies a la menthe, sorbet orange sanguine
Gariguette strawberries "swimming" in mint and blood-orange sorbet

Château de Cardaillan, Graves, 1999

❦

Mon Mari

Et il marche dix kilomètres tous les jours! "And he walks ten kilometres every day!" enthuses the older woman next to me. Tonight is her wedding anniversary and somehow we have ended up as part of the celebration at a restaurant deep in the 20th Arrondissement.

It is all coincidence, of course. In restaurants, Parisians manage to create an invisible wall between themselves and the next table, only inches away. Their eyes don't wander around the room, but stay focused on their dining partner across from them as they lean forward and talk intensely but softly. They have learned to live a private life in small spaces by ignoring the people right next to them. But somehow on this trip, all that has changed. It's as if Paris collectively has decided that we are now French-worthy. This is the second meal in as many nights where our neighbours strike up a conversation with us.

It was a long ride out to Maraîchers, the nearest Metro station. I found the restaurant located in the ground floor of an early 20th century brick building, with an attractive storefront. Not so attractive is the block of distressingly modern apartment buildings across the street, looking like they were built in the none-too-fabulous '70s.

But once inside we relax into the comfortable contemporary design. The menu is *typique français* and we order things like roast duck, a salad of fresh greens, and a lobster *fricassée*. Not knowing anything about the wines on the restaurant *carte du vin* I randomly choose a Margaux from *Château Paveil de Luze*.

When the wine is poured I notice the man at the next table eyeing our bottle. He is in his sixties, with a bristling moustache, almost stately, and dressed in his finest, like a farmer for a wedding. With an approving nod he indicates that we have made a good choice. I puff with pride at being so clever and ask Monsieur if he would like a taste. I am a bit surprised when he accepts, sips the wine with approval, and mutters a low-key *"Merci"*. His wife chips in to tell us that her husband is certainly *un connaisseur de vin,* well known in their district for having a superb nose. I ask them where they live.

"The 20th is the best neighbourhood in Paris and I'll tell you why," he begins. His wife and I pay rapt attention as he continues. "There is everything you could ever need in our neighbourhood, the best *boulangeries,* the best *fromageries*; but there is also the country feel, where one can walk and breathe fresh air. I feel sorry for those poor buggers who have to live with all that smog and congestion down in the 6th. In fact, we rarely leave our Arrondissement. You are fortunate to be dining at a very good restaurant."

Madame turns her eyes downward like a schoolgirl. "We're celebrating our 43rd anniversary tonight," she blushes, "and we're at our favourite restaurant." She clearly adores and cherishes her husband, as if she were married to Gerard Depardieu himself. Every sentence begins and ends with him.

"Everyday, he walks! He's so fit and healthy," Madame brags. With her grey hair up in a knot, she looks more like an adoring mother than a wife, but I keep that thought to myself.

It's time to introduce ourselves. *"Je suis Mark"* I say to him, *"et quel est votre nom?"*

"Je suis Monsieur Blanche et ma femme s'appelle Madame Blanche." We politely shake hands.

In the pleasure of our conversation, I momentarily forget French formality, which has its place even among new dining companions. First names are to be shared only with family and lifelong friends. After the business of introductions, the formality breaks down and they once again become the friendly country folk we have known and loved for twenty minutes.

"You must come visit us at our apartment. We can give you a tour of our neighbourhood to convince you this is the best district in Paris!"

We are interrupted by a diner on the other side of us, two tables removed. He shouts a greeting to M. Blanche and jumps up to shake his hand. It is Fabien (we hear him say), who knew Monsieur Blanche years ago. While the two *Parisiens* catch up, Madame Blanche supplies the commentary.

"He knows *everyone*. Wherever we go, he is always surrounded by friends." I am getting the picture, to know him is to love him. While she shares with Diane the admirable qualities of her husband, I find the waiter and order a bottle of the Graves for our new friends to help them celebrate their anniversary.

Fabien returns to his table, but the conversation continues between the two men, over our heads so to speak, complemented by plenty of gesticulation. They discuss the good and bad qualities (mostly the bad) of people they have known, complain about the mayor, and, for all I know, comment on the unfortunate proliferation of tourists in their neighbourhood.

The waiter delivers the wine to the celebrants and speaks softly into the ear of M. Blanche. Monsieur performs that delicate shrug, that in France says nothing and everything, and nods our way to give thanks.

We are back in Formal Paris, where effusive thanks are simply not done. By now, I am familiar with the custom, and know he is grateful.

The evening continues with more bantering, kvetching and reminiscing: M. and Mme. Blanche; Fabien, his wife and daughter; and us, right in the middle; participants in an unplanned party celebrating old friends and long marriages and the best neighbourhood in Paris.

Salade de mâche avec tranches de parmesan
Lamb's lettuce salad with slices of parmesan

Fricassée de homard et lotte, caramel de homard
Fricassée of lobster and monkfish with caramelized lobster

Canette rôtie, cannelle et compote de figues
Roasted duckling with cinnamon and figs

Château Paveil de Luze, 1999, Margaux

December 20, Paris

Walking through Paris is my favourite kind of hiking. There's always something new to see. After an afternoon at the Musée D'Orsay, we decided to walk home the long way, winding through crowds of shoppers, down deserted streets, past statues and monuments, through small parks. By 9 o'clock we were ready for a meal.

We stayed in the neighbourhood and went to a favourite local bistro, *Le Petit Lutétia*. Just up the street from the *Le Bon Marché*, it is a classic 1900 Art Deco bistro with plenty of stained glass dividing the bar from the seating area. It's rarely mentioned in guide books and I'm glad for it.

Outside the bistro was the oyster station you find at many Paris restaurants in the winter. It was a cold night, but I stopped to chat with the oyster man in his Cossack hat. He explained to me how important oysters are to Parisians at Christmas time, *La Saison des Fêtes*. He told me how they are shipped daily from Brittany to arrive in time for lunch in Paris. Many Parisians eat oysters once a day throughout December. I knew what I would be eating that evening.

He gave me a tasting tip: it's best to eat oysters without any sauce so you can taste the brine of the sea. I decided then and there to stop using the vinaigrette that often is served with fresh oysters. He even recommended not to eat them with a squeeze of lemon. "You need to taste the sea!" he said.

I started with six oysters, #3 size, followed by *moules farcies* (although they are called stuffed they are more like little mussels put into their own tray filled with basil pesto arriving piping hot to your table). Mark loved his *foie gras*, house made, with a glass of *Muscat de Beaumes-de-Venise*.

As we walked back to the apartment, I once again marvelled at what Paris has to offer.

Polenta Soufflé au Chèvre à la Crème
POLENTA SOUFFLÉ WITH GOAT CHEESE CREAM

Soufflés may be the Greatest Culinary Show on Earth. Hot out of the oven they are huge, steamy puffs of wonder. But get them directly to the table so your guests can watch Act Two, as the soufflés slump within moments to create a concave top where you then place a spoonful of the *Chèvre Crème*.

When making the polenta for soufflés, I've experimented with everything from water to cream to a combination, but I've finally settled on milk as the best for this dish. In order for the soufflé to rise properly, the polenta should be neither too thin nor too thick, but something like creamy oatmeal.

Individual dishes of polenta soufflé make for an surprising entrée or an unexpected side for a main course.

2 T *Parmigiano-
  Reggiano*, grated
¾ cup milk
⅓ cup polenta
2 T butter
pinch sea salt
freshly ground pepper
2 eggs, separated
½ cup soft goat cheese
½ cup heavy cream

Preheat the oven to 370° F.

Thoroughly butter four 1-cup ramekins and then grate in some *Parmegiano* to coat the insides. Gently shake out any excess cheese.

In a heavy pot bring the milk to a boil. Whisk in the polenta, then stir as it cooks. If it gets too thick, add a bit of water. Stir almost continuously to ensure the polenta doesn't stick to the bottom of the pot, a wooden spoon works well. Cook until it is creamy thick, about 10 minutes.

Remove from heat, add a tablespoon of butter and salt and pepper to taste, then stir in the 2 egg yolks. Stir to mix thoroughly.

Place the egg whites in a small mixing bowl and beat them until they form peaks. Then gently fold them into the polenta, using a spatula. If the pot you've used to make the polenta is large enough, you can fold the egg whites directly into the polenta mixture. Otherwise, and this is my preference, transfer the polenta to a mixing bowl and then fold in the egg whites; the curved sides of the mixing bowl make the blending easier. Don't beat or stir the egg whites, but use a motion that gently folds the mixture together.

Pour the mixture into the buttered soufflé dishes. Grate a small amount of parmesan on the top and bake for about 30 minutes, until the soufflé has risen and the top is browned.

While the soufflés are baking make the *chèvre crème.* Nothing could be simpler, just mix the goat cheese and the cream together. I like to mix them in a small pot that I have slightly warmed on the stovetop; the heat makes the goat cheese soften into a cream-like texture that blends perfectly with the cream. If you have a bit of fresh herbs (basil, thyme) chop them and add them to the *chèvre crème.*

Before you take the soufflés out of the oven the table should be set and guests should be seated. Place the soufflés on heat-proof plates in front of each diner. (The soufflé dishes will be hot, hot, hot.) After your guests *ohh* and *ahh* for a few moments the soufflés will start to collapse. When they do, spoon some of the *chèvre crème* into the crater that forms on the top of each soufflé.

Pour a crisp white Sauvignon Blanc. Makes 4 individual servings.

Coquilles Saint-Jacques
THE FAMOUS FRENCH SCALLOP DISH

One Sunday afternoon at *Fermette Marbeuf 1900*, a stylish Paris *belle époque* restaurant, I was served *Coquilles Saint-Jacques*. The simplicity of their version captured me. No mushrooms or ring of mashed potatoes, just silky scallops bathed in cream with a hint of lemon.

This can be served as an appetizer (one shell) or as a main course (two shells) with a salad and crusty bread. Don't overcook the scallops - they should still be a bit translucent when you remove them from the pan.

6 large scallops
1 T extra-virgin olive oil
1 tsp lemon juice
2 T butter
¼ cup unbleached flour
1 shallot, finely chopped
½ glass white wine
3 T heavy cream
pinch sea salt
freshly ground pepper
3 T *Reggiano-Parmigiano*
Preheat the broiler.

Cut the scallops by slicing them in half horizontally. In a non-reactive dish marinate the scallops for 30 minutes in the olive oil and lemon juice. Drain them, dredge them in the flour, and cook them gently in one tablespoon of butter, for about a minute. Remove the scallops from the pan and set aside. Divide them among four shell-shaped baking dishes.

In the same pan, cook the shallots at medium heat in another tablespoon of butter until they are almost caramelized. Add the white wine and a few drops of lemon juice. Cook until the mixture is bubbling and reduced. Add the cream and then season with salt and pepper. Let it simmer for another 2 minutes until the cream has thickened.

Pour the shallot-cream mixture equally over the baking shells of scallops and grate on the *Reggiano-Parmigiano*. Place under a broiler at high heat until bubbling and browned, no more than 5 minutes. Serve immediately.

n, les traou-mad. Des biscu
e, beurre et salive. Ça n'à l'arae
inquer à l'unisson, ya mat!
hantant la Breiz, voguer l'Oue
e à nous les chasseurs d'horizon, ja
eds sur terre. A quoi sert le traou-mad
e le dernier verre ou le regard des fi
ur la marée montante. Supprimons
n ne salive plus, kenavo.

Yann Bucffelec

THE FOUR CHEFS *PLUS* ONE

Staging our dinner reservations in Paris to meet our mood and appetite is almost a second job. I spend hours poring over reviews of Paris restaurants, booking, cancelling, rebooking; all in the attempt to get it just right. It's even more of a challenge when choosing restaurants with particular friends in mind. Friends who are, in fact, particular.

Tom and Jos will be in Paris to join us for a few days. Tom is a hard guy to please. He's not swayed by trends and fancy presentation, such as fish wrapped in cellophane or beef tenderloin shipwrecked on a beach of mashed turnips. He's a man of simple, but distinct, pleasures.

One year we dragged Tom to the trendy restaurant *L'Entredgeu* in the far reaches of the 17th Arrondissement where he was able to spot this place for what it is; a busy cash machine. There literally was no room to turn. You couldn't hear a thing; yelling was the norm. I don't like to yell in restaurants. The waiters forgot about us and our order and by the time the food arrived I was exhausted. At the end of the evening it was like being freed from a trapped, crowded elevator full of partying Danes.

Given the Tom Factor, I've upped my research and learned that *L'Os à Moelle* is open this week, even though it's the beginning of August when many restaurants in Paris close for vacation, and they have a table for four.

Restaurants come and go; restaurants change, sometimes for the better, too often for the worse; but *L'Os à Moelle* has remained one of my favourites, and I haven't eaten there enough over the years. It's way out in the fifteenth and we've often stayed in apartments where a long metro ride with several changes would be required. But this year *L'Os* is only a ten-minute walk from our place. We can practically skip there.

Tom and Jos meet us at the apartment where I have a lovely 16-Euro Champagne on ice. I take delight in finding bargain Champagne in Paris. As usual, Tom takes charge of the Champagne opening; this bottle is a live one! The cork caroms off the ceiling as we all duck.

"How much did this one cost?" he says, raising an eyebrow. He knows my ways.

We say goodnight to Alexandre and Colette, the babysitter, and walk out into the warm summer evening, heading south on Avenue Félix Faure. As we walk Tom marvels at the neighbourhood; he hasn't been here before. "I could live here," he says as we pass the second of four local *boulangeries.*

Coming up to the corner of Rue Lourmel and Rue Vasco de Gama is very familiar. We're only a couple of short blocks from the busy highway of the *Périphérique*, but it's serene here and the restaurant looks especially appealing in the fading summer light. I've usually been here in the winter, when it's dark well before nine, and haven't really noticed the neighbourhood or the building until now. It's in the pointy end of a flatiron building where, tonight, the windows and doors have been flung open and the interior beckons with warm light. We are seated next to the tiny bar that has a hidden staircase built into the cabinetry, leading to the *cave* below and so typical of Parisian bistros. The yellow walls and the chalkboard menu with the small Sanskrit-like print are like familiar friends.

The restaurant, too, is tiny, with tables tucked wherever there is space, yet it doesn't feel crowded. The wall-size mirror on one side helps to make the room feel bigger and they've done a good job of arranging the room so diners feel comfortable and at ease. From my seat I can see, through the open double doors, the wine store across the street, *La Cave de L'Os à Moelle,* where very casual meals are served at communal tables.

It was the early 1990s when four young chefs rocked the Paris culinary scene by breaking away from the *haute cuisine* practiced at such restaurants as *Les Ambassadeurs* at Hôtel Le Crillon (where they all trained under master chef Christian Constant) to open their own small bistros scattered across Paris. There was Yves Chamborde and *La Régalade* in the 14th Arrondissement, Thierry Breton with *Chez Michel* and *Chez Casimir* in the 10th, Rodolphe Paquin of *Le Repaire de Cartouche* and, in the 15th Arrondissement, Thierry Faucher's *L'Os à Moelle.* These guys set the tone for the generation of chefs to follow; using traditional French ingredients to express their own style of cooking and show us something new, as if we've never tasted it before.

All four restaurants have been, at one time or another, on our circuit. Each of the chefs, it seems to me, returned to their roots to feature cooking from their native region, Brittany in the case of *Chez Michel.*

I ate at *La Régalade* many times in the years before Chamborde sold the restaurant, and before he seemed to burn out after years of nightly hectic activity. The food was country southwest France hearty, including the best rice pudding and the best cherry *confiture* I've ever had.

Of the four, *Le Repaire de Cartouche* offered the most basic cooking, I've never been able to remember much about the food. But I do remember the night we were there with our friends Michelle and Eddie, who were visiting us from California. Mark was sporting a new linen jacket of a beautiful pale blue. I don't know how it happened, but at the table behind him a bottle of red wine was knocked off the table. The wine splashed into the air and time seemed to slow down as I watched a deep crimson tidal wave, made from the reddest, most linen-hungry grapes, fly up off the floor on onto Mark's new jacket, completely soaking the back of it.

The waiter sprang into action. He hurried across the restaurant shouting out, *"Quelle catastrophe!"* and, ignoring our table, rushed to the people sitting behind Mark. *"Je vais vous apporter une nouvelle bouteille de vin immédiatement!"* With that he scooped the fallen soldier from the floor and scurried off to find the diners a replacement bottle of wine. Later, when I asked the staff what they were going to do about Mark's damaged jacket they shrugged their shoulders in that "what can we do?" way. A customer seated at the bar turned to me, "Things happen," he said, and then he actually added, *"C'est la vie."* I was both astonished and delighted at hearing this wonderful *cliché*. I could say nothing else.

It's easy to understand how chefs cooking at their own restaurants can burn out. The signature food requires their personal attention night after night, year after year. This burden can cause them to withdraw from customers, taking refuge in their kitchens, and eventually leads them to sell or close down their restaurants.

But at *L'Os à Moelle* Chef Thierry is still in the kitchen and he's definitely a presence in the restaurant. Tonight, his impressive menu for 35 Euros offers four courses with a small supplement for a cheese course if I want it.

Both Tom and I choose the cream of mushroom soup to start. It is served the way I like it, with both drama and art: a large soup bowl arrives with a scattering of fresh herbs, toasted pine nuts and crispy *lardon*.

Then the server brings a pitcher of the soup to ladle into the bowl, in this case a billowy mushroom broth is poured. Tom and I take a taste and turn to look at each other in surprise, saying simultaneously, "The soup is cold!" My taste buds, expecting warmth, are jolted awake with cold, silky, wonderful soup! This cold mushroom soup, I learn, is a signature dish invented by Chef Thierry.

Across the table, Jos and Mark are eating a fish soup, this one hot and steamy. The night goes on like this, one superb plate after another, *boudin noir, foie gras, lapin, pintade*; accompanied by the white *Saumur* and the red *Saint-Joseph* that Tom has selected.

As can happen on a summer's night, there is a sudden rain, a shower that lasts a long time. We watch the night rain through the open doors as we enjoy our courses, the room, and the company.

Over coffee Tom tells me he is impressed and I sigh with relief. Chef Thierry is out on the floor, shaking hands while carrying his young daughter, a halo of curls and little golden earrings. We *ohh* and *ahh* over the baby and compliment the chef, applauding him for keeping his restaurant scrumptious for nearly twenty years.

ᢞ

Brother Michel, Sister Casimir

I didn't get it.

We were at Gare du Nord to pick up train tickets for Russ and Mary-Lynn, who were arriving in a few days. Before we left the apartment I leafed through Rosa Jackson's guide looking for restaurants near the *gare* and circled the review of *Chez Michel*. But when we arrived at Gare du Nord just past noon, I couldn't imagine anything nice was to be found in this neighborhood.

It was a grey day, and the stained, grimy façade of the station looked even grimier. We wound our way through a maze of illegally parked cars, past drunks, beggars and the *Quickly Burger*. When we came to the *St Vincent de Paul* church we took the side stairs up the hill as the main steps were held hostage by a group of thuggish men smoking cigarettes. By the time I stepped into the wood-timbered interior of *Chez Michel*, with windows on two sides, I didn't know what to expect.

The place wasn't hopping at lunch time; a few businessmen were interrupted when we jostled the communal table to move into our corner. The waiter seemed friendly and eager to converse in English, all the while answering the phones and booking reservations.

The menu was based on the food Chef Thierry Breton grew up with in his native Brittany, in the west of France on a peninsula that sticks out into the Celtic Sea. So, I started with the fish soup. The broth was aromatic, pungent, pureed, tasting of the sea. This soup was a healing elixir: the kind of soup that knits your mitochondria together to cure any major illness. Suddenly the neighbourhood seemed beautiful. Was that the sun I saw breaking through the clouds?

The rest of the meal was equally magical. After that lunch I vowed I would cross town any day just to have a taste of Chef Thierry's cooking.

Today is one of those days. It's sunny and Paris is positively shining. We're back in the 10th Arrondissement to meet up with Tom and Jos, who are arriving at the Gare du Nord on the Eurostar, the high-speed train that runs through the Chunnel to connect London and Paris. We're using it as another opportunity to have dinner at Thierry Breton's restaurant. But this time we're going to eat at *Chez Casimir*, the sister restaurant next door to *Chez Michel*. And they *are* brother and sister, one being named after Chef Thierry's son, the other after his daughter.

The Gare du Nord has undergone a facelift since my last visit, its beautiful ochre stones gleam in the light of the sunset. The streets in front of the *gare* are, not unusually, frantic. Police swarm like wasps around the area, moving traffic along, blowing whistles. Here, at one of the busiest train stations in Europe there is absolutely no chance of parking within five hundred meters. Dozens of desperate drivers are anxious to "just stop for a minute" while they drop off their passengers, or run inside to meet a train.

Gendarmes write tickets as fast as their pens can pass over paper, while desperate housewives with tears in their eyes pour out improbable stories of woe. One conversation I overhear goes something like:

Housewife: *"Ma mère est handicapée, paralysée, et j'étais seulement parti pour deux minutes ... "*

Gendarme to his partner: *"Eh, Pierre, venez,* ever hear this story before? Paralyzed mother, just left her car here for a moment?"

Partner: "Oh, yeah, the paralyzed mother. Heard that one about five minutes ago. Book her!"

We skirt the tangle of traffic, pass the *Quickly Burger,* and walk toward St Vincent de Paul. The same thugs still control the church steps. We wave at them and they wave back. Solidarity. This time they have a child's backpack as hostage. We follow the clues of the backpack heist up the hill: an empty pencil case, a Star Wars duo-tang, a pair of children's scissors. I only hope the child escaped.

The bell tower rings eight times. It's time to leave the church gang to their work and head to the restaurant. At *Chez Casimir* we're greeted by the black and white stripes of the Breton flag. We check out the sidewalk seating and decide to take a table indoors. The server motions with her head to take a table over there. Her hands are piled high with dishes as she bustles to the kitchen. I like the simplicity of the service, just a nod will do. No "I'm Hilary and I'll be your server tonight" sort of nonsense. The room, too, is simple, but comfortable enough. It's small, maybe thirty-five seats, with a few tables outside.

The busy server buzzes by and drops off the blackboard that features an amazing four course menu for twenty-nine Euros. I shake my head in disbelief at the low price and delectable selection. Mark goes out to search for Tom and Jos. The blackboard is taken away a few times as I wait, but no matter, I'm enjoying the atmosphere. This is real life Paris, people eating fantastic looking meals, drinking nice wines, and having a great time. Everyone is in a good mood and so am I.

Mark returns with Tom and Jos, pulling their luggage behind. They're a little disheveled from the travel, but Tom puts on a Texas accent and says, "Gawd I love this city!" The waitress sweeps their luggage off somewhere and we greet each other with a glass of Champagne. Tom takes a moment to look around and to study the blackboard, and then begins nodding his head in acceptance and appreciation of the convivial setting I've chosen. I smile to myself. He likes *Chez Casimir.*

And what's not to like at only twenty-nine Euros for four courses: *entrée, plat, fromage et dessert?* The food is regionally hearty, flavourful, and perfectly done. There are five choices of *entrée*, including *bouillon de homard avec petite légumes, rillettes de maquereau*, and a salad of heritage tomatoes; and an equal number of *plats*. Between us we order *pot au feu de cochon*, slow-cooked, rich pork stew; *filet de rascasse*, the Mediterranean scorpion fish used in *bouillabaisse; fricassée de veau*, veal cooked in a white sauce; and *médaillon de lotte et ratatouille*.

Our desserts, too, are perfect and totally of the season; a bowl of fresh strawberries, *crème fraîche* and mint. As we linger over the last of the wine, we express our gratitude to Brother Michel, Sister Casimir and Papa Thierry.

∽

Birth of a Classic

Walking along a Paris market street at night is different than in daytime. The food shops are closed; shuttered with metal pull-downs covered in graffiti. You don't see the graffiti during the day, but at night the street becomes a sort of museum of modern street art.

I pass *Poissonnerie Soguisa* which we visited on the Marais market tour; except for the store sign it is unrecognizable. It's the same for the other food shops along Rue Montorguiel, they've turned into colourful, metal-clad walls of art. There are not many pedestrians. Except for an occasional restaurant, there is nothing open. A solitary man passes by pulling a wire shopping trolley filled with bottles.

We cross over busy Rue Réaumur, where Citroëns speed on their way to the Marais, and come to Rue de Nil. Street of nothing? It seems that way; a dark, narrow alley with no sign of life. But I know that this is the place to be for those in the mood for great French cooking. People like me.

I feel a like real Paris insider when we turn into the constricted street and walk toward the patch of soft light coming from the restaurant. The sign on the building is like the those you see on abandoned *boulangeries* in rural France; dark, faded, hard to spot in the dimness. When I get to the door I'm surprised we don't need to give the password or secret handshake. The place is that hard to find. *"Frenchie"* reads the sign above the door.

This is a seriously small restaurant; eleven tables, twenty-six seats. No wonder it's next to impossible to get a reservation. They don't seem to answer the phone, you can't reach them by email, and the restaurant's website is a study in minimalism: a single page with the restaurant's name and a link to a Google map. I silently thank our Parisian friend Sarah who persevered to get us a table.

As we enter we go through the familiar Paris seating dance; we're offered the worst table. This one is in the annex room the size of a closet, wedged between the bathroom and a table with a nervous young mother and a mammoth stroller. We reject it and the Head Guy shows us to a better table set against the wall and close enough to see the chef in action. Gregory Marchand, a young chef from Nantes with the celebrity of a rock star, has trained in New York City and with Jamie Oliver in London, where he acquired the nickname *Frenchie.* Anywhere else the name would be absurd, but here it all makes sense.

This is the *It* restaurant of the year. When it opened in the spring of last year, *Frenchie* immediately received favourable reviews, including one in the *New York Times.* I've been worried that the Big Mention might be damaging to the food or service, such as I have seen happen at *Aux Lyonnaise* on Rue St Marc, where too much hype turned that restaurant into a noisy, tourist destination. I wonder what to expect at *Frenchie.*

For young chefs starting their first restaurants in Paris the norm has been to find a low-rent location in the outlying Arrondissements, the 12th, the 14th, the 15th; and then count on good reviews to tempt customers to make long Metro rides to reach them. *Frenchie* has gone a different route. Marchand's restaurant is in an expensive neighbourhood in the 2nd Arrondissement, but at the end of this insignificant street where, I presume, the rent is more affordable. Here Marchand has found two tiny rooms and a kitchen just big enough to turn around in.

The waitress is a calm young woman, and she starts us out with generous *coupes de Champagne* while we survey the menu: three courses for thirty-five euros. The choices are simple: two starters, two main courses, two desserts and one cheese plate.

So few diners can fit in the small space that I start to feel like part of a family. A table of four next to us: the mother is in her late seventies, slim, coordinated, done-up like a *Parisienne*, with her grown daughter. They are chatting to friends, two women who spend much of their time popping in and out of the restaurant for cigarettes. On the other side a couple swoon over each other between bites and snatch kisses between courses. I wonder if they are paying proper attention to the food. Don't they know how precious their reservation is? Where are their priorities?

While the waitress effortlessly glides around the restaurant, the Head Guy is staccato, head down, ignoring the ringing telephone, but always rushing, rushing, rushing. He spends most of his time turning away hopeful diners who are begging him for a table. No, sorry, he says, we're booked all week. Don't bother coming back till September. His other job is to keep the door slammed shut, presumably to make the restaurant less inviting to casual passers-by, but also turning the room into a sauna, since the air conditioning is (here's a big surprise) not working. Together they comprise the entire front staff.

All the dishes are good. *Really good*. But there are three dishes that, together, make up a meal that is right up there with the best I've ever eaten.

The smoked trout *entrée* is one of those last-meal-in-my-life choices. In fact, it is so delicious it might be able to revive me for another day or two. Think of it as restorative trout. I am a fan of slow-cooked food and this dish is a perfect example of what can happen when you use top quality ingredients and gently warm them to release the flavours and aromas. The blend of the smokiness of the fish with the roasted peppers and oils is a wonder.

The main course of *bar* makes me wonder why I don't order fish for every meal. Cooked to a crispy skin, yet with a delicate white flesh, it is served over a handful of beans accompanied by one perfect beet and one perfect potato.

With the one-two punch of trout and *bar*, I wonder if it can possibly get better. The answer is yes, in the form of the *tarte aux fruits de la passion*. In my life I have not often crossed paths with passion fruit, so I ordered it not knowing that I was about to experience the best dessert I have ever had in my life. *Ever*. Marchand's creation is a relative of a lemon tart, but one that was sired by Zeus himself. It is served partially cooked, still soft and unctuous. Beside it is a puddle of the most miraculous sauce, *caramel au beurre salé,* a blend of caramelized sugar, *fleur du sel* and plenty of cream. It's the kind of sauce I can imagine pairing with everything: chocolate, cakes, cookies, my morning toast.

Frenchie demonstrates what inspiration combined with training and experience can produce. This chef knows about cooking, and his meals are like fine art. In the half door of the kitchen we watch Chef Marchand tending to every single dish, bent down to get eye level with the food to make sure all is perfect. Only then does he send it out. He is able to maintain this perfect control because the restaurant size is manageable: one seating a night, twenty-six tables, seventy-eight plates, and that's it.

Art is created every day in Paris and tonight we are lucky enough to witness the creation of a culinary classic.

Truite fumée, chou rave, oignons pickles
Smoked trout, kohlrabi, pickled onions

Gaspacho, cèleri, chorizo, burrata
Gazpacho, celery, chorizo, fresh Italian cheese

Bar, coco de Paimpol, moules, salicorne
White fish, Paimpol coco beans, mussels, sea asparagus

Faux-filet, betteraves chiogga, groseilles
Sirloin steak, Italian candy-stripe beets, red currants

Ossau Iraty, miel, truffe d'été, piment d'Espelette
Ossau Iraty cheese, honey, summer truffle, mild chili pepper

Panacotta a la verveine, fruits rouges
Panacotta with verbena, red fruit

Tarte aux fruits de la passion, caramel au beurre salé
Passion fruit tart, caramel and salted butter sauce

Caramel au Beurre Salé
CARAMEL BUTTER SAUCE WITH A TOUCH OF *FLEUR DE SEL*

The blend of caramel with *Fleur de Sel* is the perfect combination to heighten the flavours of apple tarts, chocolate cakes, and lemon desserts. Or try it on its own, with a spoon! For easy clean-up, add water to the pan once the sauce has been cooked and removed. Bring it to a boil and all leftover sauce will melt away.

½ cup granulated sugar (brown sugar will not work)

2 T butter, diced

1/8 tsp *Fleur de Sel*

⅓ cup heavy cream

In a heavy-bottom sauce pan, melt the sugar over high heat. Gently shake the saucepan in circles; don't be tempted to use a spoon to stir it. Carefully watch the pan; as soon as the edges of the sugar start caramelizing immediately lower the heat to a medium-low. Once the sugar has melted and is an amber colour, remove the pan from the heat.

Let the sugar cool for about a minute, then slowly add the butter and salt, stirring constantly with a wooden spoon. Put the pan back on the stove at the lowest heat possible. Pour the heavy cream little by little while continuing to stir.

The sauce can be served warm or cooled to room temperature and heated again just before serving.

The Elevator on the Right Bank

" This is the roller for pastry, like so," he flourishes the thin wooden cylinder and reaches for the next item. "These knives are of a professional quality. The pots, see, are heavy, *inoxydable.*"

Our Parisian landlord is displaying his purchases nervously, as if he were presenting a report in front of the class at the *lycée.* We look in wonderment at the collection of culinary wares he has spread out on our kitchen counter; professional-quality, extensive, and wonderful.

It's the first week of our four-month stay in Paris. Our apartment was his family home until a month ago and now they are renting it to visitors, like us, their first tenants. On move-in day, we complimented him on the newly fitted kitchen and talked about our love of food and cooking. This was interpreted as meaning we are *serious cooks,* and so here we are, a few days later, looking in amazement at our landlord and his offerings.

Christophe, clearly, is not the typical jaded landlord. Learning of our interests, he set out to make his apartment as perfect as possible for us. It is so kind it nearly brings tears to my eyes. Or maybe it's just the sight of the heavy-bottomed cooking pots.

While we examine our kitchen treasures, out on the balcony six-year old Alexandre tends to his new garden of potted flowers. Looming behind him is the mass of the *Arc de Triomphe,* so close I feel I can touch it. Our building is just steps away from *Place Charles de Gaulle,* the eleven-street star-shaped intersection with its famous monument. So star-like that Parisians refer to the *place* as *l'Étoile.*

But that isn't all we see from our *terrasse.* To the right of the *Arc,* in the near distance, is Gustave Eiffel's iron-knit wonder. At night the *Arc* is spotlighted in a golden effect, while the Tower sparkles behind with its own light show. Some people live with a view of only *one* major monument, but I just don't know how they do it.

Our building is *typique Parisien,* built in the latter part of the 19th-century to strict design guidelines. There are thousands of these five-storey buildings lining the grand boulevards laid out by Baron Haussmann. Today, most of the boulevards are busy thoroughfares with plenty of traffic all day long. Avenue Carnot, though, is quiet. From the massive traffic circle at *l'Étoile,* only the first block of Avenue Carnot was demolished by Haussmann and rebuilt into a wide boulevard. The rest was never completed, meaning that today Carnot's traffic is minimal.

Like all Haussmann-era buildings, ours was built at a time when elevators were as rare as space shuttles. As elevators were eventually installed in many of these buildings, they were made to fit into odd spaces such as vacant corners or the inside of a curved stairway. Now at the beginning of a new millennium, many of the early elevators are being upgraded.

The upgrade in our building is the reason we are able to rent this particular apartment for such a bargain, by Paris standards. The elevator is to be demolished soon and replaced by a larger one. For most of our stay we will live like authentic Parisians of 1890, *sans* elevator. We will haul our daily shopping up and down three creaking, twisting flights of fifty-seven steps for one hundred twenty-seven days. But who's counting?

I know from experience that the elevators in these buildings are small. We still talk about the elevator in our first Paris apartment: so small my shoulders would only fit in one spot, so small that a friend refused to get in it and walked the five flights every time she visited.

Yes, I thought I knew small, but it turns out I don't know anything. One ride in the Avenue Carnot elevator turns me into a dedicated stair climber. It is *small.* To operate it you reach in to push the floor button before you step in because, to fit in at all, you have to press your face against the far wall to allow the door to close behind you. During the ride up you mutter prayers to the gods of elevation that this cramped box will not become your coffin since, in case of trouble, the chances of reaching the emergency button are slim. Did an emergency button even exist? You forgot to check before you got in. Finally, to add insult to claustrophobia, during the ride your nose is pushed up against a sign limiting the number of passengers to three people. Three two-year olds, maybe. Stacked on top of each other.

It is almost a relief when the elevator is demolished. We become resigned to hiking up and down, hauling everything we need. Luckily, in a previous existence Diane was a Sherpa. How else can you explain the daily treks she makes up the perilous slopes of Mount Carnot carrying the loaded shopping trolley on her back.

Alexandre will start first grade in Paris, in a school by Parc Monceau. Before we arrived we solicited the help of our friend Denis, who lives in Paris, to scout out the private schools in the city. He researched and visited several schools, including one institution that he memorably described as a warren of long narrow hallways governed by a severe Russian headmistress.

Finally, though, it was the golden gates of Parc Monceau that signalled to Denis he had found the right school for Alexandre. *École active Bilingue*, or EaB, is set just inside the park gates and, in fact, the park is used as the children's school playground. It is an international school with students from Spain, Africa, Australia, and Trinidad, although French is the language of instruction. Madame Knightly, enthusiastic and fresh from New York, is in charge.

School starts in one week and today we have to attend a final screening to determine if Alexandre is fit to start Grade One. Months in advance we scheduled this interview for him, one-on-one with the headmistress, and planned our travel around the date. Poor Alexandre is so nervous that he can't eat breakfast and clings on tightly to me during the Metro ride.

We meet the young headmistress at the school's reception and she takes Alexandre to her office, alone. He gives me one last forlorn look over his shoulder as he is led away. It feels like he is going to the warden's office to find out what cell he'll be put in. I think I'm as nervous as he is.

Ten minutes later the two of them come back and Alexandre is all smiles, singing and skipping along. He is in! There are handshakes and cheek kissing all around and I promise to bring Alexandre back for the first day of school next week. On the way back to our apartment he tells me about one of the questions Madame asked him.

"There were four pictures," he says, "and I had to choose the one that didn't fit in the group. There was a horse, a bicycle, a car, and a train. I chose the bicycle because it was the only one you have to pedal."

He reflects a moment. "It was a close one," he says. "It could have gone either way."

಄

Each day lunch is prepared for students at EaB. The menu is posted just outside the classrooms and every morning parents gather around to read the *carte*. It is France, so there are always three courses, usually starting with *crudités* and a dip, followed perhaps by *une pièce de boeuf sauce béarnaise* with some stuffed tomatoes, and finishing with dessert: *crème caramel, mousse au chocolat* or a fruit tart. Lunch for the primary grades is an hour long but increases to ninety minutes for the older children. The meals are served at a table in the dining area with supervisors nearby to ensure the cutlery is used continental style and the meals are finished.

A week into classes I notice Alexandre is increasingly anxious about school. Are the teachers are too strict or is instruction in French too difficult for him? Finally, one day as we walk hand-in-hand to school, he pulls me aside and begs, "Daddy, tell them I don't like stuffed tomatoes! Please tell them I don't have to eat them!"

After dropping off their children parents gather at the local café for a morning coffee and to discuss the finer points of the day's school lunch menu. There is always a lively debate with plenty of differing opinions on the matter. One mother claims it has turned her child into a gourmand. I, however, have the feeling that long-term therapy might be in Alexandre's future.

I do talk to Alexandre's teacher about the stuffed tomatoes. She isn't happy about it, but she finally agrees to let him eat only what he wants, which pretty much boils down to lots of baguette, water and French fries on *frites* day Friday. Alexandre is one member of our family who clearly isn't fond of three-course lunches.

∽

His parents are a different story. On the way home from school drop-off, I pick up croissants at our local bakery and, over several Nespressos, map out the day. We spend an hour or so reviewing correspondence, check to see which museums have special exhibits, and then refer to our lunch bible, Rosa Jackson's *Time Out Paris: Eating & Drinking.* Once we decide on the museum or *Arrondissement* we are going to visit, we select a neighbourhood restaurant for today's lunch.

In addition to the fabulous view another thing I love about the apartment is the Metro station located right outside the door, where I can catch three of the most useful Metro lines in Paris: line 1, which takes me to the Louvre in nine minutes and then all the way to woods of Vincennes on the east side of Paris; line 2, which connects west and east via a half circle arcing to the north, and gets me to the bustling, narrow streets of Belleville; and line 6, which arcs to the south, passing through all the important neighbourhoods of the Left Bank.

At our Metro station I can also choose to go deeper underground and ride RER Line A. This convenient transport can take me from our station to Opera (which might be considered the centre of Paris) in only five minutes. Staying on the A train for ten minutes more gets me all the way across Paris to the suburb of Vincennes. In fifteen minutes. Beam me up, Scotty.

And when I discover the buses I feel I have unlocked another secret of Paris. It seems that half the bus routes in Paris make a stop at Place Charles de Gaulle and it is very easy to connect to the remaining routes.

Every day, equipped with camera, maps and credit cards, we head downstairs to our Metro station or bus stop and start the day's itinerary. Sometimes we make a short visit to a museum, sometimes we stroll around a new neighbourhood, but we always arrive at the restaurant in time for lunch. I don't even try to resist the *coupe de Champagne* offered when we are seated. I'm learning how to lunch the Parisian way.

Most restaurants offer daily *prix fixe* lunch menus; a three-course meal at a reasonable price. I try to be sensible and order the *menu* but sometimes my eyes wander to other side of the *carte* to the more expensive items: *foie gras poêlé, morilles fraîches et asperges blanches, poularde de Bresse*.

These leisurely lunches give me a front row seat to daily life in Paris. There is a certain voyeuristic delight in watching people interact, in noting what they are wearing, in identifying the bureaucrats and the elegant ladies who lunch. While the bureaucrats and the ladies seem to take this experience for granted, I savour it because I know I only have a season's pass. The four-month clock is counting down.

From the far reaches of the 19th Arrondissement, with walks through Parc Butte Chaumont; to the suburbs of Vincennes for a *foie gras* extravaganza at a local bistro; to restaurant *La Gare* in the classy 16th where I save a little time for the *Musée Marmottan* to view the Monets; the restaurants became the connecting dots of my life. My *raison d'être à Paris*.

Each day I imagine a leisurely lunch with plenty of time for museums, shopping, and exploring. The reality is that by the time coffee arrives I am madly consulting the Metro map to find the quickest way to get back to Parc Monceau to pick up Alexandre. I gulp down my coffee and rush off because, at three o'clock sharp, the school doors open and all the children run out to the street to meet their parents.

Imagine little Alexandre waiting. In Parc Monceau. In Paris. All alone. I don't need any further reasons for his future therapy. So while Diane lingers to pay the bill, I race towards the metro.

∿

Wednesday is early dismissal at school and we pick up Alexandre at noon, catch the #92 bus to the 7th Arrondissement, disembark at Rue de Grenelle, and walk over to Rue Cler. Wednesday means lunch at *Café du Marché*.

Café du Marché is a model Parisian bistro. The good food and reasonable prices ensure that it is absolutely packed at lunchtime. And I mean packed: the waiters can't squeeze between the chairs, so customers are recruited to pass plates full of *steak frites* and *salade composée* from table to table.

Alexandre always orders *confit de canard*. Duck *confit* is to Paris what hamburgers are to Pittsburgh. It is the standard lunch fare found at almost every café in the city. At its best, it is crispy on the outside with flakey, tender meat inside, served with pan-fried potatoes cooked in goose fat.

At six years old, Alexandre loves *confit* but he is more of a *frites* guy than a goose fat connoisseur. One Wednesday I ask our waiter if Alexandre can have his *confit de canard* served with *frites*. "It is not possible," the waiter responds in a typically Parisian service provider kind of way. "What if everyone wanted *frites?*"

On sunny days we sit outside of *Café du Marché* at one of the tables along Rue Cler to watch shoppers, strollers and gawkers pass up and down one of Paris' most famous market streets: a group of three schoolboys, all smoking; a business man in a tailored suit, designer glasses and chic pink tie, talking on his cell phone; a baby in a stroller gnawing on a two-foot-long baguette.

Rue Cler is all about food. In the two *rue piéton* blocks of this street are vegetable stalls, a seafood store, wine stores, butchers and fishmongers, a bakery, restaurants and even a shop that specializes in honey and honey products. It's just one of the incredible market streets scattered across the city, integral parts of Parisian life

After eating and looking at so much food, we are ready to walk the few blocks to the American Library in Paris. Wednesday is children's story day. We pull our shopping trolley behind us, filled with books and DVDs checked out last week.

The American Library is another reason Paris is so liveable for Anglophones. Its large English-language collection is funded entirely by individuals. It's only open to members, for a small annual fee. While Alexandre listens to the stories I browse the books and magazines, or stroll over to the Eiffel Tower, less than a block away. The library is something of an anchor, a connection to our language after a week of struggling with my fractured French.

One evening in October the library hosts a Halloween party for children. As we leave, Alexandre exclaims, "Hey guys, turn around!" We turn around and look, and then lean back. Way back. There is the Eiffel Tower glittering like a gaudy chandelier, like a monstrous glass of Champagne, shining right in our astounded faces. Behind the tower is a gigantic harvest moon.

Our life in Paris is punctuated by such wonder.

AUGUST 17, PARIS

It's the first day of our four-month stay in France! Paris was just waking up as we arrived at our apartment; a dense fog covered the city. The *Arc de Triomphe* was barely visible from our *terrasse*, even though it's only meters away. As the morning progressed the fog burned off and it turned into a gloriously sunny day. A gloriously sunny day in Paris! I can't think of anything better!

We spent the afternoon in the Latin Quarter, walking along narrow streets lined with rough stone walls and flanked by the spires of churches and the dome of *L'Observatoire*. We looked at the second-hand offerings in the window of *La Brocante du Val-de-Grace* and passed by the red storefront headquarters of the socialist party on our way to visit friends who had helped us find Alexandre's new Parisian school. Afterwards we wandered the labyrinth of streets in the 5th Arrondissement until it was time to think about dinner.

On Sundays Parisian restaurants are usually closed, and in August many are shuttered for the annual summer holiday. Without reservations or hope, we walked down Rue Mouffetard when I remembered we were close to bistro *L'Ourcine*. We had been there once before and the food was amazing. In fact the chef, Sylvain Daniere, is one of Yves Camdeborde's protégés from *La Régalade*. I didn't have the address but I thought I knew the way.

Travelling down a desolate avenue I was beginning to think my instincts were failing, when, suddenly, ahead of us I saw a pool of warm light shining on an otherwise deserted street. The bistro was open, on a Sunday night in August! But the biggest miracle of all was they had a table for two available.

This was our first experience in a Parisian restaurant since the smoking ban and the room seemed open, fresh, more friendly somehow. Just outside the door of the restaurant an impromptu smoking area had formed, where friends gathered to drink their aperitifs while having cigarettes.

Frothy *amuses bouches* in shot glasses arrived at the table, setting the tone for this modern bistro meal. I started with marinated fresh mackerel served on a salad with a tangy Thai-influenced vinaigrette. Then roasted sea bream, crispy-skinned fish on a bed of vegetable couscous, and with it a chilled red wine from the Auvergne. The meal seemed to be a reward for making it to Paris!

It was eleven o'clock when we got back to the apartment. Alexandre was asleep and the babysitter was knitting. After she left we spent a few minutes out on the *terrasse* watching Paris by night. This time the *Arc* was sharp, golden and very, very near.

Crème de Tomate en Croûte
TOMATO SOUP IN PUFF PASTRY

This tomato soup is so impressive that it could have its own fan club! It arrives at the table encased in a bubble of puff pastry and as you break the crust, flakes of pastry fall into the creamy tomato soup below.

I like to serve the soup in white French *latté* bowls or French onion soup bowls. Make sure to choose oven-proof bowls.

2 T butter

1 large onion, sliced

6 garlic cloves, whole

1 bay leaf

1 tsp dried thyme

1 tsp black peppercorns

¼ cup tomato paste

2½ lbs ripe tomatoes, cored and quartered

2 cups chicken stock

1 cup heavy cream

1 tsp salt plus extra to taste

1 lb puff pastry, thawed

1 egg

1 T water

Preheat oven to 400° F.

In a large stockpot, melt the butter over medium-low heat. Add the onions, garlic, thyme, bay leaf and peppercorns. Stir and cover; cook at low heat for about 5 minutes, do not let the onions brown.

Add the tomato paste and let the mixture lightly toast, stirring constantly for another 5 minutes. Add the tomatoes and simmer partially covered over low heat for 30 to 40 minutes, until the tomatoes and onions are very soft.

Using a blender or handheld immersion blender, process until completely smooth. Return to the heat and add the chicken stock, cream and salt. Bring to a simmer and then remove from the heat.

Roll out the pastry to about 1/8-inch thickness. Cut out into 6 rounds slightly larger than your oven-proof bowls.

Ladle the soup into each bowl and place the bowls on a baking tray before proceeding.

Mix together the egg and water. Paint one side of the rolled dough with the egg wash and then place over the soup-filled bowl, egg-wash side down, pulling slightly on the sides to make the dough tight, like a drum.

Do not allow the pastry to touch the soup, it should be tight across the top of the bowl. Lightly paint the top of the pastry with egg wash, being careful not to push the pastry down.

Bake for 10 to 15 minutes, until the dough is golden brown. Do not open the oven during cooking as the pastry may fall. Let the bowls cool for about 5 minutes before serving. Serves 4 to 6.

Gâteaux aux Miel et Amandes
ALMOND HONEY CAKES

These puffy cakes are filled with almonds, butter, honey and just enough flour to bind them. They are inspired by *madeleines*, the famous French cookie that, in turn, inspired Marcel Proust. Use a *madeleine* pan if you have one, but a small-muffin tin works as well. I use a cast-iron *ableskiver* pan (made for a type of Scandinavian apple pancake). The cakes benefit from browning the melted butter.

¼ cup butter
¼ cup finely ground almonds
½ cup sugar
¼ tsp sea salt
½ cup unbleached flour
½ tsp baking powder
2 egg whites
1½ T honey

Preheat the oven to 450° F.

Butter your muffin tin or specialty pan very well. The batter will stick to any spot that is missed! In a small, heavy-bottom saucepan, heat the butter at medium until it melts and begins to bubble. Let it cook for a few minutes until it becomes slightly brown. Be careful not to burn it. Set it aside to cool.

In medium bowl stir together the almonds, sugar, salt, flour and baking powder. When blended, add in the egg whites and honey and mix gently. Now add the melted butter and continue to mix until the batter is smooth.

Distribute the batter evenly over 9 or 10 of the muffin holes, or fill the molds in your specialty pan. Place the pan in the oven. In about 10 minutes the cakes will have risen and have turned a dark, golden brown. Gently lift the cakes out of the molds and cool them on a rack. Serve while they're still warm.

HOW TO COOK BOUILLABAISSE
IN 37 EASY STEPS

O ne night, long before Vaison-la-Romaine became our second home, the celebrated French *chanteur*, Claude Nougaro, stumbled into the Vaison pizza shop on *Place Monfort*, an unlit cigarette dangling from his lips. He had been celebrating after finishing a performance at the Roman amphitheatre. Now he was hungry, and he needed a match.

The young pizza maker, who thought of himself as a creative problem solver, didn't have matches, but led Nougaro to the blazing oven. The singer stuck his head in, trying get a light from the flames, but the powerful heat, combined with too much alcohol, overwhelmed him and he fell to the floor, unconscious.

The creative pizza maker, who had also taken CPR lessons, was able to revive Nougaro, saving his life. They became friends, and Nougaro, who was also a noted artist, would later present the young man with a special drawing.

And that was why, on a bright day in December, I am in Avignon, the City of the Popes, where I will learn the fortune of the young pizza maker.

꩜

We arrive on time for that most important of appointments in France: a cooking class in the kitchen of a renowned chef. Avignon is a bustling, crowded city, crammed within medieval walls. A modern road surrounds the city, and the only way to enter is through narrow stone archways called *portes*, or gates. We circle the medieval walls, driving in through one *porte* and out another, until I finally spot the restaurant and a miraculous parking place nearby. On foot, we hurry along the narrow street to Le Jardin de la Tour and enter through a small garden used as a *terrasse du café* in the summer months.

A man dressed in the whites of a chef greets us. "Ah, you English, you are always on time!" he says, with a certain amount of disdain. "We are having a birthday party for my father-in-law. Please, please, sit here. I will be back shortly." Gesturing to a couple of chairs at the front, he hurries off to rejoin the party.

The restaurant is a long, narrow room, deserted except for the birthday party at the far end, in front of a fireplace. We watch as the family continues to celebrate; a cake is wheeled out, candles are lit, birthday songs sung. Small children (*clearly* his second family) ride plastic tricycles around the party group. Meanwhile, we are feeling like members of the lonely heart's club.

While we wait, we read faded newspaper clippings posted on the wall that tell the story of that fateful night in the Vaison pizza parlour. Jean-Marc was haled as a hero for saving Claude Nougaro's life, although it seems to us that having the singer stick his head in a 700-degree oven is something less than heroic.

I wonder if being treated like lowly apprentices is part of the experience of this French cooking class. But, after the twenty-minute mark, I move from feeling ignored to angry to thinking about leaving. Finally, and perhaps taking pity on the loneliest people in the room, Jean-Marc's wife (*clearly* his new, younger bride) brings us Champagne and birthday cake, two things that always make me feel better!

Then Jean-Marc himself arrives, this time in professorial mode and carrying linens. "First, we learn how a chef ties his apron." With that he garbs us in the traditional kitchen whites and demonstrates the proper way to tie an apron. "It ties around your waist, like so. No, no, it must be tighter. How you say, snug? Then you fold it down so, two times. And your kitchen towel tucks into the left side, so." He does this with the precision of a Wushu master.

Satisfied with our attire, he leads us through the dining room, past the party table, and into the kitchen. As we walk he tells us the history of the restaurant. Back in 1988, when he found the space, it was an abandoned "workshop for precision mechanics" and in the rafters we can still see the pulleys and central drive shaft. Above the fireplace is the drawing by Claude Nougaro that is now *Le Jardin de la Tour's* logo.

By this time, I am doubting the credibility of this "cooking school". It seems odd that the Chef would be hosting a party at the time of the cooking class. But, we are in Provence after all, where *les temps* move at a different pace. He leads us into the chilly kitchen where the first thing I see is a Vespa parked next to the walk-in cooler. The cracked linoleum countertops and dangling light bulbs do nothing to build faith in our leader.

I am used to a different style of cooking class. There was the *Le Cordon Bleu* in Paris, with its dedicated classrooms, its pristine kitchens, its translators, and a formal approach to the art of cooking. In Châteauneuf-du-Pape we worked as kitchen assistants to prepare the lunch menu at a hotel restaurant. The owner of the inn and his chef greeted us as honoured guests when we arrived and gave a tour of the modern, stainless-steel kitchen.

Back in Jean-Marc's dilapidated kitchen in Avignon, my thoughts are interrupted by our host. "Today, we make *bouillabaisse*," Jean-Marc proclaims. "It's a pity you weren't here this morning when I went to the market to choose the fish." He shows us a huge colander filled with the brightest collection of small Mediterranean fish I had ever seen. Ever. At this point I don't know that these fish are used only for the stock; we will eventually strain them out completely and use larger, beautiful fresh *rascasse* in the final dish. Jean-Marc calls for our attention.

"When we are here we are not just working in a kitchen," he says, gesturing around the space. *"But enjoying as happy cooks what you want to attain."* We spend a moment absorbing this cryptic statement.

Jean-Marc seems to be going through the motions of cooking and teaching with a certain amount of weariness. He has been working as a chef for nearly forty years, cooked in Hong Kong and Australia, and now has been in the kitchen of *Le Jardin* for eighteen years. He is like an eccentric artist nearing the end of a glorious career.

"Bouillabaisse is complicated and every chef has his own particular way," Jean-Marc went on. "But today I show you the real bouillabaisse." Jean-Marc, as it turns out, is the only chef in all of Avignon who is a recipient of the *Charte de la Bouillabaisse Marseillaise*, a recognition awarded by a group of chefs who promote and protect the traditional bouillabaisse made in the *méthode marseillaise*. I thought that bouillabaisse was simply some kind of fish soup. I am about to be proven wrong.

Jean-Marc begins by throwing handfuls of unpeeled garlic gloves into olive oil sizzling in an enormous cauldron, so big that I couldn't begin to wrap my arms around. Then, a few minutes later, we add the jumble of colourful fish.

"We want the fish singing, we don't want them swimming." Jean-Marc holds his hand up to his ear and leans over the cauldron. "What do we cook with? Eh?" Clearly I don't know the correct answer. He snaps out, "With our ears! Listen. Listen to the fish and the garlic singing."

I listen. And I do hear a kind of sizzling, snapping sound. "You see? You hear?" Jean-Marc beams. When the fish has sizzled to his satisfaction, he adds chopped onions and fennel along with a *bouquet garnie*. Jean-Marc sets us to chopping more vegetables: carrots, onions, and, of course, leeks. Then, in a separate skillet we begin to sauté them.

While the mixtures cook, I peel an orange and toast the rind. From another cauldron that holds the heated stock, I begin ladling liquid into the fish mixture, adding the orange rind. I think this is an unneeded affectation. How can you possibly taste the peel from one orange in this giant, fishy concoction?

As the broth begins to boil Jean-Marc calls us over. "The cooking food is alive," he says. "You must ensure that the broth can breathe, otherwise she chokes." He grabs his throat for emphasis. Before adding the sautéed vegetables to the broth he drains off the oil on a perforated tray. "Too much oil and the food cannot breathe."

He shows us how to remove the foam and scum that rises the top of the broth as it cooks. Then he gathers other ingredients, including saffron and turmeric, and tosses them into the cauldron. And a secret ingredient: a large splash of *Pernod*.

While the bouillabaisse simmers Jean-Marc sets us up at a station to carve mushrooms and radishes into fancy shapes. As we carve, his staff begin to arrive with *bisous* all around. A well-dressed woman stops in to gather fancy hors d'oeuvres for a party. She glances our way, imagining that we are just part of the kitchen staff.

Next is our truffle lesson. He hands me one giant black truffle and asks how much I think it costs. "A mere 25 Euros," is the answer. It is a truffle on steroids from China. It looks bloated for a reason. Chinese "truffles" are only a distant relative of the real thing from Europe.

Then he delicately fills my palm with three dusty, midnight-blue balls and asks me to guess again. "800 Euros per kilogram for the real thing." I am holding over $200 worth in my hand.

"Today, we make truffles two ways, one with the Chinese and one with the real French truffle. *Vous-êtes prêt?*"

"*Oui,*" I weakly reply. It has been slowly occurring to me that I am, in fact, learning a lot from Jean-Marc. I am in the presence of someone who knows his stuff. He is Chef, the chief.

The pace picks up considerably. When I'm not skimming scum from the bouillabaisse cauldron, I am bubbling cream and infusing it with honey and lavender and egg yolks for *crème brûlée*. Or I am at the giant Cuisinart whirring garlic and vast quantities of olive oil into *rouille* while toasting fresh croutons with the other hand.

Then Chef steps in for the final stages of the bouillabaisse. He lifts a giant hand-cranked food mill from the shelf and places it over a battered stainless steel bowl. With a slotted spoon he ladles in the fish, vegetables, orange rind and spices from the cauldron. With the strength of a thousand men he mills the whole fishes and cooked vegetables, straining with the effort of turning the crank, extracting the essence of the fish. Chef then returns the milled liquid to the cauldron and discards the rest.

I have lost track of time and are surprised when the first customers arrive. The food we have made will be served to the restaurant's guests! Chef is transformed. His ennui lifts, the circles under his eyes seem to disappear, and I can see that he retains his passion for the kitchen. His people, his followers, have arrived to partake of his creation.

While he adds a final pinch of salt to the *rouille*, he orders his assistant to bring a bottle of white wine to be opened at the stove. Then he welcomes me to dip the fresh croutons into the wildly delicious *rouille*. The crisp white wine is miraculous with the creamy, garlicky concoction. We are now comrades. He toasts our good work and then attends to the fresh batch of fish that are simmering in the delicious bouillabaisse. But first, open another bottle!

When the waiters return to the kitchen with customers' orders, Chef carefully eases two of the exquisite *rascasse* into the boiling pot of bouillabaisse. After a few minutes of simmering, he removes each fish with a large slotted spoon to a cutting board, where he nimbly filets the tender meat. Grabbing a couple of heated flat serving bowls, he drops some croutons in each, places the filets next to them, and then carefully ladles in some bouillabaisse, getting just the right mix of broth and solids. After garnishing the bowls with parsley, he passes them to the waiter to serve.

Like all novices, we gather at the round window in the kitchen door to watch the customers' faces. Some diners dip baguette into the *rouille*, while others mix spoonfuls directly into their soup. When he sees them *oohing* over the bouillabaisse, Chef goes out to greet his guests and to accept their praise.

My eight-hour shift is over. I take off my apron, hat, and whites to revert to a civilian. Chef invites us to sit at our own table and be served the bouillabaisse that we have laboured over. I don't want to leave. I want to curl up on a cot in the kitchen and start again tomorrow as Chef's assistant. This could be the beginning of a beautiful adventure.

The food is delicious, and the *bouillabaisse* is like nothing I have ever eaten. And, amidst the riot of amazing flavours, I can clearly pick out the orange rind! After the meal I am as tired as any restaurant apprentice, I just want to go home and sleep. Jean-Marc gives us a fond farewell; he compliments us on our stamina and respect for the trade. We will miss him, mentor and friend.

Close to midnight we leave through the now-dark *terrasse* and find our car. It is pitch black in the Provençal countryside, so dark that I am sure we are lost. But soon we come upon familiar villages with their welcoming Noël lights. The long drive home takes us back to other dark nights, and to our very first Christmas in Provence.

Crème Brûlée Infusée au Miel de Lavande
LAVENDER AND HONEY CRÈME BRÛLÉE

Chef Jean-Marc turned this classic dessert into a distinctive Provençal version with the addition of lavender and honey. I have experimented using half milk and half cream, but the texture was disappointing. Use all heavy cream for the best results.

2 cups heavy cream
½ stalk fresh lavender or
3 T dried cooking
lavender
¼ cup honey
6 egg yolks
¼ cup granulated sugar

Preheat oven to 275° F.

In a small saucepan, bring the cream to a boil, but don't let it boil over. Remove it from the heat, add the lavender and infuse for one hour at room temperature. Using a fine sieve or cheesecloth, strain the mixture and return it to the same saucepan. Heat to a simmer and then remove from the heat immediately. Stir in the honey until dissolved.

In a medium-size mixing bowl, whisk the yolks until they are combined. Continue to whisk while slowly adding a small amount of the warm lavender cream. Add a little bit at a time so the yolks don't cook, until all the cream is mixed in.

Divide the liquid custard among 6-ounce ramekins. Place them in large baking dish. Fill the baking dish with hot water to halfway up the sides of the ramekins and put the baking dish in oven. Bake for 40 minutes and then check every 5 minutes. When fully baked the *brûlées* will be almost firm but will jiggle just slightly when shaken. Remove the ramekins from the water bath, let them cool and then refrigerate for at least 2 hours.

To prepare for serving, sprinkle each dessert with 1 tablespoon of sugar. Next, brown (*brûlée*, or broil) the sugar using a kitchen torch. Sugar can burn quickly, so use the torch carefully until the top is a deep golden brown. Serve immediately.

Bouillabaisse
THE FAMOUS FRENCH FISH SOUP

Bouillabaisse is filled with mystery and intrigue. There are no two recipes alike and each cook seems to think their recipe is authentic. But in fact, there is an organization dedicated to preserving the recipe for traditional Marseilles bouillabaisse. Here it is.

The Fish
8-10 pounds firm white-fleshed fish, (choose 4 varieties):
Ocean perch, red snapper, rockfish, monkfish, cod, halibut, haddock, or
 turbot
4-5 pounds oily fish, (choose 2 varieties):
bluefish, eel, mackerel, striped bass, sea bass, kingfish, Spanish mackerel,
 mahi-mahi

Part One, the Fish Stock:
5 T butter
2 onions, sliced
8 cups cold water
2 *bouquet garni*: (4 sprigs fresh parsley, 6 sprigs fresh thyme, 10 black
 peppercorns, and a bay leaf, tied in cheesecloth)
1 cup dry white wine
½ cup extra-virgin olive oil
6 garlic cloves, finely chopped
fish heads, tails, carcasses

Part Two, the *Rouille*
1½ cups French bread, white part only, diced
½ cup hot water
4 garlic cloves, peeled
1 tsp sea salt
½ tsp cayenne pepper
pinch of saffron
1 large egg yolk

freshly ground black pepper to taste

1 cup extra-virgin olive oil

Part Three, the Croutons

5 T butter

¼ cup extra-virgin olive oil

1 garlic clove, minced

40 to 50 slices of a French baguette

Part Four, the Bouillabaisse

Saffron threads, steeped in ¼ cup of hot water. Set aside.

1 cup olive oil

2 large onions, finely chopped

3 leeks, white and light green part, well cleaned and thinly sliced

3 stalks celery, finely chopped

2 pounds ripe plum tomatoes, peeled, seeded and chopped

1 long thin strip of orange zest, no pith

1 T. fennel seeds

½ tsp saffron threads steeped in ¼ cup dry white wine until needed

Sea salt to taste

Freshly ground pepper to taste

Extra boiling water as needed

2 T tomato paste

2 T Pernod or other anise flavoured liqueur

1 cup fresh parsley, finely chopped

1. Prepare the *bouquet garni* and set aside.
2. Prepare the batches of vegetables and set aside.
3. Peel a long strip of orange strip and lightly toast it over an open flame for about one minute, be careful not to burn. Set aside.
4. Clean the fish. You will need the heads, tails and carcasses for the stock. Cut the fish into 4 x 2-inch pieces and marinate the fish pieces in a large ceramic or glass bowl with 1/4 cup of the olive oil, half of the chopped garlic, and the saffron threads for 2 hours in the

refrigerator. Keep the firm fleshed fish and the oily fish marinating separately, as they require different cooking times.

5. Begin to prepare the fish stock: rinse the fish heads, tails, and carcasses in cold water.

6. Meanwhile, in a large stockpot, melt the butter over medium heat, and add the sliced onions and cook until soft but not brown, about 6 minutes, stirring occasionally.

7. Add the fish heads and bones and cover with the cold water.

8. Place one of the *bouquet garni* and the wine. Bring to a boil, skimming occasionally, then reduce the heat to low, partially cover, and simmer for 2 hours.

9. Strain the fish broth through a conical strainer and set aside to cool. Press firmly to get as much fishiness as possible. Put some muscle into it!

10. Discard all the fish heads, carcasses, *bouquet garni* and vegetables. You will have about 10 cups of fish stock when finished.

11. Clean the stockpot because you will need it in step 13.

12. You are now ready to start making the bouillabaisse.

13. In the large stockpot, heat the remaining 1 cup of olive oil over medium heat, then cook the chopped onions, leeks, and celery for 15 minutes, stirring often.

14. Add the tomatoes, the remaining garlic, the remaining *bouquet garni*, the orange zest, and fennel seeds.

15. Stir in the reserved fish stock and the saffron steeped in wine and season with salt and pepper.

16. Bring to a boil, then reduce the heat to medium-low and simmer for 40 minutes. The broth can be left like this, covered, for many hours, over very low heat.

17. While the stock simmers, make the *rouille*.

18. Soak the diced bread in water. Squeeze the water out.

19. Mash the garlic cloves in a mortar with the salt until mushy.

20. In a food processor, place the soft bread, mashed garlic, cayenne, saffron, egg yolk and black pepper and blend for 30 seconds.

21. Then slowly pour in the cup olive oil through the feed tube in a, thin, steady stream while the machine is running.

22. If the *rouille* separates, add 2 to 3 tablespoons of the fish stock and whisk it in until smooth and emulsified. Refrigerate for 1 hour before serving.

23. Now, make the croutons. Prepare the bread slices by cutting the baguette into slices of equal thickness.

24. In a large skillet, melt the butter and ¼ cup of olive oil. Add the minced garlic clove.

25. Lightly brush both sides of each bread slice with the melted butter and oil and set aside.

26. When all the slices are brushed place them back in the skillet in batches and cook until they are a very light brown on both sides. Set aside until serving.

27. When you are ready to prepare the final stages of the bouillabaisse, bring the broth back to a rapid boil. The boiling liquid helps to emulsify the oil.

28. Add the oily fish and boil, uncovered, over very high heat for 8 minutes. Stir often to prevent sticking.

29. Now put the firm-fleshed white fish in and boil hard for 6 minutes. Add more boiling water if necessary to cover the fish.

30. Carefully remove the fish from the broth with a slotted spoon and spatula or skimmer and transfer to a large bowl or deep platter.

31. Arrange the fish on the platter more or less in the order in which you put them into the pot. Keep them warm by covering with a sheet of aluminum foil.

32. Strain the stock through a fine mesh strainer into a soup tureen or large bowl, discarding what doesn't go through.

33. Whisk in the tomato paste-and-anise mixture.

34. Sprinkle the platter and soup tureen with the parsley.

35. On a separate plate, serve the croutons alongside with a bowl of the *rouille*. Some people prefer to mix the *rouille* with their stock, while other prefer to spread some *rouille* on the croutons.

36. Place the fish into the soup tureen and pour over the hot fish stock.

37. Serve immediately and *bon appetit!*

PARIS CULINARY ADDRESSES

Although I love the monuments and museums of Paris, it's the search for the best baguette, hidden food shop and traditions of French food that really excites me. Here's a list of our favourite culinary addresses, that we never miss when I'm in Paris.

॰॰

Maison Prunier

Everything I thought I knew about caviar was wrong. It took a visit to the elegant dining room of *Prunier* on Place de la Madeleine, to set me straight.

My first shock was to learn that it is now illegal to import caviar into France; the diminishing numbers of wild sturgeon are now protected. Goodbye Russian caviar. But that's not really bad news for the *House of Prunier* who were the first French producers of farmed sturgeon and the caviar they produce. They've been doing it for almost a century.

Today, *Prunier* continues to farm sturgeon in giant tanks in the Dordogne region. It takes two years of feeding and caring for the 200,000 sturgeon before it can be determined which fish are female. Then the female sturgeon are groomed for another six years before they begin to produce eggs. A fish obstetrician is on hand to carefully monitor their growth before the eggs are harvested.

The James Bond style caviar tasting room with its smoky glass walls (probably bullet-proof) surround the central tasting island. My caviar hostess brought out a small tin and told me to hold my hand in a fist like I'm playing *One Potato, Two Potato*. With a silver spoon, she placed an almond-sized dollop of caviar on the fleshy part of my fist. This, she explained, is the best way to taste caviar, without interference from other flavours.

I'm surprised by the taste. It's not salty like I was expecting; it's smoky, subtle and silky. Don't miss the *Prunier Héritage,* this rare caviar is prepared according to Persian methods, with large grains and a low salt content.

15, Place de la Madeleine, 75008

৩৯

Fauchon: Home of the Éclair

This food emporium has been around for over a hundred years and it dominates a complete corner of Place de la Madeleine. It was Madame Fauchon who first had the idea to put their name on every tin of tea, cookies and jam that they made. The world's first luxury brand was born.

But what they are really famous for is the éclair. What *Ladurée* did for the macaron, *Fauchon* has done for the éclair. An entire case, the length of a Citroën, is dedicated to their vast array of éclairs. There are even bite-size éclairs for the slender clientele to enjoy. Don't miss the *foie gras* éclair; this delicate, savoury is filled with *foie gras* cream and coated with a hazelnut glaze.

24-26, Place de la Madeleine, 75008

৩৯

Hediard

From *Fauchon's* windows, you can look across the Place de la Madeleine and see their main competitor, *Hediard*. In 1850, Ferdinand Hediard began selling exotic fruit out of wheelbarrow on *Place des Victoires.*

Although their offerings are similar to *Fauchon*, don't miss *Hediard's* luxurious exotic fresh fruit and vegetables. Their meticulous produce displays are a riot of colour and variety.

21, Place de la Madeleine, 75008

৩৯

Albert Ménès

Bigger is not always better and this tiny shop on Boulevard Malesherbes proves the point. They manage to cram four hundred French-made specialties onto the shelves of their tidy gourmet store.

It's not surprising to learn that the jams and marmalades are the company's best sellers. There are forty different types and all are made by hand. A row of pretty *confit de fleurs de violettes* (violet jam) and *confit de pétales de rose* (rose petal jam) are as dazzling as precious gems. The roses for the rose jelly are harvested in the month of May at dawn near Grasse in the south of France.

Don't miss their fish soup sold in cans, it's what has put them on the map since 1921.

41, Boulevard Malesherbes, 75008

❦

Le Grande Épicerie de Paris

As soon as you enter this emporium of gourmet shopping your heart will beat faster; you will want to put the entire contents of the store into your shopping cart. Their selection of *fleur de sel* is mind blowing, their rows of extra-virgin olive oil, mustards and chocolate will send you into a gourmet frenzy.

Don't miss their *foie gras* sandwiches, found in the deli. Great, thick slabs of *foie gras* are wedged in a crusty baguette with onion confit. To die for!

38, Rue de Sèvres 75008

❦

Lafitte

Foie gras is a traditional food of France and link to their ancestry. In 1920, Pierre Lafitte, started selling game - partridge, woodcock, *ortolan*, hares and *foie gras* from his small town in Landes, the southwest of France.

Today, Lafitte works with a small group of farmers all within a forty km distance of their farm. The tradition of small scale farming is honoured; all the ducks are kept outdoors in a natural, grassy environment and are fed a diet of corn, oats and grass.

All their foie gras is made by hand without any preservatives. Their sole shop in Paris is found on Île Saint-Louis. Don't miss their *foie gras d'oie entier truffe*, (made with goose whole liver and truffles).

8 rue Jean du Bellay, Île Saint-Louis

❦

Huilerie J. Leblanc

This family-owned company has been making small-batch, handcrafted toasted nut oils since 1878. Today, Jean-Charles Leblanc, the grandson of the founder, runs the mill at its original location in a sleepy village in Burgundy. The oils are still pressed in the *huilerie's* original granite mill.

For each batch of oil, fifty pounds of nuts are ground into a thick paste, then transferred to a roaster, and stirred constantly for about ten minutes. Once pressed, the oil rests for up to two weeks before bottling to allow the sediment to settle. The oils are pure, unadulterated, unfiltered, unrefined and are made-to-order.

J. Leblanc has only one store in Paris and it's smaller than most people's walk-in closet. Don't miss the roasted almond oil; its intense, nutty flavour capture the essence of almonds.

6, rue Jacob, 75006

❧

L'Épicerie de Bruno

Bruno Jarry is passionate about pepper. His Paris shop carries 34 varieties of pepper (and over 200 spices) from around the world and he treats them with the same respect as the best aged *Bordeaux*.

"They must be matched to the dish like wine," Bruno enthuses. The Ceylon black pepper, has a delicate spicy fragrance and subtle citrus notes. It's a superb every day pepper which goes well with most savoury dishes except fish or dessert.

For dessert, Bruno prefers the Sarawak black pepper from the island of Borneo. "It's fresh and mildly spicy with notes of forest and fauna. It's surprisingly good on fruit desserts, on melon, over honey or to accent dark chocolate."

Don't miss the *Kari Gosse*, a mild curry, from Bruno's home town in Brittany. This gentle curry with notes of ginger, cloves and cinnamon matches the subtle flavours of scallops, fish, and lobster.

30, rue Tiquetonne, 75002

❧

Premier Pression Provence

Olivier Baussan, the man behind *L'Occitane*, the mega-popular skin care line, has a new twist on olive oil. He's gone back to its roots to tell the story of the people who grow and produce olive oil.

Olivier works directly with small olive oil growers to bottle and bring their oils to a wider audience in his shops in Paris. There's plenty of tasting and a fantastic selection of olives, olive oils, and all things related: soaps, tapenades, and gift boxes.

35 rue Charlat, 75003

∽

A La Mère de Famille

In French baking, there is a special category called *patisserie sec*, which refers to cookies, pound cakes, *tuiles, palmiers, meringues* and *macarons*. This is the world of *A La Mère de Famille*: part *chocolatier*, part *pâtisserie sec*, part candy maker. In their 250-year-old location in the 9th Arrondissement they've created an adult version of a kid's candy store.

Chocolates, caramels, marshmallow, nougat and almond *calisson* line antique wooden shelves. The floor has heaved over the centuries, and the entire port side of the store leans towards *le grand magasins*. Don't miss their *floretins*, made with both dark and milk chocolate and a touch of honey.

33, rue du Faubourg Montmartre, 75009

∽

Maison de la Truffe

Since 1932, *Maison de la Truffe* has been specializing in *diamant noir*, black diamond truffles, from the Perigord and Provence. In the shop you can find both fresh and dried truffles, as well as sauces made with summer truffles and with black truffles. And while you're there enjoy a three-course truffle-themed meal in their restaurant. The staff really rolls out the red carpet presenting the best of their dishes, all featuring truffles.

Don't miss the *tagliatelle* with everything delicious: cream, a generous amount of shaved truffle, and on top, a beautiful piece of seared *foie gras*. I'm not making this up!

19, Place de la Madeine, 75008

14, Rue Marbeuf, 75008

❦

Maiffret Chocolate

It all started in 1883, when Jean Maiffret, in charge of candied fruits production in a large factory in Grasse was refused the pay raise he asked for. He resigned and left Grasse to set up on his own making candied fruits, chocolates and sweets. Today, *Maiffret* is still a family company, run by son and grandson.

At their new location in the 15th Alain le Gouedec explained to me that all the chocolates are made in their own factory, even the praline is made by hand. Fresh chocolates like these have a short shelf life of one month. All the chocolates are openly displayed and shoppers are invited to sample before they purchase. The service is impeccable. There are no wrong choices at Maiffret.

57 rue du Commerce, 75015

❦

Au Grand Richelieu

The oldest bakery in Paris, dating back to 1810.

51, rue de Richelieu, 75001

Du Pain et des Idées

Christophe Vasseur, the world's most interesting baker, can be found in his shop Monday to Friday.

34, rue Yves Toudic, 75010

Le Grenier à Pain Abbessesess

Best Baguette 2010. It's worth a metro ride to Montmartre (Metro: Abbesses) to sample the official best baguette of 2010. Don't be surprised if there's a line snaking down the street.

38 rue des Abbesseses, 75018

Debauve & Gallais

The oldest chocolate shop in Paris.

30, Rue des Saints-Pères, 75007

Patrick Roger
Paris' bad boy of chocolate.
108 boulevard Saint-Germain, 75006

Pierre Marcolini
The godfather of chocolate.
89 rue de Seine, 75006

Fromager Beillevaire
Jérôme's shop is worth making the trip out to Belleville.
140, rue de Belleville, 75020

Fromagerie Quatrehomme
This famous cheese shop has been run by Marie Quatrehomme for over 20 years. Don't miss her *Beaufort* and *St-Marcellin*.
62 Rue de Sèvres, 75007

Cooking Classes

École Ritz Escoffier
Nothing tops a cooking class in the professional kitchens of the world's most famous hotel.
38, rue Cambon, 75001

Le Cordon Bleu
Offers many half-day and full-day classes that are perfect for those wanting a taste of traditional French cooking.
8, rue Léon Delhomme, 75015

Marguerite's Elegant Home Cooking
A trip to the suburbs is worth it for Marguerite's casual cooking classes.
35, rue Rouget de Lisle, Suresnes, 92150

Cook n' with Class

A very intimate cooking class. Creative design and top-notch instruction make for a perfect pause in Paris.
21, rue Custine, 75018

La Cuisine Paris

Overlooking the Seine, this cooking school offers many options for morning, afternoon and evening classes.
80 Quai de l'Hôtel de Ville, 75004

Restaurants

Le Dôme du Marais

Lovely food served under a stylish dome in the Marais.
55, bis des Frances-Bourgeois, 75004

Brasserie de l'Isle St Louis

A favourite during the winter months, when pork and sauerkraut hits the spot.
55 quai, de bourbon, 75004

La Bastide Odeon

A stylish restaurant near to the Jardin du Luxembourg.
7, rue Corneille, 75006

Brasserie Lipp

Not the place for a quiet dinner, but go with a group of friends for a loud, fun evening out.
151, boulevard St. Germain, 75006

La Closerie des Lilas

Classic service in a historical setting.
171 boulevard du Montparnasse, 75006

Le Petit Lutétia

One of our favourite small bistros near *Le Bon Marché*. Service can be hit and miss but their *cassolette d'escargots* are divine.
107, rue de Sèvres, 75006

Café Constant

A casual spot for lunch or dinner. Part of the Christian Constant empire on Rue St. Dominique.
139, rue St-Dominique, 75007

Les Fables de la Fontaine

A classic seafood restaurant right next door to an adorable fountain and close to the Eiffel Tower. Another Christian Constant restaurant.
131, rue St-Dominique, 75007

Le Violon d'Ingres

Christian Constant's luxury restaurant on rue St-Dominque.
135, rue St-Dominique, 75007

Le Boeuf sur le Toit

A big restaurant for when you're in the mood for hearty, French fare.
34, rue du, Colisée 75008

Fermette Marbeuf 1900

A charming restaurant perfect for a casual lunch. Just be sure to reserve your space *sous le dôme*, under the dome.
5, rue Marbeuf, 75008

Senderens

An elegant restaurant on the *place*.
9, place de la Madeleine, 75008

Chez Casimir

Great food at very reasonable prices.
6, rue de Belzunce, 75010

Chez Michel

Chef Thierry has been turning out Breton classics for close to twenty years.
10, rue de Belzunce, 75010

L'Ourcine

A gem!
92, rue Broca, 75013

L'os a Moelle

Another of the four chefs restaurants.
3, rue Vasco-de-Gama, 75015

Le Marcab

Not a bad choice if you're in the 15th and wanting a quiet, elegant meal.
225 Rue de Vaugirard, 75015

La Table de Lauriston

Though unassuming, this restaurant turns out some delicious food.
129, rue de Lauriston, 75016

La Gare

A nice lunch spot before or after your visit to the *Marmatton Monet Musée*.
19, Chaussée de la Muette, 75016

L'Astrance

If you're lucky enough to get a reservation here, bring only your serious foodie friends.
4, rue Beethoven, 75016

Le Huitrier

The best platters of oysters in town. It's a small restaurant, so make sure you make reservations.
16, rue Saussier-Leroy, 75017

The Long Lunch

Le Meurice

"I try to think of what people will like" says Yannick Alléno. And here, a meal orchestrated by Yannick (who was awarded three Michelin stars) and his staff can seem magical. The *Meurice* dining room's 90 € lunch menu is probably the best Euros you'll spend in Paris.
228, rue de Rivoli, 75008

Le V

More spa than restaurant, a lunch here can revive your senses better than a 90 minute massage.
Hotel Four Seasons George V
31 rue de George V, 75008

Le Bristol

We've been following Eric since his heydays out in the 19th. We've watched the boy grow into a man at *Le Bristol*.
112, rue du Faubourg-St. Honoré, 75008

Merci Mille Fois

Thanks to everyone who made our adventures possible:

Tom Medcalf & Jos Gill of The Cotswolds, who showed us the ropes. Jane "Commander" Reeves, who found the hideaway and taught us how to be prepared; her husband Chris Blewden; and the girls, Isabelle & Tamsin, *les amies* of Alexandre. Ed & Michelle Muscat. Colette de Castro. Joe Crachiola, who opens a mean bottle of wine and who taught us what a photo of France should look like. Jean & Paul Denman of Greenville, South Carolina, for lending us their house in Nyons when we were in need. Bob & Elizabeth Rafloski who let us stay in their place in the *haute ville* and taught us what it means to be citizens of the world. (Thanks, Bob, for that road in Vietnam.) Rana Shaskin, for being an excellent student. Russ Willms and his lovely wife, Mary-Lynn Bellamy-Willms, who are always game for an adventure.

All of these people are smarter, funnier and better looking than we make them appear in the book.

Thanks also to: Rebekah Lee & Muriel-Marguerite of *Marguerite's Elegant Home Cooking*. Chef David Goulaze and Frances Laure at the *Ritz Paris*. The chefs and staff at *Le Cordon Bleu*. Gerri from *Paris on Your Plate*. Diane de Sédouy at *Fauchon Paris*. Nathalie Roze at *Albert Ménès*. Julie Puyssegur at *Lafitte Foie Gras*. Jean-Michel Leblanc at *Huilerie J.Leblanc*. Jane Dolfi of *La Mere de Famille*. Pauline Ferrero-Quevreux at *Maiffret*. The staff at *La Truffe Marbeuf*. Nicolas Paradis of *Ô Château*. Christelle Delaunay at *Café Prunier*. Bruno Jarry from *L'Epicercie de Bruno*.

Another big *merci* to Russ Willms who spent hours with us poring over materials, and made magic with his illustrations and cover design. Tami Moritz who graciously volunteered her time to make sure the recipes were just right. Rosa Spricer, Greg Hollingshead and Karin Ivand for taking the time to read and comment on our manuscript. And to Chris Shaskin for telling us it was good enough.

Most of all, thanks to our son, Alexandre, who has shown us what the adventure is all about!

This book is dedicated to Françoise & Laurent Gaud of Puyméras, who taught us human kindness.

Diane Shaskin and Mark Craft have lived the French dream. They've shopped the food markets from rue Poncelet to Vaison-la-Romaine; dined at the best French bistros, brassieres, and restaurants; learned to cook from top chefs in Paris and Provence; frequented the wineries of the *Côtes-du-Rhône*; and have cooked and eaten their way through a small fortune.

When they're not in France they live on Vancouver Island with their son Alexandre.

Diane and Mark lead week-long gourmet food tours in Paris and in Provence.   Visit their website at www.paristoprovence.ca or contact them at info@paristoprovence.ca

11241627R00176

Made in the USA
Charleston, SC
09 February 2012